ABAP™ Performance Tuning

 **PRESS**

SAP PRESS is a joint initiative of SAP and Galileo Press. The know-how offered by SAP specialists combined with the expertise of the Galileo Press publishing house offers the reader expert books in the field. SAP PRESS features first-hand information and expert advice, and provides useful skills for professional decision-making.

SAP PRESS offers a variety of books on technical and business related topics for the SAP user. For further information, please visit our website: *www.sap-press.com*.

Horst Keller, Wolf Hagen Thümmel
Official ABAP Programming Guidelines
2009, app. 350 pp.
978-1-59229-290-5

James Wood
Object-Oriented Programming with ABAP Objects
2009, 357pp.
978-1-59229-235-6

Dominik Ofenloch, Roland Schwaiger
Getting Started with Web Dynpro ABAP
2009, app. 480 pp.
978-1-59229-311-7

Frank Föse, Sigrid Hagemann, Liane Will
SAP NetWeaver AS ABAP System Administration
2008, 648 pp.
978-1-59229-174-8

Hermann Gahm

ABAP™ Performance Tuning

Galileo Press

Bonn • Boston

Galileo Press is named after the Italian physicist, mathematician and philosopher Galileo Galilei (1564–1642). He is known as one of the founders of modern science and an advocate of our contemporary, heliocentric worldview. His words *Eppur si muove* (And yet it moves) have become legendary. The Galileo Press logo depicts Jupiter orbited by the four Galilean moons, which were discovered by Galileo in 1610.

Editor Florian Zimniak
English Edition Editor Justin Lowry
Translation Lemoine International, Inc., Salt Lake City, UT
Copyeditor Lori Newhouse
Cover Design Jill Winitzer
Photo Credit Getty Images/Max Oppenheim
Layout Design Vera Brauner
Production Editor Kelly O'Callaghan
Typesetting Publishers' Design and Production Services, Inc.
Printed and bound in Canada

ISBN 978-1-59229-289-9

© 2010 by Galileo Press Inc., Boston (MA)
1st Edition 2010

1st German edition published 2009 by Galileo Press, Bonn, Germany

Contents at a Glance

Contents

7 Processing of Internal Tables 253

8 Communication with Other Systems 287

Foreword

SAP® provides software applications that support process and business modeling innovations, flexibility, and fast adaptability. Our customers implement standard processes but also carry out targeted extensions of the SAP standard using the SAP NetWeaver Development Infrastructure to customize software to their individual requirements and to be distinguishable in the market. Many enterprises use the service-oriented architecture and the openness of SAP backbones to accelerate innovations and simplify business processes. SAP has an ever-expanding ecosystem of partners who implement these extensions. Scalability, performance, and throughput of these customer extensions in conjunction with the SAP standard must meet the expectations of business process owners and end users.

SAP Active Global Support is regularly commissioned to review and optimize ABAP customer applications. The extensive experience of Hermann Gahm, the author and SAP support employee, in the analysis of ABAP programs for major SAP customers ensures that this book will considerably contribute to the success of your projects. This compendium about ABAP tuning provides details about everything you require for the analysis and optimization of your specific developments, including tried-and-tested tools integrated with a systematic procedure of how you can detect and resolve performance problems in your ABAP programs and practical recommendations on how you can consider the performance already in the architecture of ABAP developments.

On that note, I would like to thank the author and all persons involved who provided their experience, which they gained in hundreds of service deliveries. I'd also like to thank our customers and partners within this book. As for you, dear readers, I hope that this book provides you with valuable information regarding the optimization procedure and tools for ABAP performance tuning and that you can efficiently incorporate this information in your programming and optimization scenarios.

Best regards,
Uwe Hommel
Executive Vice President Active Global Support

When all you own is a hammer, every problem starts looking like a nail.
–Abraham Maslow

Preface and Acknowledgments

Questions such as "What are the most essential points that you must consider regarding performance issues of your specific developments?" are frequently asked in SAP consulting. One of my former colleagues and I therefore had the idea to write an SAP Press Essentials guide on this topic. We submitted this proposal to Galileo Press about 14 months ago. As fate would have it, Florian Zimniak, the responsible editor, was looking for an author on this topic exactly at that time. The discussions that followed on the concept of such a publication quickly showed that a book would be the appropriate format for this topic. Therefore my small project became a book project that accompanied me throughout the year of 2008.

In the same year, as I visited many customers on virtually every continent within the scope of my work in Active Global Support (AGS) of SAP Aktiengesellschaft (AG), I gradually developed the manuscript of this book. I included personal experience that I've gained in current and past projects, as well as content from customer, partner, and colleague dialogues.

This book imparts method knowledge and background information on the different tools and questions on ABAP performance tuning. When things take a while, I hope that this book helps you meet the challenges.

All the information, statements, menu paths, and screenshots in this book are based on SAP NetWeaver AS ABAP Basis Release 7.00 if not otherwise explicitly stated (for example, in Chapter 10).

The terms used in this book are all masculine, but they represent both men and women. If the terms "developers," "administrators," or "users" are used, they also include the female developers, administrators, and users.

Acknowledgments

This book was possible only with the support of numerous people.

I would like to thank Stefan Kuhlmann and Karsten Bach for their support and the possibility to implement this book project in addition to my daily work.

Furthermore, I would like thank my editor, Florian Zimniak from Galileo Press, for his competent support and help during the entire project duration. I thank him, Alexandra Müller, and Iris Warkus for their review and corrections of the manuscript.

Also, I would like to give my thanks to my girlfriend, Kathleen Piskol, for her support, motivation, and inspiration.

I also owe thanks to the many colleagues who supported me with their valuable answers regarding questions on content, their reviews, expert discussions, and advice. My thanks go to Franz-Josef Stortz, Tobias Wenner, and Dr. Sigrid Wortmann from the development department for their helpful feedback and expertise.

I also thank Axel Treusch from the training department for checking the book content against the trainings available for SAP customers on ABAP performance tuning.

I thank my former colleagues at SAP SI AG, Bernhard Borutta and Frank Föse, for their review of the chapters and their invaluable comments.

With regard to technical reviews and valuable comments, corrections, and remarks, I thank the following colleagues of the PDMS group (Performance, Data Management & Scalability): Ingo Bohn, Dr. Randolf Eilenberger, Dr. Heiko Gerwens, Dr. Manfred Mensch, and Hartmut Willy.

In addition, I thank my colleagues from the Active Global Support department (AGS): Hans Bäßler, Martin Frauendorfer, Jochen Hartmann, Dr. Nikolaus Hertz-Eichenrode, Rinat Kaipov, Jan Kritter, and Tin Ling for their valuable feedback on database-specific topics, as well as Bernd Bayerlein, Michael Biehl, Wenbo Chen, Martha Cooney, Tony Fitzgerald, Thomas Holz, Andreas Kiriljuk, Claudia Langner, Jens Otto, Simone Schabert, Siegfried Schmidt, and Pete Zhou for their reviews and helpful discussions. It is always great fun working with you!

Hermann Gahm

ABAP performance tuning is an essential part of performance management for the development and maintenance of software.

1   Introduction

In computer science, the concept of *performance* usually describes the performance of a data processing system. It is used both for hardware and software.

For software, you usually use the two most critical metrics, *response time* and *throughput*, to describe the performance.

- *Response time* is the elapsed time between sending a request and receiving the results.

- *Throughput* generally refers to the data volume processed within a specific time unit (for example, order items per hour).

Another important property is the *scalability* of software. For example, a "good scalability" is present if an application requires twice the time for processing the double dataset. A "poor scalability" is if the double dataset requires an amount of time that was four times (or more) higher than usual.

Response time, throughput, and scalability are the most important goals of performance tuning.

1.1   Tuning Methods

This book focuses on the optimization of ABAP programs. Within the scope of performance management, you are provided with further options to achieve the mentioned goals whose characteristics and effects are briefly described in the following comparison to ABAP tuning.

ABAP tuning requires both expertise and time because it involves testing, among other things. With regard to expertise, you should have a sound technical understanding of the SAP NetWeaver Application Server, the ABAP programming language, and accesses to databases. Changes to ABAP applications always entail risks, which you must minimize through testing. The sphere of influence usually is limited to the optimization of the application, whereas positive effects, for example, in the form of released system resources, can also positively influence the entire system. The optimization of an ABAP application generally is a sustainable measure (for example, for increasing data volume).

Application tuning refers to an optimization of the application's business logic. By means of application tuning, you can deactivate entire program parts that are not required for specific tasks or use alternative or more efficient data accesses, for example, to other tables. Application tuning is similar to ABAP tuning with regard to expertise, time requirement, sphere of influence, and risk. Regarding expertise, application tuning requires a more detailed knowledge of the application and the business process.

System tuning (system configuration, parameter changes, load distribution, and so on) requires yet another type of expertise and usually less time than the previously mentioned tuning methods. System tuning is the configuration of an SAP system. Changes to the configuration involve a certain risk that can be reduced through testing. System tuning changes not only affect an application but also the entire system or an application server.

The last method presented here is the *adding of hardware*. This approach is also playfully referred to as the *kiwi approach* (*kiwi = kill it with iron*). Some performance problems can — or, in some situations, must — be resolved by adding hardware. This approach usually requires less expertise. Time requirement, risk, and test effort depend on the type of hardware expansion. For example, system migration to another hardware platform can take a lot of time and test effort. Of course, more simple expansions, for example, main memory expansions, are not very comprehensive. Adding hardware is also a system- and application server-wide approach.

Successful performance management is characterized by taking and managing the right actions at the right time. Usually, successful performance management cannot be implemented with one single tuning method.

This book provides a detailed description of the ABAP performance tuning topic.

1.2   Structure of the Book

An understanding of the SAP system architecture forms the basis of ABAP tuning. *Chapter 2* presents the *architecture* of SAP NetWeaver Application Server ABAP and details the performance-relevant aspects of this architecture.

Chapter 3 describes the use of the most essential tools available for ABAP performance analysis and provides general tips for performance analysis.

Chapter 4 outlines parallel processing. You will learn about prerequisites for parallelizable programs and the methods to parallelize programs.

Chapter 5 describes the tuning options for database accesses. For this purpose, you obtain a description of the database architecture and the technical background of database accesses. It details the execution of SQL statements using execution plans, the read data volume, bundling techniques for the reduction of executions, and further special topics, such as database- or database interface hints.

Chapter 6 describes the most important buffer options to avoid unnecessary database accesses. You will get to know the different buffers that are available on the SAP NetWeaver Application Server ABAP.

Chapter 7 outlines the performance-optimized processing of internal tables. It details the basic principles of the organization of internal tables and the performance-relevant aspects of their processing.

Chapter 8 discusses the data transfer to other systems via Remote Function Call (RFC). It outlines the most important performance aspects for RFCs.

Chapter 9 details further special topics that play roles in certain cases — for example, the local updates or parameter transfers — or are of secondary importance.

Chapter 10 provides an outlook of the essential innovations of some of the topics discussed.

Figure 1.1 shows a graphical display of the chapters.

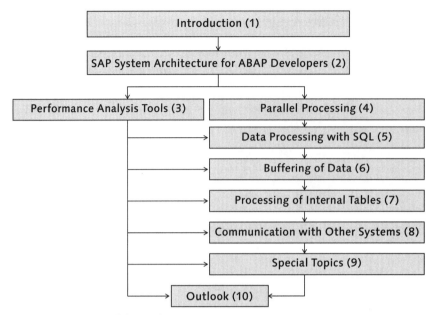

Figure 1.1 Structure of the Book

1.3   How to Use This Book

Figure 1.1 indicates that you can read the book in two different ways.

The first way is to read the introduction and description of the architecture and then the analysis in Chapter 3. Here, you are presented with the most essential tools for performance analysis, and the respective results screens of the tools refer you to the background information and optimization options in Chapters 4 to 10. This way is advisable if you focus on the analysis of performance problems.

The second way is to first read the introduction and description of the architecture, and then read Chapters 4 to 9. This approach focuses on the optimization of ABAP coding and the background knowledge for the individual topics, not on performance analysis. This way is advisable if you are primarily interested in basic optimization techniques and background information for performance tuning.

The performance of an ABAP program also depends on the architecture of an SAP system. This chapter describes at which points the architecture plays a role for you as the ABAP developer.

2   SAP System Architecture for ABAP Developers

The following sections describe the architecture of an SAP system and which aspects are relevant for you as an ABAP developer with regard to performance.

Let's first discuss the different layers of an SAP system and their tasks.

2.1   SAP System Architecture

An SAP system extends over multiple logical layers. From the end user's point of view, software runs on the computer, the *client*.

This client is connected to the *server*, an SAP NetWeaver Application Server.

This application server, in turn, is connected to the database server. From the view of the database, the SAP NetWeaver application server, or more precisely, a process or thread of the application server, is a client of the database server.

In the simplest case, an SAP system comprises the following three layers: *presentation layer, application layer*, and *database layer.* Internet accesses may include further layers.

The aim of these different layers is to distribute user requests across multiple application servers. The following takes a closer look at the traditional *three-layer architecture*. All performance aspects of this architecture also apply to models with more than the three mentioned layers with regard to ABAP development.

The load distribution across the software layers plays a central role in SAP administration. For more detailed information on this topic, refer to the current editions of the two books, *SAP Performance Optimization Guide (5th edition)* by Thomas Schneider and *SAP NetWeaver AS ABAP System Administration* by Frank Föse, Sigrid Hagemann, and Liane Will (both Boston, SAP PRESS 2008).

2.1.1 Three-Layer Architecture

The three different logical layers of the three-layer architecture are the following.

- ▶ Presentation layer
- ▶ Application layer
- ▶ Database layer

These three layers take over different tasks for the processing of user requests.

Presentation Layer

The *presentation layer* establishes the connection between the user and the SAP system. Here, the system receives the entries of users and presents the results of queries.

From a technical standpoint, the presentation layer is a program, for example, SAP Graphical User Interface (SAP GUI), SAP NetWeaver Business Client, SAP Business Explorer (BEx), or an Internet browser. It can also be programs that access the SAP NetWeaver Application Server as a Remote Function Call (RFC) client or a Web services consumer.

While in older SAP releases (older than 4.6) virtually every interaction of the user resulted in a request in the system, releases higher or equal to 4.6C use control elements that enable the execution of actions on the user's screen without starting a request to the application layer. The expansion of nodes in trees, for example, is one of those actions that doesn't require a new call to the application layer if all data was transferred to the presentation layer. Another example is the editor that executes many actions at the presentation layer that don't require any requests to the application layer (roundtrip).

Application Layer

From a technical point of view, the application layer consists of one or more SAP NetWeaver Application Servers (SAP NetWeaver AS). An SAP NetWeaver AS can consist of two *stacks*. There is an ABAP stack (SAP NetWeaver AS ABAP) and a Java stack (SAP NetWeaver AS Java), which are responsible for the execution of the ABAP or Java programs, respectively.

Depending on the used SAP solution, you only require one or both stacks (double stack). A majority of the business logic still runs on SAP NetWeaver AS ABAP, while AS Java uses middleware and applications for data formatting at the frontend (for instance, SAP NetWeaver Portal, Web Dynpro Java).

SAP NetWeaver AS ABAP consists of multiple processes that assume different tasks. Section 1.2, Performance Aspects of the Architecture, discusses some of these processes in greater detail.

The actual processing of the ABAP source code is carried out in the application layer on SAP NetWeaver AS ABAP. An ABAP Virtual Machine (VM) executes all ABAP commands in the application layer. Only the database commands that must be executed in the database are excluded because they are passed on to the database.

Database Layer

The database layer executes the data retention; all data of the SAP system are stored permanently. In addition to the application data, for example, the customer or order data, you also store technical data of the SAP system in the database. For example, the source code texts of the ABAP programs as well as their binary, executable units (*ABAP loads*) are stored in the database.

From a technical viewpoint, the database — similar to SAP NetWeaver AS ABAP — is a collection of processes or threads that fulfill different functions, whereas the processes or threads have access to a common main memory.

2.1.2 Distribution of the Three Layers

Figure 2.1 shows a schematic diagram of the SAP architecture.

The diagram includes the three layers: presentation, application, and database. At the application tier, you can view a *double-stack system*, an SAP NetWeaver Application Server (SAP NetWeaver AS), which includes both an ABAP stack (AS ABAP) and a Java stack (AS Java).

The figure shows a logic display of the layers and of the SAP NetWeaver AS. The following two sections describe how you can distribute the layers across multiple computers.

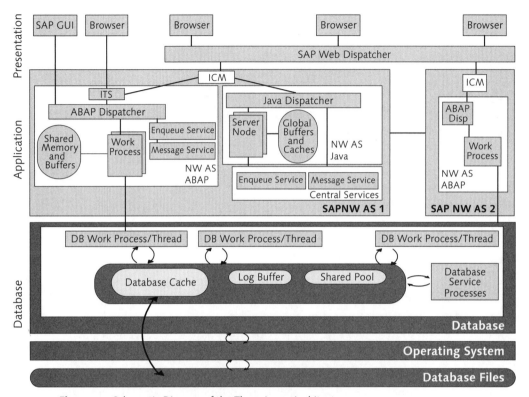

Figure 2.1 Schematic Diagram of the Three-Layer Architecture

A distinction is made between vertical distribution and horizontal distribution.

Vertical Distribution

In theory, all layers could run on one single piece of hardware, for example, a laptop. However, this is only an option for demonstration systems; for larger systems, a *vertical distribution is required*. For smaller systems, the presentation layer is usually localized on a user PC, while the application layer and the database layer run on a server. For larger systems, you have the option to separate the application layer from the database layer.

Horizontal Distribution

For the presentation tier, one frontend runs for each user on a PC or laptop; the presentation layer or the various frontends are distributed horizontally across multiple computers. A single frontend is not scalable because it cannot be distributed across multiple computers.

The application layer is distributed across one or more computers in the form of multiple SAP NetWeaver Application Servers. The number of necessary SAP NetWeaver Application Servers is specified depending on the capacity of a server and the number of users or the throughput a system must provide. This is the central task of sizing and SAP system administration. You can find further information in the SAP Service Marketplace under *http://service.sap.com/sizing* or in the SAP PRESS Essentials Guide 27, *Sizing SAP Systems*, by Susanne Janssen and Ulrich Marquard (Boston, Galileo Press 2007).

Usually, the database runs centrally on a server. In special installations, it can also be distributed across multiple servers. Currently, this type of distribution of the database across multiple servers is not supported by every database manufacturer and cannot be found often. The distribution of databases across multiple computers is not further discussed in this book because it is independent of the subjects detailed here.

2.2   Performance Aspects of the Architecture

As mentioned previously, you can distribute the respective layers vertically across different computers; the horizontal distribution, however, has some limitations. For example, you cannot distribute a single frontend across multiple computers. Furthermore, there are central resources for the application layer that cannot be distributed.

2.2.1 Frontend

The frontend is limited by the resources of *one* PC because it runs on a PC and cannot be distributed across multiple computers. The network connection to the frontend (bandwidth) is also limited. Therefore, the application developer must take into account that a sub-optimally programmed application can result in resource-intensive operations (memory, CPU, bandwidth) to and at the frontend.

Because an SAP system can include a high number of frontends, high resource utilization at the frontend possibly requires the expansion of the hardware resources of many frontend computers.

Section 9.5 in Chapter 9 describes in more detail which influence you as the developer have on the resource utilization to and at the frontend.

2.2.2 Application Layer

SAP NetWeaver AS ABAP consists of multiple processes that have access to the same main memory. The application layer always has a central instance in which you have some processes that perform special functions that are of such high significance that they cannot be distributed. These include the message service and the enqueue service. Furthermore, the application layer may have further instances across which the work processes can be distributed. Each of these instances has a dispatcher that manages the calls to the respective instance and distributes them across the free work processes.

Message Service

The message service assumes the load distribution in the SAP system and sends messages between the application servers. For example, it ensures communication and sends important status information between the application servers. This way, you can transfer enqueue messages to the enqueue service and to the remote instances.

Enqueue Service

The enqueue service receives lock requests for SAP lock objects and checks whether they collide with an already set lock in the enqueue table. As you must keep all logical SAP locks at a central point in the system (the enqueue table), the enqueue service can result in a bottleneck. As it must be ensured that the enqueue information remains consistent in the enqueue table, only one single process may change the enqueue table at a specific time.

Section 9.6 in Chapter 9 describes in more detail which influence you as the developer have on the use of the message service, the enqueue service, and the dispatcher.

2.2.3   Database

The database of the SAP system is another central point. Even if it can be distributed across multiple computers to a certain extent by means of special technologies in the case of IBM DB2 (Parallel Sysplex) and Oracle (RAC, Real Application Cluster), the database is still a resource that can be a bottleneck in an SAP system. Therefore, many tuning projects begin with the avoidance or reduction of database load.

Chapters 5 and 6 comprehensively describe the influence you as the developer have on the use of the database.

2.2.4   Summary

Scalable resources, such as the processes of an SAP NetWeaver AS, can be distributed across multiple servers. If a bottleneck emerges at this point, you can usually resolve it by adding additional hardware and expanding the resources to this hardware.

Central resources cannot be distributed across multiple computers or can have limitations for the distribution across multiple computers, as is the case for the database. For this reason, use these resources particularly sparingly and don't load them with unnecessary or inefficient queries. An overload of central resources can negatively influence the entire system in the long run. Therefore, central resources can represent the limiting factor for benchmark tests as well as in live operation.

Logic bottlenecks due to locks can be another limiting factor. These are discussed in Chapter 4.

Figure 2.2 highlights the parts of the response time that you as the developer can directly influence. All other components of the response time depend on the system configuration and system load and cannot be influenced directly by the developer. *SAP Performance Optimization Guide* by Thomas Schneider (Boston, SAP PRESS 2008) provides a detailed description of the other components of the response time.

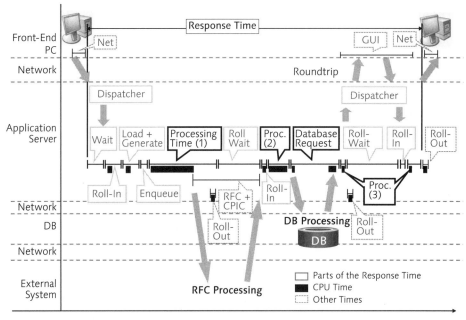

Figure 2.2 Parts of the Response Time That Can be Influenced by the Developer

To analyze the performance of ABAP applications, you are provided with different tools whose functioning and use is described in the following chapter.

3 Performance Analysis Tools

This chapter details which programs you can use for the runtime analysis, when and how they are used, and which procedure is recommended for the use of these tools.

For the performance analysis of ABAP programs, several tools that you can use for the analysis of performance problems at different points in time are given. This chapter initially provides a brief overview of the existing tools and shows when you can work with these tools. This is followed by a description of how you can use these tools to analyze the performance of ABAP programs. However, descriptions of all options of the tools are not included because this would go beyond the scope of this chapter. Instead, the most important options for performance analysis using the respective tools and the common methods and procedures of performance analysis are described.

With the respective analysis results, you can find references to the appropriate background information and the tuning tips contained in this book.

Not all tools discussed here are special performance tools. Some of them are development tools or tools for system administration that you can use to record performance-relevant data. This chapter also discusses the use of these tools to determine this data.

Section 3.3.14, E2E Trace, is dedicated to the E2E trace (End-to-End) for the analysis of SAP NetWeaver AS ABAP. This chapter concludes with tips for performance analysis.

3.1 Overview of Tools

The traditional and most important tools for performance analysis undoubtedly are the *single records statistics* (Transaction STAD) and the traces, *ABAP trace* (Transaction SE30), and *SQL trace* (one part of the performance traces — Transaction

ST05). In addition, there are other tools that contain interesting performance-relevant data. For these tools, the first part briefly discusses the usage, the second part describes at what point these tools are used, and the third part outlines their uses.

Table 3.1 contains an overview of the tools and their usage. The order does not indicate any prioritization.

Transaction	Description
SE30 ABAP Trace	With the runtime analysis, you can analyze the performance of ABAP programs.
ST05 Performance Trace— SQL Trace	With the SQL trace, you can trace which database accesses occur to the database, how long they take, and how many data records are processed.
ST05 Performance Trace— Buffer Trace	With the table buffer trace, you can analyze which accesses occur to the table buffer, how long they take, and how the table buffer is loaded.
ST05 Performance Trace— RFC Trace	With the RFC trace, you can trace which remote calls your application executes, in which direction they go, what quantity of data was transferred, and how long the calls took.
ST05 Performance Trace— Enqueue Trace	With the enqueue trace, you can determine which enqueue requests your application or the SAP system executes on which lock objects, and which parameters the system uses for these enqueues.
ST12 ABAP and Performance Trace	Using Transaction ST12, you can start Transactions SE30 and ST05 together. Furthermore, you can evaluate the ABAP trace with additional options in comparison to Transaction SE30.
STAD Business Transaction Analysis	The statistical records display enables you to display the statistic records of applications and evaluate them.
SCI SAP Code Inspector	You can use the SAP Code Inspector to check the ABAP programs with regard to performance, security, syntax, and the adherence to naming conventions.
SM50/SM66 Work Process Monitor	You can use the Work Process Monitors to obtain information about the currently running processes.

Table 3.1 Overview of the Tools for Performance Analysis

Transaction	Description
S_MEMORY_INSPECTOR Memory Inspector	The Memory Inspector is a tool to display and analyze memory snapshots.
ST22 ABAP Dump Analysis	If a runtime error occurred in an ABAP program, you have the option to access the information associated with the termination and analyze it.
OK-Code /h or /ha ABAP Debugger	The Debugger is an analysis tool that executes ABAP programs by line or by section. You can use the ABAP Debugger to display the contents of data objects and to check the flow logic of programs.
DB05 Selectivity Analysis	You can use the selectivity analysis to analyze the number of unique values of a field (or of field combinations) of a database table. Furthermore, you can use this transaction to determine the size of the tables that are supposed to be buffered.
ST10 Table Call Statistics	Based on the table call statistics, you can have the system display the call statistics for buffered or unbuffered tables. For buffered tables, the system displays the status of the table in the buffer.
E2E Trace End-to-End Trace	Based on the end-to-end trace, you can record traces across system boundaries by inheriting trace flags. It is also possible to trace non-ABAP systems (for instance, Java instances).

Table 3.1 Overview of the Tools for Performance Analysis (Cont.)

3.2 Usage Time of Tools

The tools can be used at different points in time and in different systems. For the SAP systems, you can distinguish development, testing, and production. For a program, you differentiate development, runtime, and post runtime.

Let's first have a look at the development, testing, and production phases. Figure 3.1 shows when it is best to use the tools in these phases.

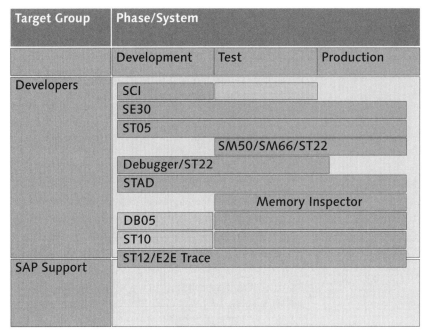

Target Group	Phase/System		
	Development	Test	Production
Developers	SCI		
	SE30		
	ST05		
		SM50/SM66/ST22	
	Debugger/ST22		
	STAD		
		Memory Inspector	
	DB05		
	ST10		
SAP Support	ST12/E2E Trace		

Figure 3.1 Use of Tools in Development, Testing, and Production

Most tools can be used in all phases. The *Code Inspector* (Transaction SCI) should ideally be used during the development. Transactions STAD and DB05 require representative test data if used in development.

The Work Process Monitors and the SAP Memory Inspector are usually used if the programs can already access certain (test) datasets. This is particularly the case in the testing and, of course, in the production phase. The Debugger is mainly used during the development and in testing, and it should therefore be used only in exceptional cases during the production phase. The selectivity analysis of Transaction DB05 should only be used in the production system in exceptional cases, for example, if no representative test data is available on other systems. In any case, it should be performed for larger evaluations in periods of low loads. All other tools are usually used in all phases.

For the development, runtime, and post runtime phases, things look a bit different, as seen in Figure 3.2.

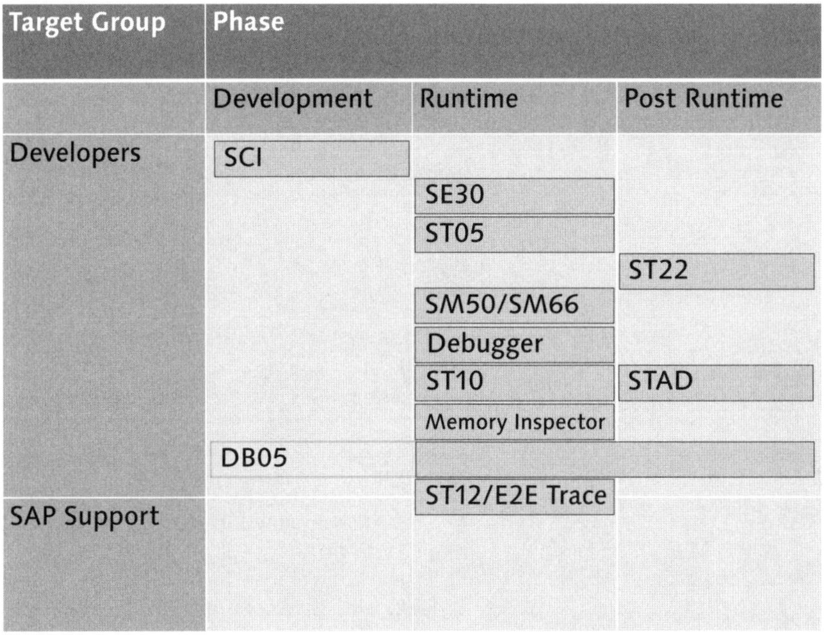

Target Group	Phase		
	Development	Runtime	Post Runtime
Developers	SCI		
		SE30	
		ST05	
			ST22
		SM50/SM66	
		Debugger	
		ST10	STAD
		Memory Inspector	
	DB05		
SAP Support		ST12/E2E Trace	

Figure 3.2 Use of Tools in Development, Runtime, and Post Runtime

The Code Inspector (Transaction SCI) can be used, for example, during development because it doesn't evaluate any runtime data but refers to the static code of a program. Most tools can be used during the runtime of a program only. These are either traces that record the execution of various commands or certain monitors for analyzing data only available or of significance at runtime. Only the selectivity analysis (Transaction DB05) can be used independently of the phases; however, representative test data should be available.

Transaction STAD is a very important tool because it is always available (doesn't need to be activated) and provides a good overview of the runtime of applications.

In performance analysis, the traces provide the information content with the highest level of detail because they measure the runtime information for individual statements. Figure 3.3 shows the architecture overview and indicates for which areas traces are available.

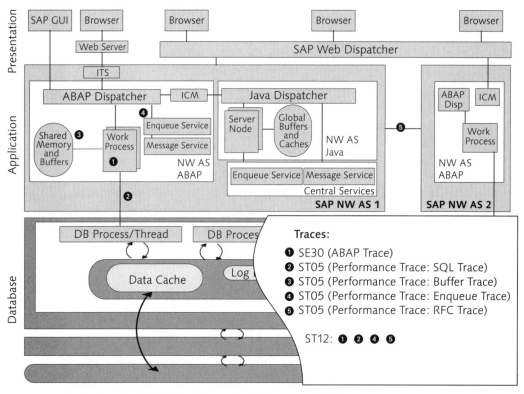

Figure 3.3 The Most Critical Traces for Performance Analysis

The next section describes the respective tools and procedures in detail.

3.3   Analysis and Tools in Detail

Let's start with the tools that you use during development.

These include the *SAP Code Inspector* (Transaction SCI) and the *selectivity analysis* (Transaction DB05).

3.3.1   SAP Code Inspector (Transaction SCI)

The Code Inspector enables analyses of the static definition of ABAP code and further repository objects. Within the scope of automated performance tests using Transaction ST30, the Code Inspector also supports the analysis of SQL traces, that is, dynamically executed code. This option is not further detailed here; the following discusses the analysis of the static definitions.

In comparison to the dynamic test tools (traces), the SAP Code Inspector benefits by examining the entire coding, while the traces only examine the executed code parts. Due to the static tests, the notifications of the SAP Code Inspector provide information about potential problems, while the results of the traces are measured values that indicate definitive problems.

The Code Inspector is based on an extensible test framework and can be used for single object analyses or mass testing. The SAP Code Inspector has been generally available since Release 6.10 of AS ABAP. A version also exists for Release 4.6C, which is available via SAP Note 543359. The target groups for which the SAP Code Inspector was developed are ABAP developers and quality managers.

The SAP Code Inspector covers different categories of tests. These include, for example, general checks, performance checks, security checks, syntax checks/generation, programming conventions, metrics and statistics, user interfaces, search functions, application checks, and so on.

You can select, configure, and store the individual tests within a category in a *check variant*. Furthermore, you can create object sets (ABAP programs and other repository objects). An inspection executes the check variant on the object set. The online help provides you with documentation on how you create check variants, object sets, and inspections. The following focuses on the checks from the performance category. An extensive description of all functions provided by the SAP Code Inspector would go beyond the scope of this chapter. The online help describes how you can create inspections with check variants and object sets.

However, there is also a direct approach for the individual developers who want to check the program with the Code Inspector. They can select the OBJECT (PROGRAM, FUNCTIONAL MODULE, CLASS, …) • CHECK • CODE INSPECTOR menu in the ABAP Workbench (or the other developer Transactions SE38, SE24, SE37) or use Transaction SCII, which directly navigates to the ad-hoc inspection. The system executes the global check variant with the call from the respective development transactions by default if the developer hasn't created any user specific default variant. By contrast, for the ad-hoc inspection, you can select another check variant using Transaction SCII or configure a temporary check variant.

The Performance Check Category

The following briefly discusses the performance checks that the SAP Code Inspector implements. You can find a corresponding reference for topics discussed in other chapters. For topics that are not explicitly detailed in other chapters, here is a brief description.

- **Analysis of WHERE condition for SELECT, UPDATE, and DELETE**
  In these checks, the system examines the WHERE conditions of the SQL statements. The checks refer to the existence of a WHERE condition (see Section 5.5 in Chapter 5) or to the index support of the fields in the WHERE condition (see Section 5.4 in Chapter 5). It does not consider buffered tables, joins, and views.

- **Analysis of the SELECT statements that bypass the SAP table buffer**
  Here, it is checked whether accesses bypass the table buffer. The check refers to the keywords in the coding or the key fields in the WHERE condition as well as the comparison condition (= or EQ). Section 6.4.3 in Chapter 6 details which checks the SAP Code Inspector implements.

- **Analysis of the SELECT statements** with **subsequent CHECK**
  This check examines the CHECK statements after the opening SELECT for SELECT/ENDSELECT statements. This retroactive filtering of data can often be changed into the specification of the condition in a WHERE condition. As a result, less data is read from the database (see Section 5.5 in Chapter 5).

- **Analysis of the SQL and DML statements in loops**
  These checks refer to the communication effort that arises in case of many database queries (see Section 5.7 in Chapter 5).

- **Nested loops**
  This check refers to nested loops. Depending on the access type, nested loops may result in a nonlinear runtime behavior (see Section 7.4.10 in Chapter 7).

- **Copy large data objects (nested tables, structures more than 1,000 bytes)**
  This check refers to the incurring overhead for copying for large data objects, for example, of nested internal tables (for which no table sharing is possible; see Section 7.4.9 in Chapter 7) and structures that have a width of more than 1,000 bytes (see Section 9.2 in Chapter 9).

- **Low performance operations on internal tables**
  These checks refer to non-optimized read accesses to internal tables (see Sections 7.4.1 to 7.4.4 in Chapter 7).

- **Low performance parameter transfers**
  This check examines whether potential performance improvements exist for the parameter transfer of a method, form, functional module, or event (see Section 9.2 in Chapter 9).

▶ **EXIT or no ABAP commands in SELECT/ENDSELECT loop**
With empty `SELECT/ENDSELECT` loops or those that only contain an `EXIT` statement, it is tried to check the existence of single records in a database table. Section 5.5.5 in Chapter 5 provides information on how you can program more efficient existence checks.

▶ **Instance creation of BAdIs**
As of SAP NetWeaver AS 7.00, you should use `GET BADI` instead of `CALL METHOD cl_exithandler=>get_instance` for performance reasons.

▶ **Table attribute check**
This check examines the technical settings (for example, transport attributes and the buffering) and the secondary indexes of database tables.

In addition, there are areas that cannot be tested statically due to their dynamics and the resulting complexity, for example, joins or views (see Section 5.4 in Chapter 5). To determine the join sequence of the tables, you usually implement a cost-based optimization at the database level. Rather, the analysis of the `WHERE` condition of the Code Inspector corresponds to a rule-based analysis. For these areas, it is still necessary to analyze the performance problems using ABAP and performance traces.

Implementing an Ad-Hoc Inspection and Results Analysis

Let's discuss the results analysis based on the example of an ad-hoc inspection. Once you've started Transaction SCII, the system displays a screen as shown in Figure 3.4.

In the OBJECT SELECTION in the upper part of the screen, you can specify the objects that are supposed to be checked. These objects can be a predefined object set, a transport request or task, or a single object. In Figure 3.4, a single object, the program Z_LONGRUNNER, was selected.

For the CHECK VARIANT, you can select a predefined check variant or configure a temporary check variant. In Figure 3.4, all performance checks were selected. A blue info button is given for each of these checks, which you can use to access the documentation on the check content. In addition to the description of the problem, in some cases, it also provides recommendations for resolving or avoiding the described problem. You can configure the individual checks with different parameters via the green button for multiple selections.

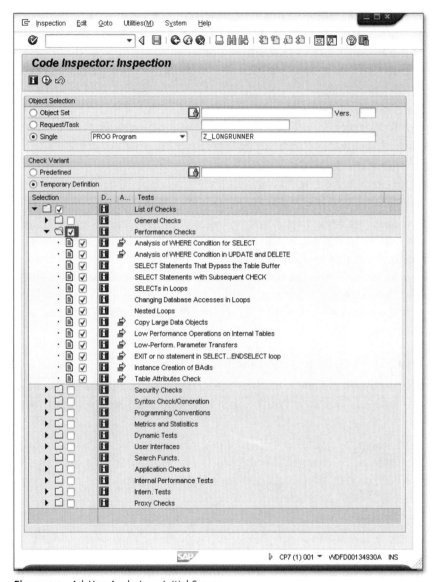

Figure 3.4 Ad-Hoc Analysis — Initial Screen

You start the inspection using the [F8] key or the EXECUTE button. The system then displays a results screen, which is similar to the one shown in Figure 3.5.

In this results screen, the results are displayed in a tree-like structure with the following layout.

1. Check category (for example, performance, syntax, etc.)

2. Check (analysis of the WHERE condition, SELECT statements in loops, etc.)

3. Error, warning, and information (depending on the severity)

4. Message code

5. Message text

Figure 3.5 Results Page of the Ad-Hoc Analysis

Here, as well, you can find the blue info button for the documentation of the check. In many cases, it provides information on when a check is classified as an error, warning, or information. If requested, change this classification in the main window of the Code Inspector (Transaction SCI) via GOTO • MANAGEMENT OF • MESSAGE PRIORITIES.

The message text contains information on the call position (program, include, row) and the actual message. By double-clicking the call position, the system directly forwards you to the call position in the respective ABAP program.

You obtain the solution to the corresponding problem in the ABAP program from the documentation (blue info button) that describes the respective problem and provides recommendations for the correction and from the additional information given in the course of this book (see the references at the beginning of this chapter).

> **Tip**
>
> If the test results are persisted or if larger sets of objects are supposed to be tested in the background (in parallel), you cannot use the ad-hoc inspection. For this case, it is advisable to use a "regular" inspection in which you combine an object set and check variant in one inspection. The corresponding procedure is described in the online help. You can repeat an inspection created this way multiple times. This option is frequently implemented in the quality assurance system within the scope of quality assurance measures for larger object sets.

Once again, the checks presented here are static checks. Regardless of the categorization into error classes, the Code Inspector doesn't provide information whether the respective program location contributes to the long runtimes significantly or not. To carry out time measurements, you must use Transaction STAD or run an ABAP or performance trace. These are discussed later in this chapter. However, this trace presupposes existing and good (production-similar) test data. Therefore, the Code Inspector is well suited to detect potential problems at a very early stage to resolve them as soon as possible (and consequently as cost-efficiently as possible). The SAP Developer Network provides some articles on the SAP Code Inspector under *https://www.sdn.sap.com/irj/sdn/wiki?path=/display/ABAP/Code+Inspector.*

3.3.2 Selectivity Analysis (Transaction DB05)

The use of Transaction DB05 assumes a representative data volume. The selectivity analysis is a tool to analyze the data distribution and to define the size of the tables that are supposed to be buffered. Usually, this tool for the selectivity analysis of fields is used for the index design and for the analysis of tables for table buffering.

To run a selectivity analysis, you must start Transaction DB05. The system displays an initial screen that is very similar to the one shown in Figure 3.6. In the TABLE field, enter the table that should be analyzed. In the lower part of the screen, specify whether the selectivity analysis is to be carried out for fields of the primary key or for freely specified fields. You can enter up to five fields. By activating the SUBMIT ANALYSIS IN BACKGROUND checkbox, you determine whether the analysis is to be implemented immediately in the dialog process or as a background job. You can find the result in Transaction SM37 in a background job, which was executed under your user name, in the job's spool.

For larger tables, select the option of the background job to not block the dialog process for too long or to not receive a timeout in the dialog.

In the example shown in Figure 3.6, the single-record buffered table T100, which contains message texts, was selected. The entered fields correspond to the fields of the primary index. Figure 3.7 shows the results screen.

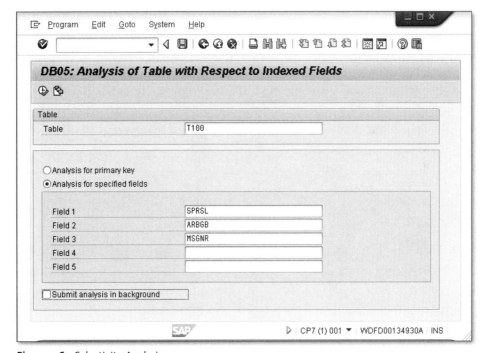

Figure 3.6 Selectivity Analysis

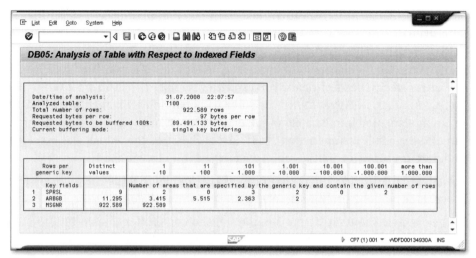

Figure 3.7 Results of the Selectivity Analysis

The upper area of the results screen contains the size analysis of the table. You can view the date, time, and the analyzed table, as well as the number of rows (cross-client) and the length of a row. Unicode and the fixed length of the fields in ABAP are taken into account here. These two values determine the memory use, which the table will require for a complete buffering in the table buffer. The last field indicates the current buffer state of the analyzed table.

For the table T100 shown in the example of Figure 3.7, this results in the values in Table 3.2.

Field	Value
Date/time of analysis	31.07.2008 – 22:08:43
Analyzed table	T100
Total number of rows	922,589 rows
Requested bytes per row	97 bytes per row
Requested bytes to be buffered 100%	89,491,133 bytes
Current buffering mode	single key buffering

Table 3.2 Size Analysis of the Table T100

Table T100 would require approximately 87.4 MB for a complete buffering.

The lower part of the results screen shows a matrix that indicates the frequency of the value combinations of the selected fields. In the example of Figure 3.7, there are nine different values for the first field, SPRSL (language key). Two out of these nine values occur between one and ten times in the total of 922,589 rows. Three values between 101 and 1,000 times, two values between 1,001 and 10,000 times, and another two between 100,001 and 1,000,000 times. The last two values are the language keys DE for German and EN for English in this system.

In combination with the ARBGB field (application area), there are 11,295 different combinations for SPRSL and ARBGB whereof 3,415 combinations occur between one and ten times, 5,515 combinations between 11 and 100 times, 2,363 combinations between 101 and 1,000 times, and two combinations between 1,001 and 10,000 times.

For the combination of all three fields, SPRSL, ARBGB, and MSGNR (message number), there are 922,589 different combinations. This equates to the total of all rows because this combination includes the fields of the unique primary key. All 922,589 combinations occur between one and ten times, in this case exactly once.

Based on this information, you can make decisions on the table buffering (see Section 6.4.2 in Chapter 6). For the changeover of the current single record buffering to a generic buffering with two fields (SPRSL and ARBGB), you run the risk to buffer two generic areas that contain between 1,001 and 10,000 records. Multiplied by the length, this results in 2 × 10,000 records in the worst case — that is, approximately 2 MB must be read for the access to a message text if it is not available in the buffer. The predefined single record buffering is finely tuned. In addition to the size, which a table would require in a buffer, the use of and accesses to the table play a significant role (see Section 6.4 in Chapter 6).

However, you can use the analysis results not only for the decisions for the table buffering but also with certain limitations for the selectivity analysis of the database accesses during the analysis of the execution plans (see Section 5.4.5 in Chapter 5). In this case, you can view, for example, that a WHERE condition of SPRSL and ARBGB contains relatively unselective areas despite a considerably high number of distinct values (11,295). There are two combinations of SPRSL and ARBGB that could return between 1,001 and 10,000 data records (~ 0.1% to 1%), while there are also 3,415 combinations that only return one to ten data records (0.0001% to 0.001%). In this case, the selectivity depends on which combinations are queried. With Transaction DB05, you cannot carry out another analysis to specify *which* value combinations occur more often than others.

The question about *which* values occur more often can be answered via an SQL statement at database level:

```
SELECT sprsl, arbgb, COUNT(*)
FROM t100
GROUP by sprsl, arbgb
ORDER BY COUNT(*);
```

This SQL statement provides all combinations of the ARBGB and SPRSL fields as well as their frequencies — in ascending order. At the end of the output, the system displays the combinations that occur most frequently.

Transaction DB05 is an indispensable tool for the decision whether tables are supposed to be buffered and with regard to the size determination. Furthermore, it also provides some support for the selectivity and distribution analyses for SQL statements. Note, however, that in a production system you should implement the analysis of large tables only in periods of low loads.

The next sections describe the tools that you can use for the performance analysis during the runtime of ABAP programs.

3.3.3 Process Analysis (Transactions SM50/SM66) — Status of a Program

Process analysis is a tool for system administration and contains many functions and analysis options whose descriptions go far beyond the scope of this chapter. But it can also be used within the scope of a performance analysis of ABAP programs; usually, when it concerns programs that have a longer runtime — for example, programs that run in the background or in the dialog for a longer period of time. Programs with a short runtime are analyzed using different tools, which are described later on.

Let's assume that a program runs longer than expected. If the program is still running, use process analysis to find what the program is doing. You can therefore specify which steps must be initiated to analyze the performance more precisely. For this approach, you only obtain information on the actions executed at the time of monitoring. So, you can neither analyze past actions nor future actions that are still to be executed in the program.

An ABAP work process can assume four statuses:

1. WAITING — The process is interactive and freely available for queries.
2. RUNNING — The process is executing an ABAP program.
3. ON HOLD — The process is idle and *waits*. This involves a real waiting, for example, for the release of a resource or termination of a synchronous RFC (Remote Function Call).
4. STOPPED — The process was aborted and not restarted.

For the analysis of an ABAP application, the following considers the RUNNING and ON HOLD statuses because they display the status of the work process during the execution of an ABAP program.

For the ON HOLD status, you can determine the reason for the wait situation of the ABAP program from the REASON column. The ⌜F1⌟ help of this field displays a list of all possible wait reasons and their descriptions.

Except for the RFC, PRIV, ENQ, and DEBUG wait reasons, all other wait situations refer to the system administration and must be analyzed by the system administration department.

For the RUNNING status, you can obtain further information in the ACTION column. In principle, there are three actions:

▶ **Database actions**
These include SEQUENTIAL READ, DIRECT READ, INSERT, UPDATE, DELETE, and COMMIT. This means that the database process or database thread that belongs to the work process is currently occupied with one of these actions. You can find the associated table in the TABLE column.

▶ **SAP system actions**
These include LOAD REPORT, LOAD CUA, ROLL-IN, and ROLL-OUT. This means that the process is occupied with an action on the SAP system side, for example, a program load. If a program is occupied with these actions for a longer period of time or repeatedly, the system administration must carry out an analysis because these wait situations should occur only rarely.

▶ **No action (the action field is empty)**
This usually involves the actual ABAP processing, and includes the execution of loops or reads in the ABAP program, for example. You can monitor it well on the basis of the CPU consumption of the work process. You can have the system display the CPU consumption of the work processes by selecting the CPU button (⊙, see Figure 3.8). Provided that increases between two updates, the process consumes CPU time, which is caused by the execution of ABAP code.

To find out what an ABAP program currently does or where the runtime is consumed, refresh the process monitor several times consecutively using ⌜F8⌟. You can then view whether the ABAP program is waiting (ON HOLD status) and possibly what the program is waiting for or whether the ABAP program is running (RUNNING status) and which actions are executed (database, SAP system, or ABAP). You can determine the next analysis steps based on this result:

If an ABAP program runs and executes database actions, you can further analyze the currently running SQL statement in the database monitor (Transaction ST04) using an SQL trace (Transaction ST05) or together with the system and database administration. In case of SAP system actions (for example, LOAD REPORT) the SAP system administrators must examine the problem in more detail.

If an ABAP program runs and shows no action, it most likely involves an ABAP processing that you can analyze more comprehensively via the ABAP trace (Transactions SE30/ST12).

Transaction SM50 is a *local* process overview of the application server to which you are currently logged on, whereas Transaction SM66 is the *global* process overview. You could use the SETTINGS button to deactivate the option, DISPLAY ONLY ABBREVIATED INFORMATION, AVOID RFC. If this setting is activated, Transaction SM66 reads the information from the message server; if this function is deactivated, however, the data is read via RFC. Only then can you view all information, as is the case for Transaction SM50.

Furthermore, the *local* process overview provides the option to view the details of an ABAP program if you double-click the respective row. There, the system displays the number of database calls, the processing records, and the required time. Further below in this screen, you can find information on the current memory use. This is a part of the data that is written to the single record statistics (see Section 3.3.15, Single Record Statistics (Transaction STAD)) after the conclusion of the transaction step.

Figures 3.8 and 3.9 show the local process overview and the details of a selected process.

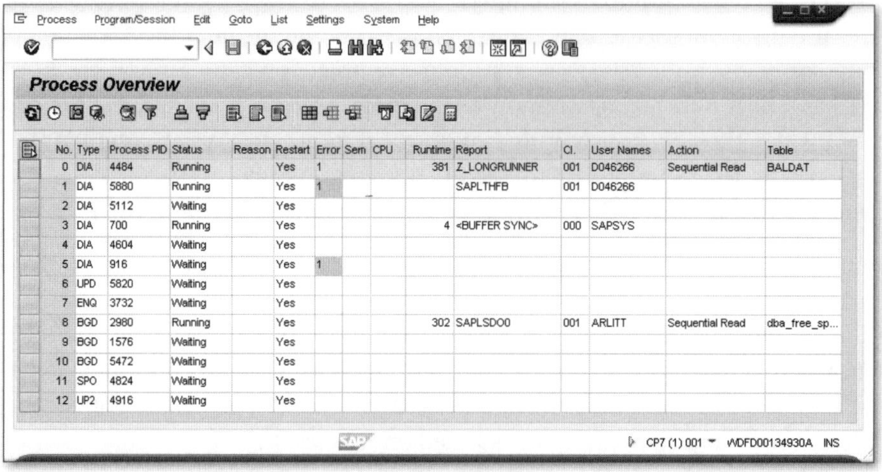

Figure 3.8 Local Process Overview (Transaction SM50)

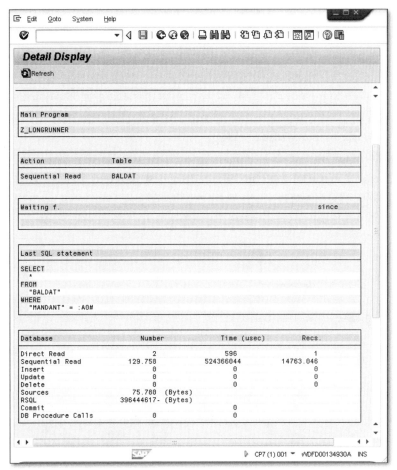

Figure 3.9 Details of the Selected Process in Transaction SM50

The process analysis enables you to find out what a program does during the analysis. You can establish whether a program is in a database action, wait situation, or ABAP execution to then continue the analysis with a more detailed tool (trace). Via the detail view (double-click on the row of the process), you obtain an overview of the previously recorded database processing (calls, row, time) and the current memory use of the program.

3.3.4 Debugger — Memory Analysis

Of course, the Debugger is mainly used for troubleshooting during the development and for the analysis of the program flow. The complete functional scope of the Debugger is not the topic of this book; it only describes how you can use it to analyze the memory use of internal tables used by a program.

Large internal tables can negatively influence the runtime (and the memory use) particularly if the accesses to the tables are not optimal (see Section 7.4 in Chapter 7).

In the Debugger, use the memory analysis to view a list of the largest data objects.

Another function of the Debugger is the creation of memory snapshots for the further analysis in the Memory Inspector.

Figure 3.10 shows how you call these functions in the new Debugger. Display the memory analysis tool by clicking on the button for a new tool and then select the memory analysis below the special tools, as shown in step 1 in Figure 3.10. The initial screen shows how much memory the analyzed internal mode allocates or uses.

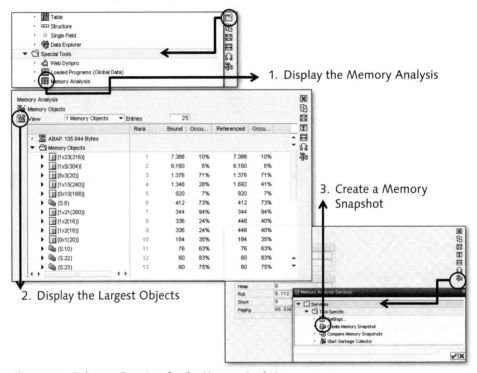

Figure 3.10 Debugger Functions for the Memory Analysis

For the list of the largest objects, you can use the MEMORY OBJECTS button to display the list of the largest memory objects (see step 2 in Figure 3.10). These memory objects may include internal tables, objects, anonymous data objects, or strings. This list indicates the largest objects in descending order.

In addition, you can create a memory snapshot for the Memory Inspector, which is detailed in the following. For this purpose, select the SERVICES OF THE TOOL button to create a memory snapshot as seen in step 3 of Figure 3.10. In the classic Debugger, you can create a memory snapshot via the DEVELOPMENT • MEMORY ANALYSIS • CREATE MEMORY SNAPSHOT menu path.

Experience has shown that large internal tables cause runtime problems for inefficient table accesses (see Section 7.4 in Chapter 7), which is why they are described more closely in this book. For inefficient access to internal tables, it is very likely that the large internal tables are responsible for the runtime problems.

3.3.5 Memory Inspector (Transaction S_MEMORY_INSPECTOR)

The SAP Memory Inspector (Transaction S_MEMORY_INSPECTOR) is used for the analysis of memory snapshots. This section presents a comparison analysis of two snapshots, which should be used to determine the tables with the most significant growth. The functional scope of the Memory Inspector is considerably larger than illustrated here; a complete overview of all functions is beyond the scope of this chapter.

The Memory Inspector considers dynamic data objects, such as internal tables, strings, objects, and anonymous data objects. This section only involves internal tables because large or continuously growing internal tables are most likely to cause performance problems in a program if these tables are processed inefficiently.

Before starting the analysis, let's first briefly discuss how you can create memory snapshots. In addition to the methods presented in Section 3.3.4, Debugger — Memory Analysis, for the creation of memory snapshots in the Debugger, you also have these other options:

1. Via the /HMUSA OK code (Memory Usage), you can create a memory snapshot at any place if the work process is available and not blocked for requests.

2. You can also use the SYSTEM • UTILITIES • MEMORY ANALYSIS • CREATE MEMORY SNAPSHOT menu path.

3. A third and last variant is the creation of a memory snapshot from an ABAP program using the method, CL_ABAP_MEMORY_UTILITIES => WRITE_MEMORY_CON-SUMPTION_FILE(...). You should only use it for debugging or testing purposes and sufficiently protect it to avoid an excessively frequent creation of memory snapshots.

To call the Memory Inspector, you can either use Transaction code S_MEMORY_INSPECTOR, the services of the memory analysis tool in the Debugger (COMPARE

Memory Snapshots), or the System • Utilities • Memory Analysis • Compare Memory Snapshots menu path.

When you start the Memory Inspector, the system displays a screen that is split into two parts (see Figure 3.11).

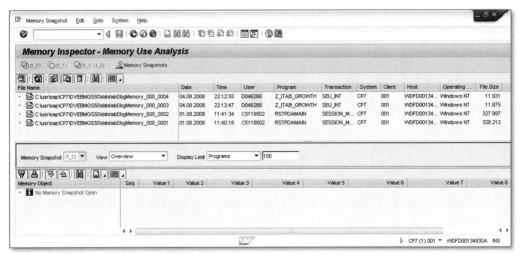

Figure 3.11 Initial Screen of the Memory Inspector

You can find the individual memory snapshots in the upper area of the screen. To be able to compare the two memory snapshots, double-click the first and second files of the memory snapshot. Select (T1-T0) in the left dropdown box in the middle area of the screen. The system displays a screen as shown in Figure 3.12.

The results screen can be read as follows.

On the left-hand side, you can view a list of data objects, in this case, the internal tables. The red names that start with a plus sign (first row below the total) are data objects that have not existed for the first memory snapshot (T0) but were created prior to the second snapshot (T1). The blue rows that start with a minus sign (fourth row below the total) are objects that existed at the time T0, but not at the time T1, that is, they were deleted in the meantime. For the black rows, the objects existed at both times. The columns for Value 1 to Value 8 indicate the changes. In this case also, the rule applies that red values stand for growth, blue values for reduction, and black values for no changes.

By means of this analysis method, you can quickly determine the large internal tables or which internal tables grow. This method can also be used for other dynamic data objects.

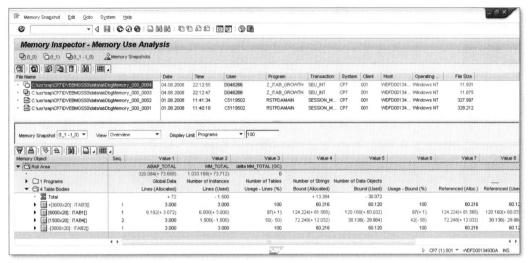

Figure 3.12 Comparing Two Snapshots

This section was supposed to describe how you can use the Memory Inspector for the analysis of large data objects based on internal tables. Chapter 7 discusses the allocation and deallocation of internal tables together with all other performance-relevant aspects.

3.3.6 Transaction ST10 — Table Call Statistics

Transaction ST10 helps you analyze the call statistics for database tables. The system administrators can analyze the buffered table using these statistics to check the efficiency of the buffer setting. Furthermore, they can then analyze unbuffered tables whether they are technically suitable for a buffering (number of changes). Moreover, the application developers must definitely provide a logic analysis for support (May tables be buffered from the business point of view?). These topics concern system administration and are discussed in detail in *SAP Performance Optimization Guide* by Thomas Schneider (Boston, SAP PRESS 2008). For ABAP developers, the check of the current buffer state of the used tables is interesting within the scope of the performance analysis. This is described in the following.

Transaction ST10 was assigned to the analysis at runtime to point out that the state of the buffered tables should be analyzed promptly, that is, at runtime, because the state of the buffered tables may change. You should not use Transaction ST10 until it is ensured that it is not the SQL statement that prevents the access to the buffer (see Section 6.4 in Chapter 6).

To determine the buffer state of a table, start Transaction ST10 and select the settings for the generically or single-record buffered tables depending on which buffer area you want to analyze. Leave the SINCE STARTUP setting unchanged and select the current application server under SERVER, which you access at the moment or another one depending on the server for which you want to carry out the analysis. Figure 3.13 shows such a selection as an example.

Click the SHOW STATISTICS button to start the analysis. Because you must analyze the respective table buffer, the analysis may take some time.

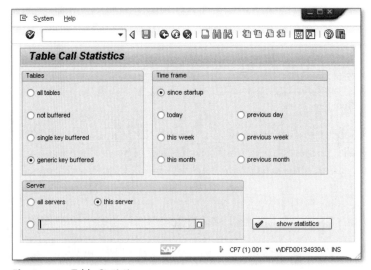

Figure 3.13 Table Statistics

You obtain a list of the generically or single-record buffered tables as shown in Figure 3.14. The system displays the buffer state for each table next to the table name. Section 6.4.3 in Chapter 6 describes the various states available. Furthermore, you can view the buffer setting (SNG, GEN, FUL) and other values about the call statistics that the system administrators require for the buffer analysis.

For example, the values of DIRECT READS indicate whether a table can be used for single record buffering, because SEQUENTIAL READS cannot be executed using the single record buffer because the unique key is not provided (see Section 6.4.3 in Chapter 6).

Based on the CHANGES values, you can view how many changing accesses exist. Relate them to the read accesses (SEQUENTIAL READS and DIRECT READS) to determine the change rate (see Section 6.4.2 in Chapter 6).

Figure 3.14 List of the Generically Buffered Tables

INVALIDATIONS enable you to specify how often the table was invalidated due to changes (see Section 6.4.3 in Chapter 6).

For you as the ABAP developer, the check for the existence of a table in the buffer is the most important check during the performance analysis of a program. For example, if you detect accesses to buffered tables in the SQL trace (Transaction ST05; see Section 3.3.8, Performance Trace — SQL Trace (Transaction ST05)), which bypass the buffer, you can use Transaction ST10 to check the existence of the table in the buffer. If it is available there, the system cannot read the table from the buffer due to the SQL statement (see Section 6.4.3 in Chapter 6).

If the table has a state other than VALID or MULTIPLE, contact the SAP system administrators for further analysis.

The MULTIPLE state indicates that a generic table buffers multiple generic areas that have different buffer states. For a more precise analysis, double-click the respective row to determine the generic areas and their states.

3.3.7   Performance Trace — General Information (Transaction ST05)

This section focuses on the performance trace. This entails the general topics that must be taken into account for the performance trace.

The performance trace is subdivided into the following areas:

1. SQL trace
2. RFC trace
3. Enqueue trace
4. Table buffer trace

The SQL trace is the most important and most frequently used trace among the performance traces.

All traces have in common that they work at the application server level. That means that only *one* user can activate the trace per application server, and the system only records the actions of this application server.

For this reason, check in the TRACE STATUS FIELD whether a trace is already active after you've started Transaction ST05. If so, you can activate your trace only when other traces are no longer active.

Figure 3.15 shows the corresponding screen. To activate a performance trace, select the trace you want to activate in the top left area of the screen. Here, you can select multiple different or all traces. In the right-hand area, you can select the ACTIVATE TRACE button to activate the trace for your own user on this server. Using the ACTIVATE TRACE WITH FILTER button, you can activate the trace for another user or specify further restrictions, for example, certain programs or transactions, or a specific process number. You also have the option to filter for specific tables or exclude tables from recording. As soon as you've activated the trace, the TRACE STATUS field indicates the activated traces and the recording starts. Currently executed actions started prior to the activation of the trace cannot be viewed in the trace; the system records all actions that started after the activation.

After the transactions that were supposed to be analyzed have been completed, you should deactivate the trace again. The trace information is written to files on the respective application server. The size of these files is predefined to prevent an overflow of the file system. If necessary, these files are overwritten at regular intervals. If this occurs during a recording, that is, the beginning of the file was overwritten, the system notifies you accordingly during the evaluation of the trace.

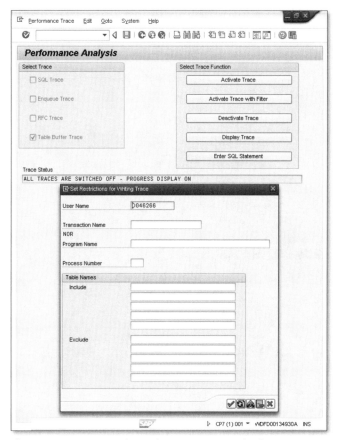

Figure 3.15 Activating the Performance Trace with Filter

To display the trace results, select the DISPLAY TRACE button after the trace was completed. The system automatically enters the start and end times as well as the filter options of the last trace recording. However, you can change them at any time to view the traces of other users or traces with different periods of time. But you must note that the trace is stored at the application server level and you must log on to the same server on which the trace was created, so you can view it again later.

In the top right area (Figure 3.16), formatting options for the basic list are given. You can also switch from the simple to the extended trace list (including more columns) later. If more than 5,000 trace records were written, the system prompts you whether you want to view only the initial 5,000 trace records or all records if you set the NUMBER OF TRACE RECORDS filter to 5,000. Of course, you can change the number of records to be displayed.

If the system wrote a high number of SQL statements, the evaluation of more than 5,000 trace records may consume a lot of time. Figure 3.16 shows the corresponding options for the display of traces.

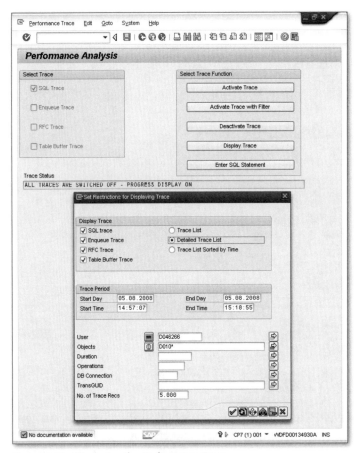

Figure 3.16 Displaying the Performance Trace

> **Tip**
>
> Via the PERFORMANCE TRACE • SAVE TRACE menu path, you can save the recorded traces. A dialog window similar to the one for the evaluation of traces opens in which you specify the data to be saved. It is then written to a new file and cannot be overwritten any longer. Via the PERFORMANCE TRACE • DISPLAY SAVED TRACE or DELETE SAVED TRACE menu, you can display or delete a saved trace.
>
> Via the PERFORMANCE TRACE • DISPLAY TRACE WITHOUT PRIOR DEACTIVATION menu, you can display already recorded trace records during the trace recording. (Note: In older support package levels, this option is named DISPLAY TRACE OR DEACTIVATE FIRST).

The following four sections discuss the respective results of the traces in detail, and you can find the references to the respective basics chapters in this book.

3.3.8 Performance Trace — SQL Trace (Transaction ST05)

Besides the ABAP trace (Transaction SE30), the SQL trace (Transaction ST05) is certainly one of the most important traces for performance analysis. For this reason, the following discusses the SQL trace in great detail.

By means of the SQL trace, you can analyze all database statements that were sent from the DBI (Database Interface) to the database. With this trace, you can log which statements were sent to the database, how long they took, and how they were formatted. Due to the translation from Open SQL to Native SQL in the DBI, you can view the Native SQL commands for the respective database in the SQL trace (see the examples in Section 5.7 in Chapter 5). Furthermore, you can view which values were used for the execution of a statement. You can also specify where COMMIT statements were triggered and which statements were executed repeatedly.

At this point, you should just note the following: The measurement data is collected by the SAP system (see Figure 3.3) and it contains all information about what happens between the database interface and the database. For example, the network communication or the time required in the database system also plays a role. However, some actions in the DBI, for example, actions on cluster tables, are not measured because they are at "higher levels" within the DBI. Usually, these times are negligible measured by the overall time. If you compare the measured times with a native SQL trace, which was created using the respective tools of the database, differences may occur due to the reasons described earlier.

The results screen of the SQL trace start with the (extended) trace list. From this trace list, you can navigate to the other details or aggregated views. The trace lists contains all details. The SQL statement summary provides the best overview. It includes a summary of all information of the trace aggregated at the statement level. The IDENTICAL SELECTS view is used for the analysis of the identically executed SQL statements. The TABLE SUMMARY view displays one row per SQL statement and table, and the aggregation of this view only displays an aggregated row per program and table. You can call all views from the menu of the trace list, whereas the aggregated table summary can only be called from the table summary. Figure 3.17 shows the options to navigate to the details or further aggregated views.

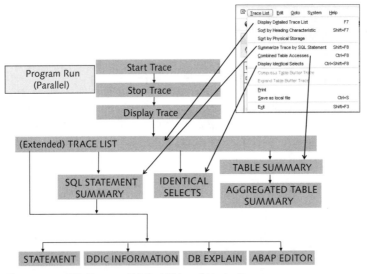

Figure 3.17 SQL Trace — Original List and Navigations

The following describes all views and the respective fields and functions. You can find references to the chapters in this book where appropriate.

Trace List

All trace lists (also the lists of the RFC, enqueue, and table buffer trace) have the block structure in common. The first row before the fields of the respective trace contains general information on the trace block. It includes:

1. The transaction that created the trace entries of this block

2. The number of the work process that executed the application

3. The work process type of this process at the time of recording

4. The client in which the trace was recorded

5. The user for whom the trace block was written

6. The transaction ID of the trace block

7. The date of the trace block

There can be one or multiple of such trace blocks in the trace. Under the trace block, you can find the respective entries of the trace regarding this block.

In Figures 3.18, 3.25, 3.27, 3.28, and 3.29, the first row shows information of the trace block before the trace information appears.

The trace list is available in a reduced and in an extended form. For the reduced form, some columns are not displayed. Table 3.3 includes all fields that are displayed in the extended list for the SQL trace.

Column	Description
HH:MM:SS.MS	Start time of the SQL statement
DURATION	Duration of the access in microseconds
PROGRAM	Name of the executing program
OBJECT NAME	Name of the table
OPERATION	Operation (see description after this table)
CURS	Number of the cursor
ARRAY	Maximum number of records that a package may contain
RECS.	Number of the processing (transferred) records
RC	Return code
CON	Connection (R/3, liveCache)
STATEMENT	The first 170 characters of the SQL statement

Table 3.3 Columns of the Extended SQL Trace List

There are different values for the operation, which are detailed in Table 3.4.

Operation	Meaning
DECLARE/ PREPARE	This concerns the compile or parse process of the SQL statement (see Section 5.2.2 in Chapter 5), which should not occur for frequently executed SQL statements because the statements should be located in the statement cache of the database (see Section 5.1 in Chapter 5).
OPEN/ REOPEN	Opens and reopens (with existing statement in the SQL cache) the cursor. You can execute the EXPLAIN function on this row.

Table 3.4 Possible Values of the "Operation" Column

Operation	Meaning
FETCH	Reading the data. Here, the system transfers the packages from database to the application server.
EXEC/ REEXEC	This is the execution of DML statements (INSERT, UPDATE, DELETE).
EXECSTA	COMMIT WORK

Table 3.4 Possible Values of the "Operation" Column (Cont.)

Figure 3.18 shows an extended trace list. It displays the executed SQL statements in their execution sequence. There are multiple rows for each statement that describe the individual operations, for instance, PREPARE, OPEN, FETCH, and so on.

Figure 3.18 SQL Trace — Extended Trace List

Multiple consecutive FETCH rows attract attention here. This is an SQL statement that reads larger sets of data records, namely 956 records (8 × 113 + 52). The return code 1403 (database-specific) indicates that there are no further records. The time required for this statement is 34.719 microseconds (~34.7 milliseconds — the total of all times from PREPARE to the last FETCH). For such a statement, check the resulting set — as it is described in Section 5.5 in Chapter 5 — for whether further restrictions of the data records are possible on the application side.

Before discussing the individual functions in this list, let's first have a look at the SQL statement summary, which offers the same functions per statement as the extended trace list. For this reason, the functions are described after the SQL statement summary.

SQL Statement Summary

The SQL statement summary provides the best overview of the trace content. For this purpose, the system writes *one* row for each SQL statement *with the same structure*, in which all information regarding this statement is aggregated. With the same structure means that SQL statements only differing in the variable are aggregated in one row.

The following information in Table 3.5 is available.

Column	Description
EXECUTIONS	Number of executions of this statement
IDENTICAL	Percentage value of identical accesses. Identical means the identical statements with the same values in the WHERE condition. You calculate the percentage as follows: Number of identical execution / number of executions × 100.
DURATION	Required time in microseconds for *all executions* of the statement
RECORDS	Number of processed records for *all executions* of the statement
TIME/EXEC	Required time in microseconds *per execution*
REC/EXEC	Number of processed records *per execution*
AVGTIME/R	Average time for *one data record* (outliers are considered as well)
MINTIME/R	Minimum time for *one data record* (best value)
LENGTH	Length of a data record in bytes

Table 3.5 Information of the SQL Statement Summary

Column	Description
BTYPE	Buffer settings of a table. All accesses to buffered tables that are listed here bypassed the buffer.
TABTYPE	Table type (transparent, pool, cluster, view)
OBJ. NAME	Table name or first table in a view
SQL STATEMENT	The first 170 characters of the SQL statement

Table 3.5 Information of the SQL Statement Summary (Cont.)

Note that the list is grouped according to the last two columns (OBJ. NAME and SQL STATEMENT). Consequently, multiple call positions of an SQL statement on a table can be combined in one row. This summary is displayed as soon as you select such a row and want to display the call position. The system then displays a small dialog window in which you can view the call positions. Because the system only displays the first 170 characters of an SQL statement, it is possible that you view some statements that appear identical but are different after 170 characters. The displayed SQL statement can deviate from the Open SQL statement. In the SQL trace, you see the statement after it was translated from Open SQL to Native SQL.

Figure 3.19 shows an SQL statement summary. For each statement, it contains a row in which the values are aggregated. You can also view the previously mentioned statement to the BALDAT table at the end of the list. It was executed once and had a duration of 34.7 milliseconds.

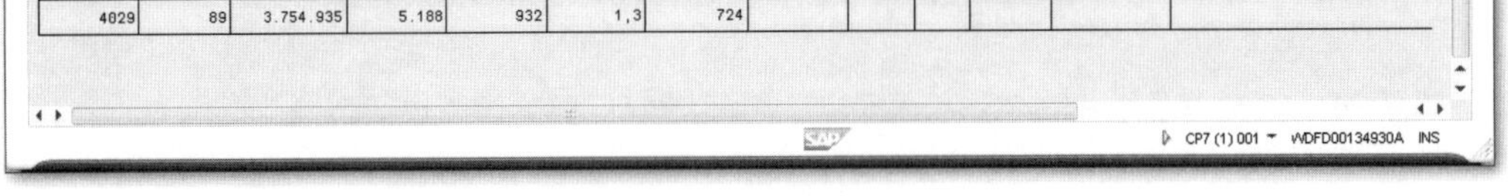

Executions	Identical	Duration	Records	Time/exec	Rec/exec.	AvgTime/R.	MinTime/R.	Length	BfTp	TabType	Obj. name	SQL statement
2.116	100	2.575.370	2.116	1.217	1,0	1.217	1.138	520		TRANSP	BALHDR	SELECT WHERE "MANDANT" = :A0
956	100	697.827	0	730	0,0	730	687	556		TRANSP	BALDAT	SELECT WHERE "MANDANT" = :A0
956	54	447.019	2.116	468	2,2	211	151	556		TRANSP	BALDAT	SELECT WHERE "MANDANT" = :A0
1	0	34.719	956	34.719	956,0	36	36	556		TRANSP	BALDAT	SELECT WHERE "MANDANT" = :A0
4029	89	3.754.935	5.188	932	1,3	724						

Figure 3.19 SQL Statement Summary

The last row shows a summary (total) of the entire trace. In total, the system executed 4,029 statements (total of executions) and processed 5,188 data records (total of records). The total duration was 3.7 seconds. All other columns in this row are average values and of less significance.

For the individual SELECT statements, check the following five columns because they have possible tuning potential.

▸ EXECUTIONS

Here, you can view the number of executions. Also, consider this value in conjunction with the number of records per execution (REC/EXEC). Are there statements that are executed frequently and return only a few, only one, or no record per execution? These could be statements that you could summarize (see Section 5.7 in Chapter 5).

▸ IDENTICAL

Here, you can view the number of identically executed SQL statements. Identical means the statements with the same values in the WHERE condition. You can implement a more precise analysis about which values are concerned here using the view of identical SELECT statements, which is described later. For these statements, check, based on the ABAP call position, which is discussed in the following, how identical accesses can occur. Often, these are SELECT statements executed in loops (see Section 5.7 in Chapter 5).

▸ RECORDS

A high number of data records raises the question whether all read data records are really required for the application (see Section 5.5 in Chapter 5). If REC/EXEC = 0 or 1, this often involves an existence check (see Section 5.5.5 in Chapter 5). You should also consider the RECORDS or REC/EXEC column in conjunction with the IDENTICAL and EXECUTIONS column. You should not execute single record queries or existence checks particularly often to avoid the communication effort (see EXECUTIONS).

▸ MIN.TIME/R

Values that are above 10,000 microseconds for SELECT statements indicate that the execution plan may be inefficient. For accesses to single tables, values above 1,000 microseconds can already indicate that the access path is not optimal. For joins and views that address multiple tables, the value can be somewhat higher even for efficient execution plans. Section 5.4 in Chapter 5 describes the access strategies. The value can be five times higher for DML statements. Also, compare the value with the values of other statements, and check the statements with the longest access times per record. The check is carried out using the EXPLAIN function, which is discussed in the following.

▸ BTYPE

If you find entries here, FUL, GEN, and SNG indicate the access to a table selected for buffering, which could not be read from the buffer (see Section 6.4.3 in Chapter 6). In this case, use the call position (SQL statement) and Transaction

ST10 (current buffer state) to check why the records could not be read from the buffer. Further entries of this column are DEFUL, DEGEN, DESNG, DEACT, or CUST. These are tables that are not marked for buffering at the moment but could possibly be buffered. Section 6.4.2 in Chapter 6 describes which tables could generally be buffered. Communicate with the system administrators to find out whether these tables can be buffered in the future.

For the individual DML statements (INSERT, UPDATE, DELETE), check the following five columns because they have possible optimization potential.

▶ EXECUTIONS
Here, the same applies for the SELECT statements (communication effort, single record processing). But, for changing statements, the effort on the database side is even higher than for a purely reading statement (see Section 5.2.2 in Chapter 5). If possible, switch the single record processing to mass processing (see Section 5.7 in Chapter 5).

▶ IDENTICAL
Avoid changing accesses that execute identical changes multiple times. In real life, however, this occurs only in rare cases.

▶ RECORDS
If you find changes here that don't change any data records, check this on the application side. Frequently, this is an error. If the application works with MOD-IFY, you often find UPDATE and INSERT pairs because MODIFY first implements an UPDATE and then an INSERT. One of these two exhibits changes. In principle, avoid MODIFY whenever possible (see Section 5.7 in Chapter 5).

▶ MIN.TIME/R
Values that are above 20,000 microseconds can entail an inefficient execution plan — otherwise refer to MIN.TIME/R of SELECT statements.

▶ BTYPE
This involves a change to a buffered table, which should occur as seldom as possible (see Section 6.4.3 in Chapter 6). In that case, check the source text. If it involves a recurring default action, scrutinize the buffering of this table.

Four functions are given for a more in-depth analysis of a statement both in the trace list and in the SQL statement summary. The following describes these four functions.

By clicking on the magnifying glass icon, the selected statement is detailed in the trace list. In the SQL statement summary, you can find details about the last execution of this statement. Figure 3.20 illustrates these details. In addition to the complete SQL text as it was transferred to the database, you can view all contents of the transferred variable. You require this variable for the detailed analysis of SQL statements, particularly if the data is not equally distributed (see Section 5.4.5 in Chapter 5). In this context, the aggregated values are given in the SQL statement summary. A single slow execution of a statement can be missed in the overview compared by the overall time.

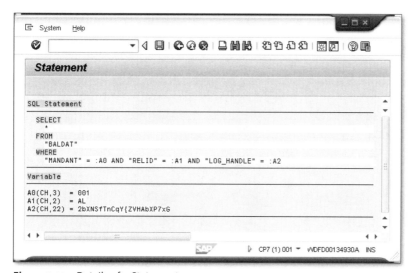

Figure 3.20 Details of a Statement

If you select the DDIC INFORMATION button, you receive further information about the table of the selected SQL statement (see Figure 3.21). For joins the system displays the first table of the join and for views the information about the views.

In the top area, you find general information on the table and their technical settings (size category, buffering, and so on) or the properties. The lower area lists the created indexes of this table. By clicking on one of these indexes (or the INDEX FIELDS button), you obtain the definition of the indexes. By selecting the TABLE FIELDS button, you navigate to Transaction SE12 for the table definition. You can use the ALL INDEX FIELDS button to obtain an overview of all indexes and their fields.

You can display the execution plan using the EXPLAIN function. Because the execution plans strongly depend on the type of the database used, you are not given examples here. Appendix A contains the execution plans for the databases supported by SAP.

All background information about the execution plan topic is available in Section 5.4 in Chapter 5.

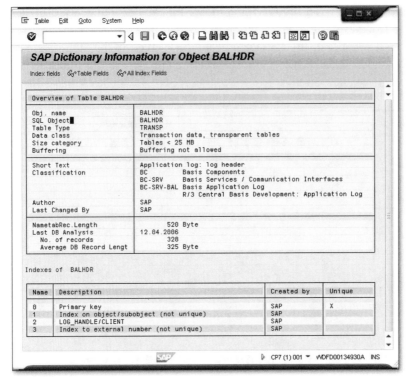

Figure 3.21 DDIC Information

Using the DISPLAY CALL POSITION IN ABAP PROGRAM function, you can navigate to the call position of the SQL statement in the ABAP program. This is possible directly from the trace list, whereas the SQL statement summary may involve multiple different call positions aggregated in one row. In this case, the system displays a dialog window that displays the respective call positions (include, row) and the number of executions per call position. From here, you can select the call position you want to view.

Identical Selects

From the basic list, you can select the TRACE LIST • DISPLAY IDENTICAL SELECTS menu path to display a list of the identical SQL statements. Here you can view the SQL statements that were combined based on their values in the WHERE clause. You can view how often a specific value (or a specific value combination) was queried from the database.

The following columns in Table 3.6 are available.

Column	Description
EXECUTIONS	Number of executions of this statement
OBJECT NAME	Table to which the statement refers
WHERE CLAUSE	The WHERE clause with the concrete values of the execution

Table 3.6 Information of the Identical Selects

Figure 3.22 shows a results list as an example.

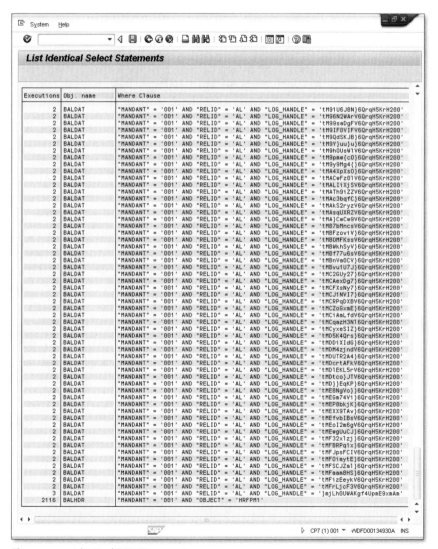

Figure 3.22 Identical SQL Statements

Table Summary

In the table summary, you obtain *one* row of execution for each SQL statement but not all details, such as FETCH conditions, in the trace list. The following information in Table 3.7 is available.

Column	Description
WORK PROC. NO.	Number of the work process that executed the queries. You can also find this information in the trace list in the header.
PTYPE	Type of the work process that executed the queries. You can also find this information in the trace list in the header.
CLIENT	Client to which the access relates. You can also find this information in the trace list in the header.
HH:MM:SS.MS	Execution time of the SQL statement
TRANSACTION	Transaction that executed the access
TABLE NAME	Name of the table
STATEMENT	SELECT/INSERT/UPDATE/DELETE/COMMIT
Σ RECORDS	Total of the read data records per statement
Σ ACCESS TIME	Total of the required time in microseconds *per statement*
DB CONNECTION	Connection (R/3, liveCache)

Table 3.7 Information of the Table Summary

Therefore, the table summary at statement level is somewhat clearer than the trace list. Figure 3.23 shows a table summary.

Aggregated Table Summary

In the aggregated table summary, there is one row per transaction for each table and each statement type. You can call the aggregated table summary from the table summary via the TABLE LIST • AGGREGATE menu.

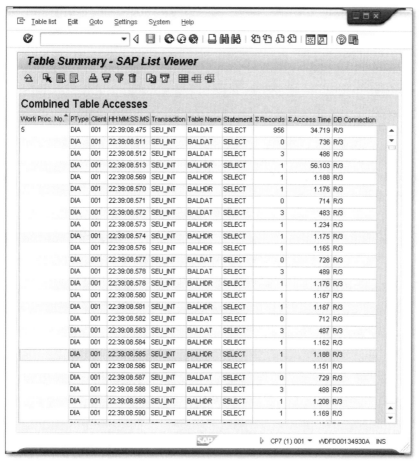

Figure 3.23 Table Summary

The following information in Table 3.8 is available.

Column	Description
Transaction	Transaction that executed the access
Table Name	Name of the table
Σ Access To Table	Number of accesses to this table
Statement	SELECT/INSERT/UPDATE/DELETE/COMMIT

Table 3.8 Information of the Aggregated Table Summary

Column	Description
Σ Records	Total of the processed data records per table
Σ Access Time	Total of the required time in microseconds *per table*
Σ Percentage	Percentage of the overall time
DB Connection	Connection (R/3/liveCache)

Table 3.8 Information of the Aggregated Table Summary (Cont.)

The aggregated table summary indicates which database tables consumed the most time or from which database table the most data records are read. Figure 3.24 shows the aggregated table summary.

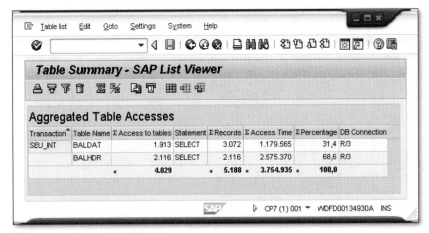

Figure 3.24 Aggregated Table Summary

Summary

Besides the ABAP trace, the SQL trace is one of the most essential tools for the performance analysis of ABAP programs. It contains all important information on the database accesses that an ABAP program executes. It is recommended to directly navigate to the SQL statement summary and start the analysis of the SQL statements with the longest runtime there and to only switch to other view if required.

3.3.9 Performance Trace — RFC Trace (Transaction ST05)

With the RFC trace, you can log incoming and outgoing RFC calls. You receive the following information in Table 3.9.

Column	Description
HH:MM:SS.MS	For the extended trace list: Specification of the execution time of the RFC call
DURATION	Duration of the call in microseconds
PROGRAM	For the client: Program that triggered the RFC call For the server: RFC module that was called
OBJECT NAME	Name of the instance where the call was executed
CURS/ARRAY/CON	Not filled
RECORDS	Not filled
RC	Return code: 0 = ok <>0 = error
STATEMENT	This column outputs the name of the local instance, the name of the "remotely" used instance, the name of the called function module, and the number of sent and received bytes.

Table 3.9 Information of the RFC Trace

Figure 3.25 shows a typical RFC trace with outgoing RFC calls.

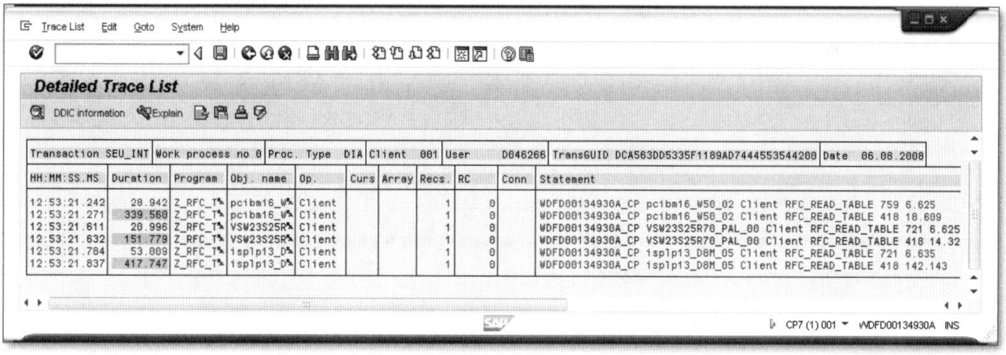

Figure 3.25 RFC Trace — Client

You can see the six outgoing (OPER = "Client") RFC calls to different target systems (OBJECT NAME) of which always two go to the same target system, one with a small and one with a large dataset. In the STATEMENT column, you can find the following information, which is directly written one after the other: local instance, remote instance, type of call, name of the function module, sent bytes, and received bytes.

By double-clicking the information, you obtain this and further information in a clearer formatting. Figure 3.26 shows the details of an RFC trace record, and Figure 3.27 illustrates an RFC trace with incoming RFC calls.

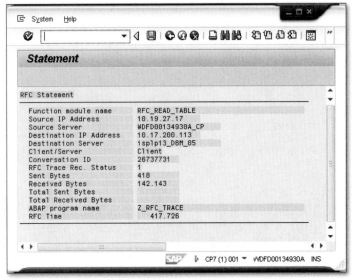

Figure 3.26 Details of an RFC Trace Record

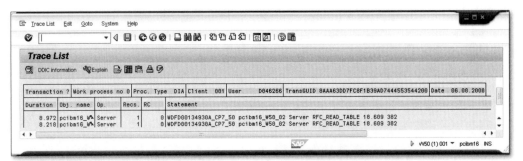

Figure 3.27 RFC Trace — Server

Using the RFC trace, you can log and analyze the number, duration of RFC calls, and the transferred data volumes. The number and the transferred data volume are significant for the performance (see Chapter 8).

3.3.10 Performance Trace — Enqueue Trace (Transaction ST05)

The enqueue trace is used to log lock requests to the enqueue service. In the enqueue trace, the following information in Table 3.10 is available.

Column	Description
HH:MM:SS.MS	For the extended trace list: Specification of the execution time of the enqueue call
DURATION	Duration of the access in microseconds
PROGRAM	Program — in this case, the enqueue service
OBJECT NAME	Name of the lock object
OPER	Function (ENQUEUE, DEQUEUE, ...)
CURS/ARRAY/CON	Not filled
RECORDS	Number of arguments of the lock object
RC	Return code: 0 = function executed correctly 2 = collision occurred 8 = internal error
STATEMENT	This is where the system specifies the arguments for the lock request. If multiple arguments exist, they are separated from one another with the | character. For each argument, the lock mode, the lock table, and the lock argument is specified.

Table 3.10 Information of the Enqueue Trace

In the trace result, you can view the type, time, and duration of the lock requests. This enables you to analyze how long a lock was kept (time between ENQUEUE and DEQUEUE for an object). This time should be as long as necessary but as short as possible (see Section 4.2.2 in Chapter 4).

For the example, in Figure 3.28, *one* enqueue call was executed on an already locked object using the _WAIT parameter (*see* Section 4.2.2 in Chapter 4). In the trace, you can view *five* lock requests that were each executed in intervals of one second. The return code 2 indicates that a collision occurred, that is, that the record is already locked.

In addition to a logic analysis (How long is the lock kept?), you can also implement a technical analysis (How long do the lock requests last?) using the enqueue trace. Here, the system also measures the complete communication stack. For lock requests from application servers that have no direct access to the enqueue table (see Section 9.6 in Chapter 9), for example, the system considers the complete communication of the lock requests. By means of this trace, you can analyze bottleneck situations with regard to enqueue requests. Note that dequeue commands are always processed asynchronously. Therefore, the measured time for dequeue commands only contains the sending of the command, while the enqueue commands are always synchronous, that is, the time covers the period from sending the request to receiving the reply.

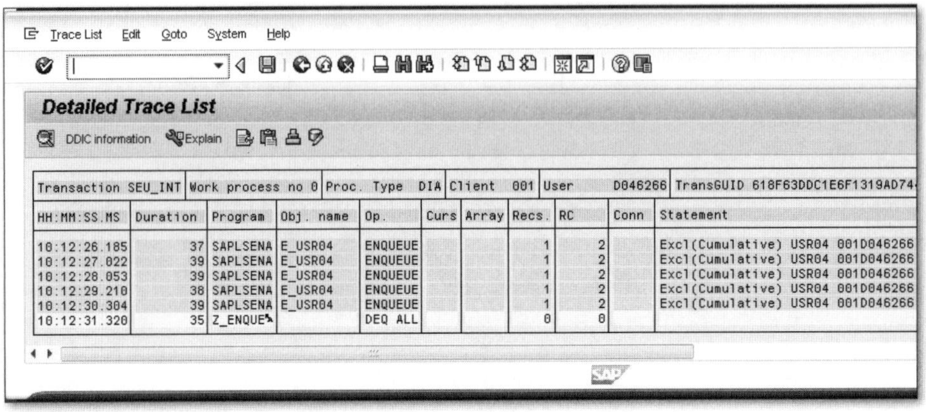

Figure 3.28 Enqueue Trace

3.3.11 Performance Trace — Table Buffer Trace (Transaction ST05)

The table buffer trace records all accesses to the SAP table buffer (see Section 6.4 in Chapter 6). Using this tool, you can analyze which statements can be handled via the table buffer and how long they take. The trace provides the following information in Table 3.11 per buffer access.

Column	Description
HH:MM:SS.MS	For the extended trace list: Specification of the execution time of the table buffer call
DURATION	Duration of the access in microseconds. For combined FETCH statements (COLUMN RECORDS > 1 and the total and average per FETCH in the statement column), this is the time for all FETCH statements. One data record is read per FETCH.
OBJECT NAME	Table name to which the access relates
OPER	Displays the function executed on the buffer for the specified table.
RECORDS	Number of records read

Table 3.11 Information of the Table Buffer Trace

Column	Description
Rc	Return code: 0 = function executed correctly 64 = no records found 256 = for table buffer access (buffering types R and P): record not available in the buffer 1024 = record not available in the buffer, buffer loading (for parallel read accesses)
STATEMENT	For OPEN function: Specifies the type of buffering: G—generically buffered P—individual table records buffered R—table fully buffered S—export/import buffering C—CUA buffer O—OTR buffer E—EMS buffer (export/import to shared memory) This is followed by the length of the key and of the queried key value. If the maximum specified duration is exceeded for a FETCH, the pattern >999999,9 is displayed. For uncompressed FETCH statements and CLOSE, no further information is displayed.
PROGRAM	Name of the ABAP program that triggered the table buffer call
CURS/ARRAY/CON	Not filled

Table 3.11 Information of the Table Buffer Trace (Cont.)

Figure 3.29 shows a typical results list of a table buffer trace. Four different buffer accesses were executed in a loop.

1. One access to a fully buffered table with complete key (table: ZBALHDR1, records: 1)

2. One access to a generically buffered table with complete generic key (table: ALCLASTOOL, records: 3)

3. One access to a fully buffered table with a selective field that is not part of the table key (table: ZBALHDR1, records: 1)

4. One access to a single-record buffered table with complete key and SELECT SINGLE (table: AUTHX, records: 1)

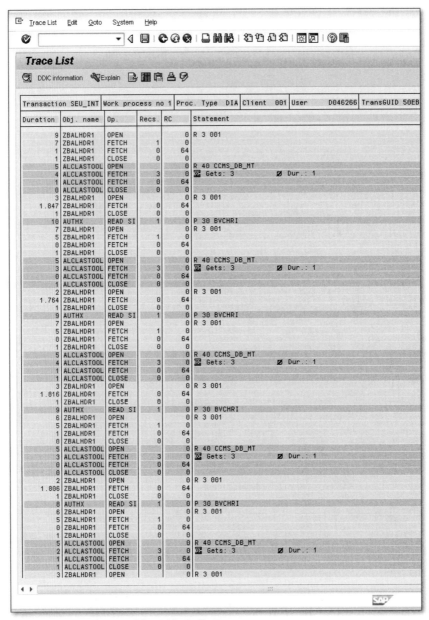

Figure 3.29 Results List of the Table Buffer Trace

Section 6.4.3 in Chapter 6 describes a scenario of how performance problems arise for fully buffered tables if you search via a field that doesn't correspond to the leading part of the primary key. In this case, the entire table must be read. In the table buffer trace, you can clearly identify the increased time for the respective second access to the fully buffered table, ZBALHDR1, although the resulting set is the same. These accesses took approximately 1.8 milliseconds. The mentioned table has 8,303 entries, which occupy approximately 4.3 MB of space. For large, fully buffered tables, you can quickly obtain access times that are common for accesses to the database. If the table is supposed to be frequently read using non-primary key fields and such access times occur due to their sizes, reconsider the buffering option, or execute the accesses that don't use the primary key via the database and a suitable secondary index instead.

3.3.12 ABAP Trace (Transaction SE30)

With the ABAP trace (Transaction SE30), you can analyze the performance of ABAP programs. The trace results are saved in files, which you can then analyze. Based on these results, you can identify long running or frequently called statements or modularization units. Apart from the database accesses, these are statements that place load on the CPUs of the application server. Transaction SE30 is primarily used for the analysis of performance problems at the application layer that runs on the application servers. Using Transaction SE30, you can also analyze the call hierarchy of a program to analyze the program flow or detect modularization units that maybe were called unnecessarily.

Before you get started with the practical use of Transaction SE30, the following provides some technical background knowledge.

All ABAP programs consist of individual ABAP statements executed by the ABAP VM (Virtual Machine) in the work process. Some of these ABAP statements are linked with *events*. These are ABAP statements that are potentially considered as performance-critical. During the execution of ABAP programs, the ABAP VM measures the performance of these events if the ABAP trace is activated (recording of the time stamps before and after the event) and writes the results to the trace file after the statement is complete. The files are written to the directory, which is specified via the `abap/atrapath` profile parameter. A specific memory space is given, which you can specify using the `abap/atrasizequota` parameter. If the ABAP trace was activated not completely but in an aggregated manner (see the following sections), the data is first collected and aggregated before it is written to the trace file. The trace file is located on the application server that executes the program respectively. The system automatically deletes the trace files after 30 days to prevent a file system overflow.

Figure 3.30 shows an overview of Transaction SE30. Just like for Transaction ST05, there are different navigation options to the different views of the data.

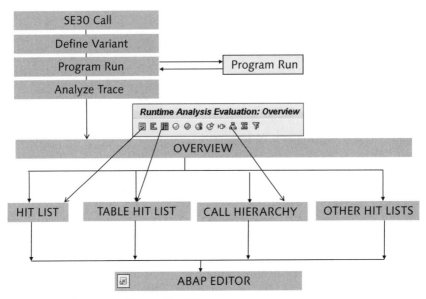

Figure 3.30 Overview of Transaction SE30

Before you record a trace, there are variants that specify which data must be recorded. You are provided with a default variant that already contains predefined settings. Depending on the usage, you must define some custom variants to obtain more details than in the default variant, for example. The variants are described in the following.

The trace is then activated. This can be carried out for the current session for which the program to be analyzed is directly started or in the parallel session for already running programs for which a section is logged in the trace. It is also possible to schedule a trace with different options. In this process, the trace requests are set in the shared memory and for each roll-in of a user context the system checks whether a trace is to be activated. Here, you can specify restrictions for the users, objects (programs), or call types (RFC, HTTP, dialog, batch, and so on).

Once the trace was recorded, the analysis takes you to the overview, which displays initial information about the trace. The most important information is the subdivision into ABAP, database, and system time. The ABAP time involves all ABAP commands except for the database accesses. These are displayed for the database time. The system time contains all system-relevant times, such as the loading of programs. If this time makes a significant difference, repeat the measurement to exclude load and initialization processes, for example. If the system time repeatedly exhibits high values, you must carry out a problem analysis in cooperation with the system administrators. The TYPE column in the hit list (see Figure 3.34) gives information about which events are assigned to which time categories.

From the overview, you can call different views. The most important view is certainly the hit list that contains all calls sorted by duration in descending order. The call hierarchy shows the program flow and the table hit list, the most expensive accesses to the database, grouped by tables. In addition, there are further hit lists for special analyses. These include the group hit list, the class hit list, the instance hit list, the method hit list, the event hit list, and the hit list of internal tables, which each provide a different or more limited view of the trace file. From each of these hit lists, you can navigate to the respective call position in the ABAP program.

Attention!

The initial screen of Transaction SE30 already shows a small traffic light icon that informs you about the reliability of the time measurement on your system. For certain platforms, for instance, DEC, HP, or AIX, unreasonable measurement values (for example, negative values) may occur for the hardware register-based method activated by default. This is indicated by a red traffic light in the initial screen of Transaction SE30. In this case, switch to the `gettimeofday` method based on the operating system function. For this purpose, select the SETTINGS • MEASUREMENT ACCURACY menu in the initial screen. The HIGH setting corresponds to the hardware register-based method and is usually more accurate and associated with less system overhead.

The LOW setting corresponds to the `gettimeofday` method based on the operating system function, which is less accurate and has a higher system overhead. Nevertheless, this method gives good information, which allows for the analysis of the biggest "time consumers." Even if the accuracy in the microsecond range is not provided, you still obtain an overview in which the time relationships to one another allow for the analysis of the time consumers. However, the CPU times are generally higher in the `gettimeofday`-based measurement, that is, the reliability of the absolute values in the statistical record in Transaction STAD (discussed later on in this chapter) is no longer ensured. For further information on the time measurements in Transaction SE30 on these platforms, refer to SAP Notes 20097 and 87447.

The following sections show how you define a measurement variant and create a trace based on screenshots. Furthermore, a description of the most important options and lists of Transaction SE30 is given.

Defining the Measurement Variant

In the initial screen of Transaction SE30, you can define a new measurement variant as shown in Figure 3.31.

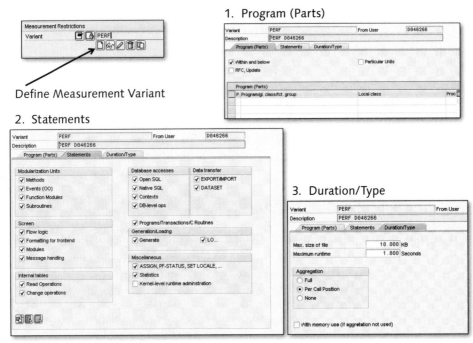

Figure 3.31 Defining the Measurement Variant

In the PROGRAM (PARTS) tab, you specify which program parts are supposed to be recorded. By default, the system records everything. Here, you can make restrictions for certain programs, classes, function modules, and so on. All program parts outside the selected ones are then assigned to the RUNTIME ANALYSIS event and mapped as system time. Moreover, you can determine whether the RFC and update calls are supposed to be recorded as well. In this process, the trace flags are inherited to these processes. This option is deactivated by default and results in a separate measurement data file for RFC or update calls if it is activated. If the RFC calls are directed to another system, the rstr/accept_remote_trace = true parameter must be set for this system, so the trace can be activated. Then the system writes the measurement data files to the remote system. The E2E trace (see Section 3.3.14, E2E Trace) also uses this functionality to activate the traces in the systems.

The PARTICULAR UNITS option specifies that the system only records commands within particular units. You can select these units via SYSTEM • UTILITIES • RUN-

TIME ANALYSIS • SWITCH ON (or SWITCH OFF), for example. Another option is the activation using the ABAP statements, SET RUN TIME ANALYZER ON and SET RUN TIME ANALYZER OFF. It is also possible to make these selections dynamically in the dialog applications or in the Debugger using the /RON or /ROFF OK code.

> **Tip**
>
> The measurement of particular units is especially useful for dialog applications with multiple screens or steps if only one specific action (dialog step) is supposed to be analyzed. It is also useful in the Debugger if you want to measure a specific coding only. In both cases, you make the start and stop selection using the /RON or /ROFF OK code or via the SYSTEM • UTILITIES • RUNTIME ANALYSIS • SWITCH ON (or SWITCH OFF), while you create a trace using Transaction SE30.

In the STATEMENTS tab, you can define which statements are supposed to be recorded. This involves the initially mentioned events, which you can activate for recording individually here. Figure 3.31 illustrates the individual groups and events. Note the database events and the internal tables in particular. Activate all database events to obtain a good overview of the database accesses also in Transaction SE30. The internal tables should be activated to analyze inefficient accesses to internal tables. Activating internal tables generates a relatively high number of entries in the measurement data file, so it can make sense for longer traces to first trace without internal tables to find the long-running modularization units and then restrict them in a second trace via the program parts and to only measure these with internal tables.

In the last tab, DURATION/TYPE, you can specify the file size of the trace file. It is preset to 2 MB by default. Increase this value considerably, for example, to 10 MB. The predefined 1,800 seconds (= 30 minutes) are usually sufficient. The maximum value you can enter here is 4,294 seconds. The trace is deactivated when the time or file limit is reached. Overwriting is therefore excluded. The aggregation is the most critical setting in this tab. Here, you specify the level of detail and therefore the extent of the trace. The three options are now described based on the following coding excerpt.

```
...
PERFORM uprog1.
COMPUTE...
DO 100 TIMES.
   PERFORM uprog1.
ENDDO.
...
```

In case of a full aggregation, you receive exactly one row in the results for uprog1 that contains the values for all 101 executions in an aggregated form. For the evaluation, only the hit list is given in this case.

For the aggregation per call position, two rows are given in the trace for uprog1, one for each call position. For the evaluation, only the hit list is given in this case.

Without an aggregation, there are 101 rows in the trace, one for each execution. For this option, all lists are available for evaluation.

The NONE option therefore provides results with the highest level of detail because every execution is measured separately. In this case, the trace file becomes the largest file, and you can usually analyze only a small source text excerpt or a short duration this way. Usually, the aggregation per call position already provides a good result, which you can use for the analysis.

Additionally, you can record the memory use of the program, too. However, this is only possible if you selected NONE.

Creating a Trace

As already mentioned, you can create traces in Transaction SE30 directly for a program in the current session, schedule a trace, or start the trace for a program that runs in parallel.

In the current session, you can create a trace for a program, a transaction, or a function module directly in the initial screen by selecting a measurement variant, entering an object name (program, transaction, function module) in the corresponding field, and then executing it. On completion of the transaction, the trace is automatically completed and can be evaluated directly using the EXECUTE button. This scenario is mainly useful to trace only a specific dialog step (for example, the click on a specific button). For this purpose, select the PARTICULAR UNITS option and choose the section to be measured, for example, by means of the /RON and /ROFF OK codes as previously described.

In the parallel session, that is, for an already running program, a process list of the current application server is given if you use the SWITCH ON/OFF button. There, you can create a trace for a selected process in which you choose the process and activate or deactivate the buttons selected in Figure 3.32. The trace cannot be activated until the currently running event is completed. For example, if a database access is taking place, you can activate the trace only when it is completed. Consequently, the system records the next full event after activation. Here, too, the general rule applies that when the recorded application is terminated, the trace is terminated as well.

To schedule a trace, in the respective dialog window, you can set the corresponding filters, for example, which process type, user, object type, object name, and so on, should be recorded. This option makes sense for incoming RFC calls or batch jobs, for example. For each roll-in, the system checks for the possibly activated trace flags and activates a trace if required.

Figure 3.32 shows an overview of the different methods.

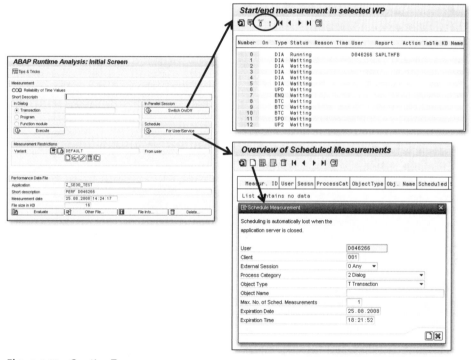

Figure 3.32 Creating Traces

Evaluating a Trace

To evaluate a trace, you must open the respective trace file using the EVALUATE button. The system displays an overview as shown in Figure 3.33. You can see which part of the runtime accounts for the ABAP statements, database processing, or actions on the system side. In the example of Figure 3.33, 161 microseconds account for ABAP processing, ~32 microseconds for database processing, and 634 microseconds for activities on the system side. The TYPE column (see Figure 3.34) indicates which events belong to which category; entries without a type belong to the ABAP category. Because the trace was recorded with the PER CALL POSITION aggregation, "only" the hit list is available for evaluation. However, this is the most important list for performance analysis by far. If the trace was recorded without an aggregation, the initial screen provides further statistic values (for example, number of conversions; see Section 9.3 in Chapter 9) and additional list views. Figure 3.34 shows a hit list as an example.

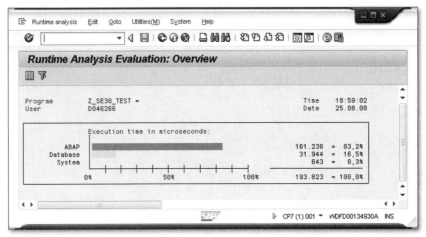

Figure 3.33 ABAP Trace — Evaluation Overview

Number	Gross	=	Net	Gross (%)	Net (%)	Call	Program	Type	No. Filter
1	193.823		0	100,0	0,0	Runtime analysis		Sys.	
1	193.787		11.150	100,0	5,8	Submit Report Z_SE30_TEST	SAPMS38T		
1	181.610		579	93,7	0,3	Program Z_SE30_TEST			
1	60.605		38.517	31,3	19,9	Loop at IT_10	Z_SE30_TEST		
5	59.706		59.042	30,8	30,5	Append IT_11	Z_SE30_TEST		
1	31.896		1.361	16,5	0,7	Fetch BALDAT	Z_SE30_TEST	DB	OpenS
5	26.250		25.878	13,5	13,4	Append IT_10	Z_SE30_TEST		
30.336	22.088	=	22.088	11,4	11,4	Loop at IT_11	Z_SE30_TEST		
100	251		159	0,1	0,1	Perform F1	Z_SE30_TEST		
101	97	=	97	0,1	0,1	Read Table IT_10	Z_SE30_TEST		
1	96		46	0,0	0,0	Load Report Z_SE30_TEST		Sys.	
1	61		57	0,0	0,0	Open Cursor BALDAT	Z_SE30_TEST	DB	OpenS
1	22		16	0,0	0,0	Event SYSTEM-EXIT	Z_SE30_TEST		
1	16		11	0,0	0,0	Perform F1	Z_SE30_TEST		
1	1	=	1	0,0	0,0	Close Cursor BALDAT	Z_SE30_TEST	DB	OpenS
1	0	=	0	0,0	0,0	Perform not found BEFORE_EVENT	Z_SE30_TEST		

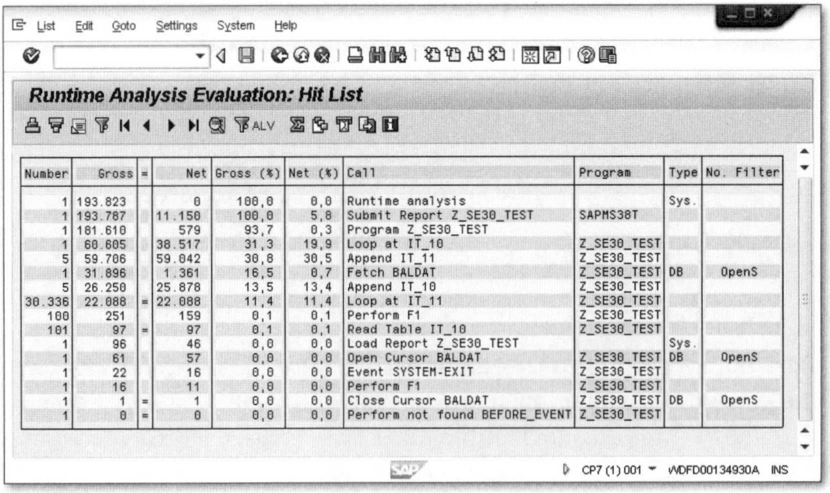

Figure 3.34 Hit List Sorted by Net Times in Descending Order

The following information in Table 3.12 is available in the hit list.

Column	Description
Number	Number of calls of this event
Gross	Used gross time for this event
=	If "=", the gross time corresponds to the net time
Net	Used net time for this event
Gross %	Percentage share of the gross time of this event in the total gross time
Net %	Percentage share of the net time of this event in the total net time
Call	Recorded event
Program	Triggering program
Type	Type of the event, for instance, Syst for system and DB for database events
No. Filter	Filter to which the event belongs

Table 3.12 Hit List Information

> **Note**
>
> By default, the system displays only those events that come from the application program itself (including the Open SQL commands). You can display further events using the 🍴 filter icon (fourth icon from the left in Figure 3.34). In Transaction SE30, you can only view the system-internal names of the internal tables. By navigating to the ABAP source text (🗐, third icon from the left in the icon list of Figure 3.34), you can have the system display the name as it is used in the application.

At this point, it is essential to describe the difference between gross and net time. Figure 3.35 shows a subroutine (f1) with further statements of which some measurable events are assigned in Transaction SE30. The gross time for the subroutine f1 corresponds to the total time including all statements within the subroutine, whereas the net time for the subroutine corresponds to the gross time *minus* all separately measured events (statements).

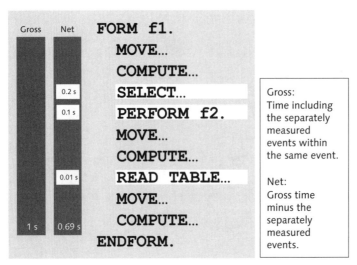

Figure 3.35 Gross and Net Times in Transaction SE30

In the analysis of the hit list (see Figure 3.34), you usually find the biggest time consumers at event level (statement level) by sorting the list by net times in descending order. This way, you obtain a list of statements that used the most time. In the example of Figure 3.34, the most expensive statement is an append to an internal table with the internal name IT_11, for example.

But the analysis of the gross times is equally important. If you sort the hit list by the gross times in descending order, you usually find the expensive modularization units. With business application know-how and based on this list, you can possibly determine whether there are unnecessary calls of modularization units or which functionality uses how much time.

For the hit list analysis, pay attention to the following event groups.

▸ **Modularization units (function modules, methods, forms, etc.)**
Check what processes run in these modularization units and how often they are called. If internal tables are processed in these modularization units, an ABAP trace with activated internal tables is highly recommended for the further analysis. Are there expensive calls of the following groups in the modularization units?

▸ **RFC calls**
These are calls in the internal or a remote system. Transaction SE30 doesn't provide any further information. But you can further analyze these calls with the RFC trace (see Section 3.3.9, Performance Trace — RFC Trace (Transaction ST05)). You obtain a separate ABAP trace in the target system only if you activated RFC for the program parts and the remote system permits the incoming trace activation.

▶ **Internal tables**
The larger they are, the more inefficient ABAP commands negatively influence the runtime. In most cases, they involve inefficient accesses (see Sections 7.4.2 to 7.4.5 in Chapter 7), sorting processes (see Section 7.4.6 in Chapter 7), or overheads for copying (see Section 7.4.7 in Chapter 7) for access to internal tables. The SAP Code Inspector also performs these checks (see Section 3.3.1, SAP Code Inspector (Transaction SCI)), but it has no information about the size of the internal tables at runtime.

▶ **Database accesses**
These can be accesses to tables in the SAP table buffer or *real* database accesses. You cannot distinguish this in Transaction SE30. The buffer settings of the tables are displayed in the database table hit list; but whether an access is implemented from the SAP table buffer can only be reproduced using the performance trace (SQL and table buffer trace, see Sections 3.3.8, Performance Trace − SQL Trace (Transaction ST05), and 3.3.11, Performance-Trace − Table Buffer Trace (Transaction ST05)). Additionally, the respective performance traces give more detailed information on the accesses. You can easily recognize an SQL statement's percentage of the total runtime in Transaction SE30, which in turn is not possible in Transaction ST05.

▶ **Further events**
These include events that are triggered by the system, for example, load and generation processes. If this event group utilizes a large portion of time, the system administrators must perform another analysis.

Let's discuss the call hierarchy as the last evaluation. This evaluation can only be performed for ABAP traces that were recorded without aggregation. The call hierarchy enables a precise analysis of the program flow. Figure 3.36 illustrates an example of a call hierarchy, which is reduced due to lack of space. The following information in Table 3.13 is available.

Column	Description
GROSS	Used gross time for this event
NET	Used net time for this event
LV	Call level for this event
CALL HIERARCHY	Name of the event
PROGRAM	Program that executed the call of the event
MEM REQM [B]	Memory requirement at the respective position in byte if activated

Table 3.13 Call Hierarchy Information

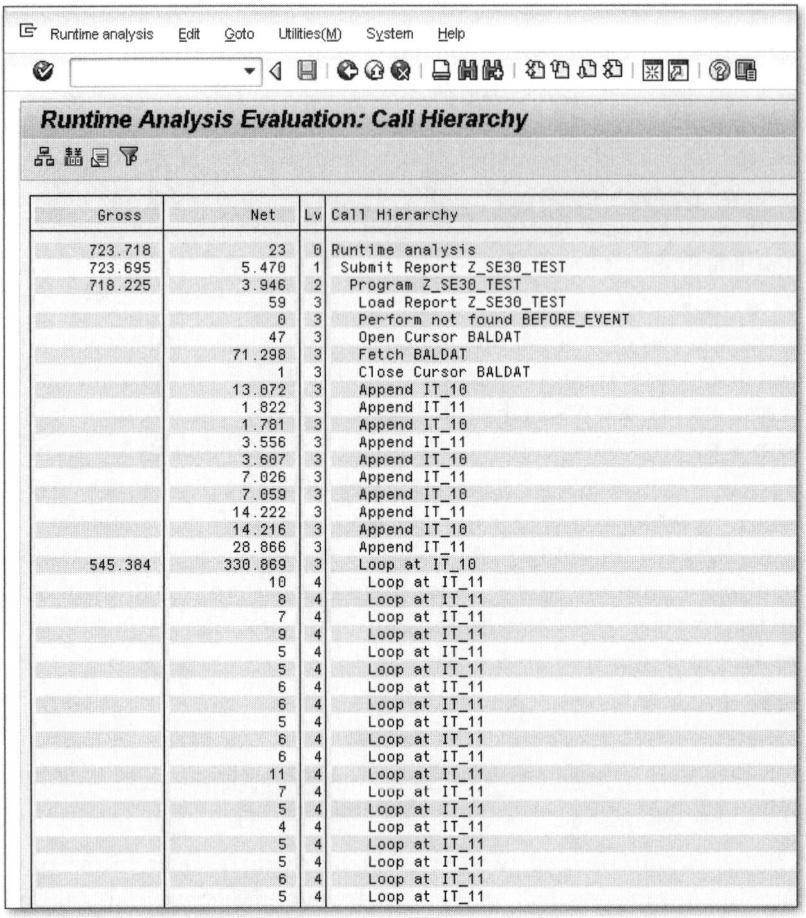

Figure 3.36 Call Hierarchy (Reduced View)

In addition to the gross and net times, the Lv column indicates the call level and you can therefore reproduce the program flow. Each call is displayed separately. For example, LOOP AT IT_11 at level 4 is called by or in LOOP AT IT_10 at level 3. Behind the events, you can find the corresponding program and the memory requirement that the program had at the time of the call (if this option was activated in the measurement variant). You can navigate to the ABAP source text ($\bigsqcup$, third icon from the left) also from this list.

Furthermore, it is possible to have the system display the absolute times or the percentages of times ($\begin{smallmatrix}\blacksquare\blacksquare\end{smallmatrix}$, second icon from the left) and have an event or a modularization unit displayed separately in the time allocation (ABAP or DB processing and system time) ($\begin{smallmatrix}\blacksquare\blacksquare\end{smallmatrix}$, first icon).

The recording without aggregation and with memory use requires the most memory space, which is why you can record only brief program parts with such a high level of detail. Usually, the hit list for the aggregation per call position is enough to determine the biggest "time wasters." If you cannot determine the cause directly (see event groups mentioned previously), you can analyze the modularization unit concerned in detail without any aggregation. Similar analyses about the program flow can also be implemented using Transaction ST12 (see Section 3.3.13, Single Transaction Analysis (Transaction ST12)).

Managing Trace Files

In the lower part of the initial screen of Transaction SE30, you can open further trace files (your own files or those of other users) using the OTHER FILE button. Here, you can use the transaction ID to open an E2E trace (see Section 3.3.14, E2E Trace), which was created using Solution Manager Diagnostics (SMD), for example. In this dialog window, an overview of which files are available on this application server is given, and you can delete files, for example. By clicking the FILE INFO button, further information is given, for example, about the storage location of the file or with which aggregation the trace was recorded. If you select the DELETE button, you can delete the selected trace file.

Examples: Tips & Tricks

In the initial screen of Transaction SE30, the TIPS & TRICKS button is in the top left corner. Once you've opened the TIPS & TRICKS, the system displays a tree structure on the left in which you can find various examples, which are grouped by categories, whose runtime you can measure. After you've selected an example, the system displays a comparison of the two examples in the right area of the window, and in the area below, a brief documentation provides details about these examples. By clicking the MEASURE RUNTIME button, you can measure the two examples. It is also possible to change the examples or to enter your own examples. These TIPS & TRICKS are referred to at different points of this book.

3.3.13   Single Transaction Analysis (Transaction ST12)

Transaction ST12 is a trace transaction that SAP Active Global Support developed for SAP employees to be used during the service delivery. Therefore, it is not subject to the usual maintenance. However, this does not mean that the transaction is not continued to be maintained, but simply that error corrections cannot be guaranteed with the usual speed. In case of an error, you can still use Transaction SE30, which was described in Section 3.3.12, ABAP Trace (Transaction SE30). However, because Transaction ST12 contains some very useful evaluation functions for ABAP traces, it is presented in this book. Despite the limited maintenance, there is nothing that stands in the way of general usage. The transaction for customer systems is delivered using the ST-A/PI add-on (standard add-on for service preparation). SAP Note 69455 provides further information on this subject.

The transaction is not translated. It is available in English only and has no official documentation. However, SAP Note 755977 includes a brief instruction.

This section presents Transaction ST12, distinguishes it from Transaction SE30, and briefly discusses its functioning. Information is then presented on the evaluation methods that are useful for the performance analysis.

Overview

In comparison to Transaction SE30, Transaction ST12 provides benefits both with regard to the recording and the evaluation of aggregated traces. For example, you can use Transaction ST12 to activate an ABAP trace together with a performance trace (Transaction ST05).

For the ABAP trace, the system uses the same functionality as for Transaction SE30. The trace is written to a file on the respective application server. However, upon completion of the trace, it is read into the database and is then available in the entire system and without time limitations. This is a major difference to Transaction SE30 in which the traces are only available on the application server on which they were created and are deleted after 30 days. Furthermore — and this is a major benefit of Transaction ST12 — you can analyze traces that were recorded with an aggregation per call position using some additional functions. These functions are presented in the following.

For the performance trace, you use the same functions as in Transaction ST05. Consequently, the same limitations apply as for the performance trace, for example, that only one user can activate the trace per application server (see Section 3.3.7, Performance Trace — General Information (Transaction ST05)). In this case, you *don't* save the trace files in the database if the trace is deactivated. Consequently, the performance trace is a real "remote control" for the operation of Transaction ST05 without extended functions. So, all information provided in Sections 3.3.8, Performance Trace — SQL Trace (Transaction ST05), to 3.3.10, Performance Trace — Enqueue Trace (Transaction ST05), also applies to the part of the performance trace within Transaction ST12; however, the table buffer trace cannot be activated using Transaction ST12. Nevertheless, the activation together with the ABAP trace is beneficial because this is more intuitive and ensures less effort.

Creating a Trace

You can define the scope of measurement also in Transaction ST12. However, this is done directly in the middle section of the initial screen as shown in Figure 3.37. In the left area, you can specify the ABAP trace options. The most important decision is whether you want to trace with internal tables, which may double the trace size. If negative times occur in the trace or the trace file size is not big enough, you can set the measurement accuracy to LOW using the FURTHER OPT. button or increase the trace file size. You can save the measurement accuracy as a default setting for your user. Moreover, you can select the aggregation (full or per call position). The remaining settings (within or below the DB or kernel-level operations) correspond to those of Transaction SE30.

In the CURRENT MODE scenario, you can set the PARTICULAR UNITS flag in the Debugger to restrict to a dialog step or a code section.

In the right area, you can activate the performance traces, SQL trace, enqueue trace, and RFC trace. Below this area, you can find the option for the context trace for RFC and update calls.

The upper area of the screen (TRACE FOR) includes various use scenarios to record the traces. Figure 3.37 illustrates that the current mode is activated. The WORK-PROCESS button corresponds to the parallel session, which you can use to trace an already running program. The TASKS & HTTP button corresponds to the SCHEDULE TRACE option in Transaction SE30, and the USER button allows for a one-time trace scheduling for a specific user.

For the USER, TASKS & HTTP, and WORKPROCESS options, Transaction ST12 lets you select the server on which the trace should be started; this is not possible in Transaction SE30. You can select the local server, a specific server, or all servers. If you want to trace incoming RFCs for which you don't know the target server (load distribution), select the TASKS & HTTP scenario with multiple trace activations and with a filter for the user. After you've deactivated the trace, the system displays a dialog window that shows all recorded traces. You must select them explicitly, so they are read in Transaction ST12.

As mentioned previously, you can activate the performance trace (for instance, the SQL trace) for all these scenarios. In case of the parallel session, you can intuitively select a specific process from the process list and click on it to (de)activate the SQL trace. This is also possible in Transaction ST05, but you must manually enter the previously determined process number from Transaction SM50 (or SM66) in the filter options (see Section 3.3.8, Performance Trace — SQL Trace (Transaction ST05)).

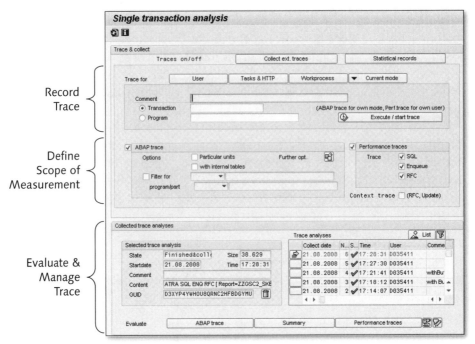

Figure 3.37 Single Transaction Analysis — Initial Screen

These recording options of Transaction ST12 are also possible with Transactions SE30 or ST05; however, you can access them more conveniently and implement them more intuitively using Transaction ST12.

Furthermore, Transaction ST12 includes a scenario for batch jobs, which is not possible in Transaction SE30. In the initial screen, you can call a dialog via the UTILITIES • SCHEDULE BATCH JOB TRACING menu (not displayed here); you can enter selection criteria just like in Transaction SM37, that is, job name, user name, time window, and program name. Two other fields are also available: CHECK INTERVAL and TRACE START DELAY. These are explained in the following. You use the ⟦ Schedule Batch job trace ⟧ button to activate the trace. The system refreshes the screen at the interval specified in the CHECK INTERVAL field, and searches for jobs that meet the entered conditions in the background. If jobs are found that meet the conditions, an ABAP and performance trace is activated for the first job according to the seconds specified in the TRACE START DELAY field. This trace is automatically deactivated if the maximum trace runtime (default = 1,800 seconds, maximum = 4,294 seconds) or the set file size for the trace file is reached or if the batch job ends. In the latest version of Transaction ST12, you can find this scenario under the UTILITIES • SCHEDULE TRACE • BATCH JOB TRACE DIALOG VERSION menu path.

Collecting Traces

The COLLECT EXT. TRACES button imports trace files that were created using Transactions ST12 or SE30 from the file system into the database. You can persist trace files in the database, which is very useful for a subsequent analysis.

In theory, this is also possible for other systems via RFC. However, it usually makes more sense to locally evaluate the traces on the respective systems via Transaction SE30 or ST12 to access the corresponding source text.

Here, you can also search for and import an E2E trace from Solution Manager Diagnostics using the transaction ID.

Evaluating a Trace

Transaction ST12 starts directly with the hit list as illustrated in Figure 3.38. In the upper area, an overview and the time allocation is given; the lower area includes the hit list. Just like Transaction SE30, Transaction ST12 also offers a hit list, which you can sort by the gross time and net time to determine expensive single statements or modularization units.

You must consider the following differences.

▶ Transaction ST12 displays the names of the internal tables in plain text; Transaction SE30 shows the system-internal names. If required, you can show them via the SHOW/HIDE • TECHNICAL DETAILS menu.

▶ For database accesses and RFC calls, the system displays only one row in case the TECHNICAL DETAILS are deactivated (default), whereas Transaction SE30 (or activated TECHNICAL DETAILS) displays one row for OPEN, FETCH, and CLOSE respectively for database accesses and the WAIT FOR RFC call (the time for the response to come back) for RFC calls.

These functions ensure a higher clarity and you have the option to show technical details if required.

For large traces, the system displays the top 500 calls. You can change this using the SHOW/HIDE • TOP 500 CALLS ONLY menu.

Moreover, you can display various other columns. The following information in Table 3.14 is also available.

Column	Description
CALL TEXT 2ND PART	If the CALL column contains text that is truncated, this column displays additional text.
CALLING PROGRAM	In addition to the PROGRAM (CALLED PROGRAM) column, which concerns the program that executed the event, this column indicates the calling program for this program.
SHORT TEXTS	These are the short texts for programs, function modules, methods, classes, and tables.
LAST CHANGED BY	Shows the last user who changed this program. Additionally, the system also displays the change date. All entries ≠ "SAP" may involve modifications or custom developments. Sometimes, only an SAP note was integrated without using the SAP Notes Assistant.
FUNCTION & SUBFUNCTION	Function and subfunction area to which the program belongs

Table 3.14 Information of Transaction ST12

By means of this additional information, which is available directly in Transaction ST12 and must be retrieved manually in Transaction SE30, you can quickly gain important insights in many cases. There are no further differences for a trace that is fully aggregated.

For traces that were recorded with the AGGREGATION PER CALL POSITION option, there are some interesting evaluation functions that are not available in Transaction SE30. You obtain a list with a summary per call position, which you can sort according to the gross and net time. You are also provided with additional information, just like for the fully aggregated traces.

In Transaction ST12, you can display the results list grouped by modularization units if the trace was aggregated per call position. For this purpose, select the PER MODUNIT button or the AGGREGATION • PER MODULARIZATION UNIT menu. This way, you obtain a high aggregation because the times of the individual statements are added to the modularization unit. But if you expand a modularization unit, you can view the individual statements that belong to the modularization unit. The individual events are sorted by the source text row and displayed within the respective modularization unit (see Figure 3.38). This way, you can easily identify modularization units with high gross times and analyze them in greater detail.

In Figure 3.38, you can directly identify that the net time (~5,607 ms) of the GET_T100 subroutine is mainly caused by the database access to the T100 table

(~4,998 ms) and a loop via the IT100 internal table (~500 ms); the same applies to the GET_R_T100SA subroutine with ~3,571 ms whose net time is mainly determined by the RFC call, RFC_READ_TABLE (~3,571 ms).

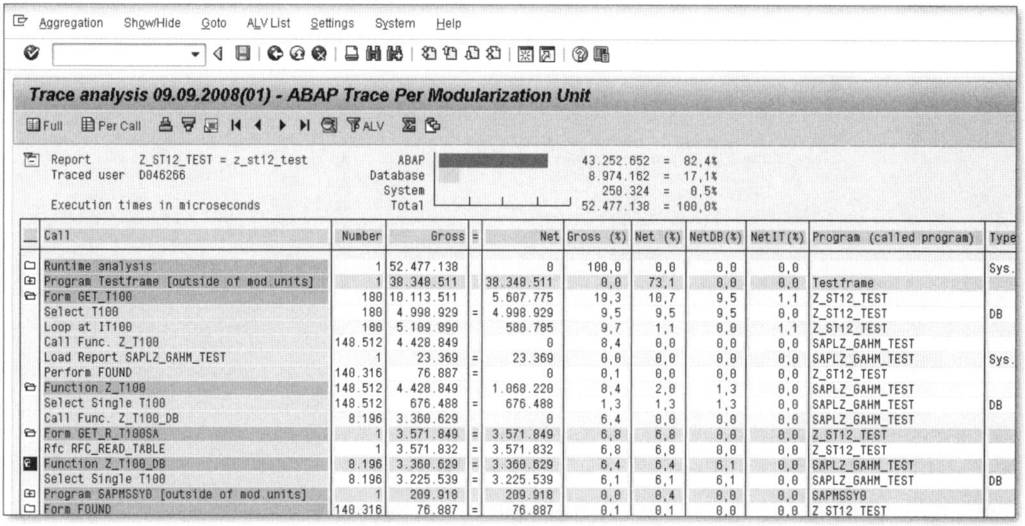

Call	Number	Gross	=	Net	Gross (%)	Net (%)	NetDB(%)	NetIT(%)	Program (called program)	Type
Runtime analysis	1	52.477.138		0	100,0	0,0	0,0	0,0		Sys.
Program Testframe [outside of mod.units]	1	38.348.511		38.348.511	0,0	73,1	0,0	0,0	Testframe	
Form GET_T100	180	10.113.511		5.607.775	19,3	10,7	9,5	1,1	Z_ST12_TEST	
Select T100	180	4.998.929	=	4.998.929	9,5	9,5	9,5	0,0	Z_ST12_TEST	DB
Loop at IT100	180	5.109.890		580.785	9,7	1,1	0,0	1,1	Z_ST12_TEST	
Call Func. Z_T100	148.512	4.428.849		0	8,4	0,0	0,0	0,0	SAPLZ_GAHM_TEST	
Load Report SAPLZ_GAHM_TEST	1	23.369	=	23.369	0,0	0,0	0,0	0,0	SAPLZ_GAHM_TEST	Sys.
Perform FOUND	140.316	76.887	=	0	0,1	0,0	0,0	0,0	Z_ST12_TEST	
Function Z_T100	148.512	4.428.849		1.068.220	8,4	2,0	1,3	0,0	SAPLZ_GAHM_TEST	
Select Single T100	148.512	676.488	=	676.488	1,3	1,3	1,3	0,0	SAPLZ_GAHM_TEST	DB
Call Func. Z_T100_DB	8.196	3.360.629		0	6,4	0,0	0,0	0,0	SAPLZ_GAHM_TEST	
Form GET_R_T100SA	1	3.571.849	=	3.571.849	6,8	6,8	0,0	0,0	Z_ST12_TEST	
Rfc RFC_READ_TABLE	1	3.571.832	=	3.571.832	6,8	6,8	0,0	0,0	Z_ST12_TEST	
Function Z_T100_DB	8.196	3.360.629	=	3.360.629	6,4	6,4	6,1	0,0	SAPLZ_GAHM_TEST	
Select Single T100	8.196	3.225.539	=	3.225.539	6,1	6,1	6,1	0,0	SAPLZ_GAHM_TEST	DB
Program SAPMSSY0 [outside of mod.units]	1	209.918		209.918	0,0	0,4	0,0	0,0	SAPMSSY0	
Form FOUND	140.316	76.887	=	76.887	0,1	0,1	0,0	0,0	Z_ST12_TEST	

Figure 3.38 ST12 — Trace Analysis Per Modularization Unit

Another interesting analysis in this view is the analysis of the NUMBER column. Figure 3.39 illustrates the appropriate source text excerpt for the GET_T100 subroutine. As already mentioned, the events (statements) within this program are already sorted by their call positions in the source text. For example, the database first accesses the T100 table and then `LOOP AT IT100`, in which the `Z_T100` function module is called. If this call is successful, the system executes the `FOUND` subroutine. In Figure 3.38, you can see that the database access is executed 100 times because the entire subroutine was executed 100 times. The loop is also executed 100 times; the call of the function module is 148,512 times, however. This means that the IT100 internal table had an average of 1,485 entries (148,512/100) at the time of execution. Because the `FOUND` subroutine was executed only 140,316 times, the function module was executed unsuccessfully for a total of 8,196 entries.

This type of analysis is extremely well suited to better understand the program flow without having to work with the Debugger. This way, you can identify the selectivities of program units. Like for the database accesses, execute the most important filters as early as possible to keep the number of follow-up activities as low as possible.

The two other groupings of the hit list (per call and full) differ only slightly. By default, you start with the grouping per call position. For the full grouping, you receive one row for each event; this list has a somewhat higher aggregation. The grouping per modularization unit has the highest aggregation level and combines the events per modularization unit.

```
 87  ⊟ FORM get_t100.
 88
 89      DATA: it100 LIKE STANDARD TABLE OF t100 WITH HEADER LINE.
 90      SELECT * FROM t100 INTO TABLE it100
 91        WHERE arbgb = it_lokal_t100sa-arbgb.
 92
 93  ⊟    LOOP AT it100.
 94        CALL FUNCTION 'Z_T100'
 95          EXPORTING
 96            arbgb       = it100-arbgb
 97          EXCEPTIONS
 98            not_found   = 1
 99            OTHERS      = 2.
100  ⊟      IF sy-subrc = 0.
101          PERFORM found.
102  ◇      ELSE.
103          write: 'Error calling function Z_T100'.
104  ┗      ENDIF.
105
106  ┗    ENDLOOP.
107
108  ┗ ENDFORM.
```

Figure 3.39 Source Text Excerpt for ST12 Trace from Figure 3.38

If you cannot find any optimization potential using the analysis methods presented so far, for example, no expensive individual statements (events), the runtime is frequently driven by the number of executions for an event. For example, it is frequently the case that optimized statements, such as database accesses or operations on internal tables, are time consuming because they are executed very often. But the individual execution is efficient. In this case, the question arises why these frequent executions occur and whether this could be avoided at a higher level, for example, by buffering the database accesses or completely preventing accesses to internal tables. To implement this analysis, you can use the bottom-up analysis in Transaction ST12, which can be executed on a trace that was aggregated per call position.

Figure 3.40 illustrates such an analysis. For this purpose, an entry was selected in the hit list and then the third button from the left (⛁, BOTTOM UP CALL HIERARCHY FOR ENTRY) was clicked. In doing so, you obtain the call hierarchy for this entry.

As you can see in Figure 3.40, the selected SELECT SINGLE on the T100 table was executed 148,512 times by the Z_T100 function module. You can identify this via the icons for CALLED PROGRAM, CALL DIRECTION, and CALLING PROGRAM (see Figure 3.40). The Z_T100 function module was also executed 148,512 times and called by the GET_100 subroutine that was executed 100 times. The GET_100 subroutine was called by the DO_WORK subroutine, which was then called by the MAIN subroutine in the main program. The rows highlighted in color (or gray) are part of the call hierarchy. Using the **Only CallHier** button, you can also hide all noninvolved entries.

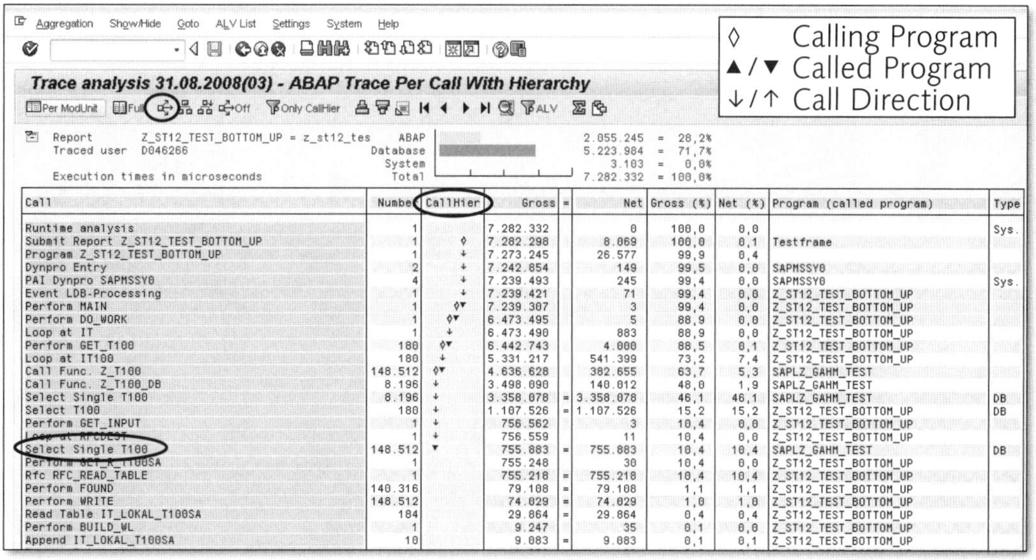

Call	Number	CallHier	Gross	=	Net	Gross (%)	Net (%)	Program (called program)	Type
Runtime analysis	1		7.282.332		0	100,0	0,0		Sys.
Submit Report Z_ST12_TEST_BOTTOM_UP	1	◊	7.282.298		8.069	100,0	0,1	Testframe	
Program Z_ST12_TEST_BOTTOM_UP	1	↓	7.273.245		26.577	99,9	0,4		
Dynpro Entry	2	↓	7.242.854		149	99,5	0,0	SAPMSSY0	
PAI Dynpro SAPMSSY0	4	↓	7.239.493		245	99,4	0,0	SAPMSSY0	Sys.
Event LDB-Processing	1	↓	7.239.421		71	99,4	0,0	Z_ST12_TEST_BOTTOM_UP	
Perform MAIN	1	◊▼	7.239.307		3	99,4	0,0	Z_ST12_TEST_BOTTOM_UP	
Perform DO_WORK	1	◊▼	6.473.495		5	88,9	0,0	Z_ST12_TEST_BOTTOM_UP	
Loop at IT	1	↓	6.473.490		883	88,9	0,0	Z_ST12_TEST_BOTTOM_UP	
Perform GET_T100	180	◊▼	6.442.743		4.000	88,5	0,1	Z_ST12_TEST_BOTTOM_UP	
Loop at IT100	180	↓	5.331.217		541.399	73,2	7,4	Z_ST12_TEST_BOTTOM_UP	
Call Func. Z_T100	148.512	◊▼	4.636.628		382.655	63,7	5,3	SAPLZ_GAHM_TEST	
Call Func. Z_T100_DB	8.196	↓	3.498.090		140.012	48,0	1,9	SAPLZ_GAHM_TEST	
Select Single T100	8.196	↓	3.358.078	=	3.358.078	46,1	46,1	SAPLZ_GAHM_TEST	DB
Select T100	180	↓	1.107.526	=	1.107.526	15,2	15,2	Z_ST12_TEST_BOTTOM_UP	DB
Perform GET_INPUT	1	↓	756.562		3	10,4	0,0	Z_ST12_TEST_BOTTOM_UP	
Loop at RFCDEST	1	↓	756.559		11	10,4	0,0	Z_ST12_TEST_BOTTOM_UP	
Select Single T100	148.512	▼	755.883	=	755.883	10,4	10,4	SAPLZ_GAHM_TEST	DB
Perform GET_R_T100SA	1		755.248		30	10,4	0,0	Z_ST12_TEST_BOTTOM_UP	
Rfc RFC_READ_TABLE	1		755.218	=	755.218	10,4	10,4	Z_ST12_TEST_BOTTOM_UP	
Perform FOUND	140.316		79.108	=	79.108	1,1	1,1	Z_ST12_TEST_BOTTOM_UP	
Perform WRITE	148.512		74.029	=	74.029	1,0	1,0	Z_ST12_TEST_BOTTOM_UP	
Read Table IT_LOKAL_T100SA	184		29.864	=	29.864	0,4	0,4	Z_ST12_TEST_BOTTOM_UP	
Perform BUILD_WL	1		9.247		35	0,1	0,0	Z_ST12_TEST_BOTTOM_UP	
Append IT_LOKAL_T100SA	10		9.083	=	9.083	0,1	0,1	Z_ST12_TEST_BOTTOM_UP	

Figure 3.40 Bottom-Up Analysis

This analysis is extremely well suited to detect problems that can be avoided at other levels in the program. For example, if identical database accesses exist (see Section 5.7) that are executed in function modules, this cannot be determined via Transaction ST05 in Version 7.00 EhP1 (where they come from or how they can be avoided) because the current Transaction ST05 doesn't indicate how this function module is called. Transaction ST12 enables you to reproduce the call hierarchy for a `SELECT` statement as described previously in the example. By means of the involved internal tables and loops, you can usually find the cause for the identical accesses or at least delimit it.

Figure 3.41 illustrates another example for the call hierarchy for an entry. Here, a function module is called multiple times from various positions in the program. To find them, you can use the call hierarchy. This way, you can identify possibly unnecessary calls.

The top-down analysis is another analysis option of Transaction ST12. There are two different views available that help you identify optimization potential.

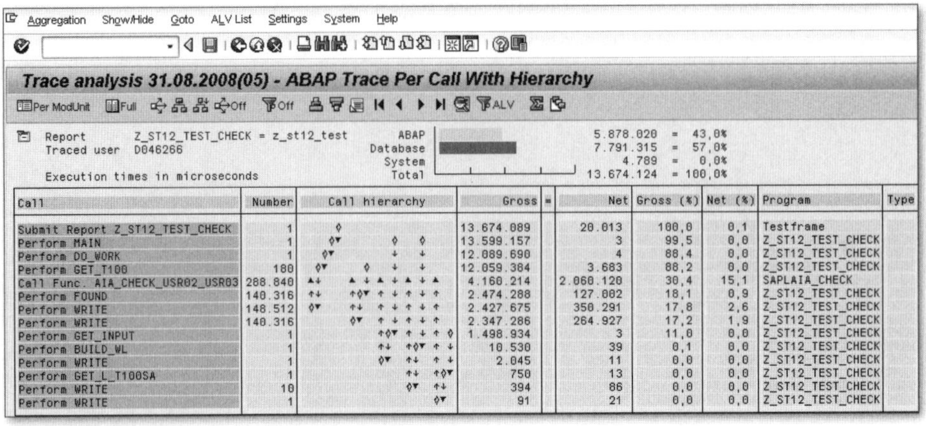

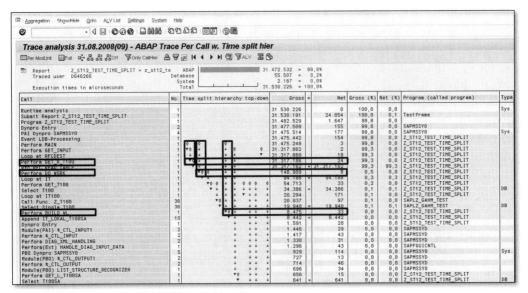

Figure 3.41 Multiple Calls in the Call Hierarchy

One view is the *time split hierarchy top-down* (Figure 3.42), which you can activate using the fifth icon from the left (⊞), after selecting a modularization unit). Using this analysis, you can identify the most important call hierarchies below the selected modularization unit. For example, you can analyze in which "time threads" the time is consumed within a modularization unit and where a "time flow" splits into different threads. These threads usually correlate with distinct functions. Therefore, the time split hierarchy is excellent for the functional analysis.

Figure 3.42 Time Split Hierarchy Top-Down

The second view is the *call tree* (Figure 3.43) which you can activate using the fourth icon from the left (🔠) after you've selected a modularization unit. Here, you can view which events can be called below the selected statement. Based on the number, you can identify how many levels below the statements are called. The view can also be understood as *show all events that can be reached from here*.

| Aggregation | Show/Hide | Goto | ALV List | Settings | System | Help |

Trace analysis 31.08.2008(09) - ABAP Trace Per Call With Call Tree

Report	Z_ST12_TEST_TIME_SPLIT = z_st12_te	ABAP	31.472.532 = 99,8%
Traced user	D046266	Database	55.507 = 0,2%
		System	2.187 = 0,0%
Execution times in microseconds		Total	31.530.226 = 100,0%

Call	No.	CallTree	Gross	=	Net	Gross (%)	Net (%)	Program (called program)	Type
Runtime analysis	1		31.530.226		0	100,0	0,0		Sys.
Submit Report Z_ST12_TEST_TIME_SPLIT	1		31.530.191		24.054	100,0	0,1	Testframe	
Program Z_ST12_TEST_TIME_SPLIT	1		31.482.529		1.647	99,8	0,0		
Dynpro Entry	2		31.477.509		155	99,8	0,0	SAPMSSY0	
PAI Dynpro SAPMSSY0	4		31.475.514		177	99,8	0,0	SAPMSSY0	Sys.
Event LDB-Processing	1		31.475.442		154	99,8	0,0	Z_ST12_TEST_TIME_SPLIT	
Perform MAIN	1	0	31.475.249		3	99,8	0,0	Z_ST12_TEST_TIME_SPLIT	
Perform GET_INPUT	1	1	31.317.862		2	99,3	0,0	Z_ST12_TEST_TIME_SPLIT	
Loop at RFCDEST	1	2	31.317.860		18	99,3	0,0	Z_ST12_TEST_TIME_SPLIT	
Perform GET_R_T100	1	2	31.317.186		24	99,3	0,0	Z_ST12_TEST_TIME_SPLIT	
Rfc RFC_READ_TABLE	1	3	31.317.162	=	31.317.162	99,3	99,3	Z_ST12_TEST_TIME_SPLIT	
Perform DO_WORK	1	1	148.909		8	0,5	0,0	Z_ST12_TEST_TIME_SPLIT	
Loop at IT	1	2	94.188	=	94.188	0,3	0,3	Z_ST12_TEST_TIME_SPLIT	
Perform GET_T100	1	2	54.713		33	0,2	0,0	Z_ST12_TEST_TIME_SPLIT	
Select T100	1	3	34.386	=	34.386	0,1	0,1	Z_ST12_TEST_TIME_SPLIT	DB
Loop at IT100	1	3	20.294		171	0,1	0,0	Z_ST12_TEST_TIME_SPLIT	
Call Func. Z_T100	36	3	20.037		97	0,1	0,0	SAPLZ_GAHM_TEST	
Select Single T100	36	4	19.940	=	19.940	0,1	0,1	SAPLZ_GAHM_TEST	DB
Perform BUILD_WL	1	1	8.475		8	0,0	0,0	Z_ST12_TEST_TIME_SPLIT	
Append IT_LOKAL_T100SA	10	2	8.442	=	8.442	0,0	0,0	Z_ST12_TEST_TIME_SPLIT	
Dynpro Entry	1		1.591		28	0,0	0,0		
Module(PAI) %_CTL_INPUT1	2		1.446		29	0,0	0,0	SAPMSSYD	
Perform %_CTL_INPUT	2		1.417		43	0,0	0,0	SAPMSSYD	
Perform DIAG_XML_HANDLING	2		1.330		31	0,0	0,0	SAPMSSYD	
Perform(Ext) HANDLE_DIAG_INPUT_DATA	5		1.296		43	0,0	0,0	SAPFGUICNTL	
PBO Dynpro SAPMSSY0	5		929		114	0,0	0,0	SAPMSSY0	Sys.
Module(PBO) %_CTL_OUTPUT1	2		727		13	0,0	0,0	SAPMSSYD	
Perform %_CTL_OUTPUT	2		714		46	0,0	0,0	SAPMSSYD	
Module(PBO) LIST_STRUCTURE_RECOGNIZER	1		696		34	0,0	0,0	SAPMSSYD	
Perform GET_L_T100SA	1	2	656		15	0,0	0,0	Z_ST12_TEST_TIME_SPLIT	
Select T100SA	1	3	641	=	641	0,0	0,0	Z_ST12_TEST_TIME_SPLIT	DB

Figure 3.43 Call Tree

Both views can display up to 28 levels below the selected modularization unit and be reduced to the called entries using the [Only CallHier] button.

For the ABAP trace, the summary ([Summary] button in the lower area of Transaction ST12) must also be mentioned. An example is illustrated in Figure 3.44; in the upper part of the screen, the times are subdivided according to CPU, DB, system, and generation time. The lower part of the screen indicates the time portions of the gross times per function and subfunction provided that they are stored in the system. For some functions, they are stored in the SAP standard and can be maintained in Transaction ST12 under the GOTO • SUMMARY CUSTOMIZING menu. This topic is not further discussed here.

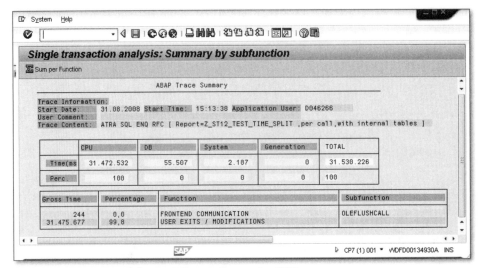

Figure 3.44 Summary of the ABAP Trace in Transaction ST12

For the SQL trace, there is another function that refers to the transactional security to evaluate the performance traces from Transaction ST12. Using the ⬚ button, you can transfer a filter for DML statements instead of the recorded performance trace (SQL trace). This filter only displays COMMIT, ENQUEUE, DEQUEUE, UPDATE, and INSERT statements. This is useful for the analyses regarding the transaction security of applications, which is not a subject of this book.

Apart from that, the evaluation of the performance trace is not further discussed now because it doesn't differ from the evaluation using Transaction ST05. Transaction ST05 is only called by Transaction ST12 with appropriate filter values for the display, so you don't have to write down on which server you used the SQL trace at what time. As already mentioned, the performance trace data is not stored in the database and hence is overwritten in the course of time, as is the case for Transaction ST05. In this respect, Transaction ST12 doesn't differ from Transaction ST05.

Another useful function of Transaction ST12 is the creation of annotations using the ⬚ icon. This is a free text that you can enter for the trace. In the ALV grid, which displays the available traces, the ANNOTATION EXISTS column is on the right, which indicates whether an annotation exists for a trace.

Tip for Annotations

For example, you can insert the copied SQL trace summary from Transaction ST05 to store the most important events of the SQL trace together with the ABAP trace in the database.

Managing the ABAP Trace

The traces are managed in the lower area (see Figure 3.37). As a basic principle, the traces are not deleted automatically and are therefore available in the database without any limitations. In the left area, you can find information about the trace file that you selected in the right area. In the left area, there is the option to delete traces.

3.3.14   E2E Trace

This section provides an overview of the E2E trace. It first presents the prerequisites, then the implementation, and finally the analysis of an E2E trace based on an example. This section cannot and isn't intended to discuss all details of this comprehensive topic, but it only provides an overview of the E2E trace, which gains in significance in complex system landscapes.

For more information on the E2E trace, refer to the SAP online documentation.

Prerequisites

The E2E trace is an important part of SAP Solution Manager Diagnostics (SMD). An SMD with connected systems is therefore a prerequisite to implement an E2E trace. The trace activation must be permitted for all systems from the outside. The activation of the traces in the systems is carried out centrally from SMD.

As you can see in Figure 3.45, you use a special browser plug-in (integral part of SMD) in the browser or the /SDF/E2E_TRACE program (Transaction /SDF/E2E_TRACE) to create a *passport* that activates the traces in the systems involved. For this purpose, you are provided with different trace levels.

For SAP NetWeaver AS ABAP, these include the following.

Trace Level / Trace	None	Low	Medium	High
HTTP log	–	yes	yes	yes
SQL trace	–	–	yes	yes
ABAP trace	–	–	aggregated	non-aggregated
RFC trace	–	–	yes	yes
Enqueue/table buffer/ authorization trace	–	–	–	yes
Application log	–	–	–	yes

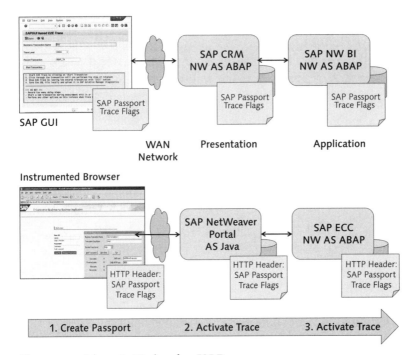

Figure 3.45 Schematic Display of an E2E Trace

The E2E trace also activates further traces (for example, BI statistics, Web services traces, and so on), which are not subjects of this book. For further information, refer to the online documentation.

To execute a performance analysis for ABAP, activate the MEDIUM trace level as a minimum. The BI statistics, the RFC, Enqueue, table buffer, and the authorization trace can only be created but not displayed in SMD. For the ABAP and SQL trace, the hit list and the statement summary are given in SMD. You can view the details of these traces or the traces that are not displayed in the respective trace transactions in the ABAP system.

The following traces are given for AS Java.

Trace \ Trace Level	None	Low	Medium	High
HTTP log	–	yes	yes	yes
SQL trace	–	–	yes	yes
Logging	–	–	–	yes
Introscope transaction trace	–	yes	yes	yes

Implementing a Trace

You can implement E2E traces both for Web applications and for ABAP applications, which run distributed across multiple systems. Figure 3.45 shows the two options. For Web applications, you use the SAP HTTP plug-in, for distributed ABAP applications the /SDF/E2E_TRACE program.

To implement a trace with the SAP HTTP plug-in, the *ie-https.cmd* script starts an instance of Microsoft® Internet Explorer™ with activated *SAPHTTPPlugIn.exe*. Enter the URL of the application to be traced. Figure 3.46 shows a screenshot.

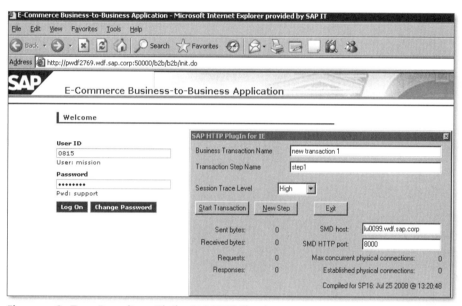

Figure 3.46 Trace Recording with the SAP HTTP Plug-in

By clicking the Start Transaction button, a new trace is started. The trace can consist of multiple steps. For each click in your application, measure an individual step by clicking the New Step button and entering a new name in the Transaction Step Name field.

Here, you can specify the trace level for each step. It determines which traces are activated in the systems involved (see last section).

The connection information about SMD is provided in the lower right-hand area. As soon as you click on the Stop Transaction button, the system automatically uploads the client-side trace to SMD. If no connection information is stored, you must enter it manually. The Exit button closes the SAP HTTP plug-in and the browser.

Once the client-side trace has been uploaded to SMD, the server-side traces are collected, depending on the set trace level as soon as you select the trace.

To start a trace of a distributed ABAP application in the SAP GUI, you can use the / SDF/E2E_TRACE report. Just like in the SAP HTTP plug-in, you specify the name and the trace level. For this purpose, you must enter the transaction that should be traced. A manual assignment of new steps like in the SAP HTTP plug-in is not possible. Each dialog step (request to the application server) is recorded as a separate step.

After the transaction is complete, a dialog window opens in which you can store the *BusinessTransaction.xml* file on your local PC. This file, which contains the client-side trace, must be uploaded manually to SMD, as is illustrated in Figure 3.47.

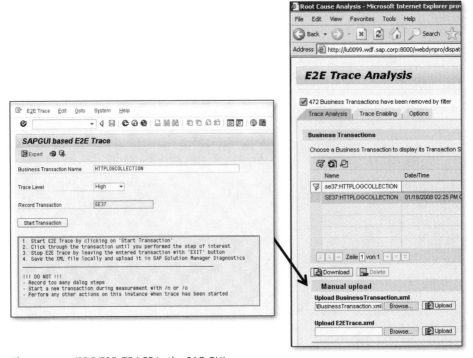

Figure 3.47 /SDF/E2E_TRACE in the SAP GUI

Analysis of an E2E Trace

This section provides an example of the analysis of an E2E trace for a Web application created using the SAP HTTP plug-in. Note that not all options of the trace analysis can be discussed here.

The lower part of the screen displays the recorded steps initially. As soon as you click DISPLAY for one of these steps, the system shows an overview of the client-side trace (see Figure 3.48).

In the medium area, the time required for this step is subdivided into the following four areas:

1. CLIENT TIME (MS)

   This time mostly contains the preparation time and the queueing time for requests as well as accesses to the browser cache.

2. NETWORK TIME (MS)

   This time contains the duration required to transfer data from the server to the front end. The data transfer time between the involved servers is not contained herein because it is a client-side trace.

3. SERVER GROSS TIME (MS)

   This is the time consumed on the server. It is the total of the times of all servers.

4. OTHER (MS)

   This is the rendering time and the time required for possible virus scans, for example. If multiple clicks were done in one step, this time also contains the "think time" between the clicks.

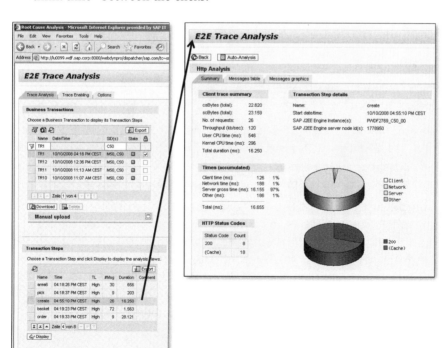

Figure 3.48 Evaluation — Client-Side Trace

In the MESSAGES TABLE and MESSAGES GRAPHICS tabs, you can analyze individual responses sent to the client for this step in more detail.

You can already determine where most of the time is consumed. The example of Figure 3.48 indicates that 16.1 seconds of 16.2 seconds were consumed on the servers.

If you open the server analysis, you first obtain an overview of the servers involved in this step (see Figure 3.49).

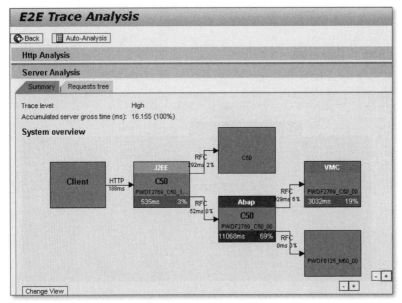

Figure 3.49 Overview of the Server-Side Trace

The example shows that the 16.1 seconds of server time are split in 535 ms Java server time, 11 seconds ABAP server time, and 3 seconds VMC server time (Virtual Machine Controller) and RFC times. In the REQUESTS TREE tab, you can track the program flow and analyze the most expensive transaction steps in more detail.

By clicking the AUTO-ANALYSIS button, the system automatically displays the most expensive call. Figure 3.50 shows an example of the requests tree. In the lower part of the screen, you can view the corresponding statistics of the transaction step. For ABAP programs, these are the single record statistics from Transaction STAD (see Section 3.3.15, Single Record Statistics (Transaction STAD)). Figure 3.50 shows the Single Statistical Record (SSR) data, which informs you that the database time of 8,411,732 microseconds accounts for the largest part of the response time.

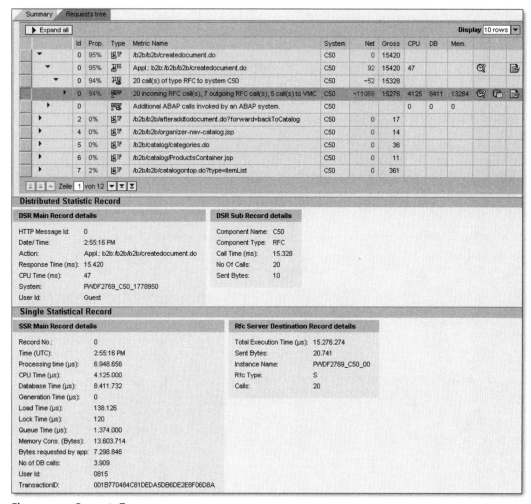

Figure 3.50 Requests Tree

For this step, you can open the ABAP trace (by clicking 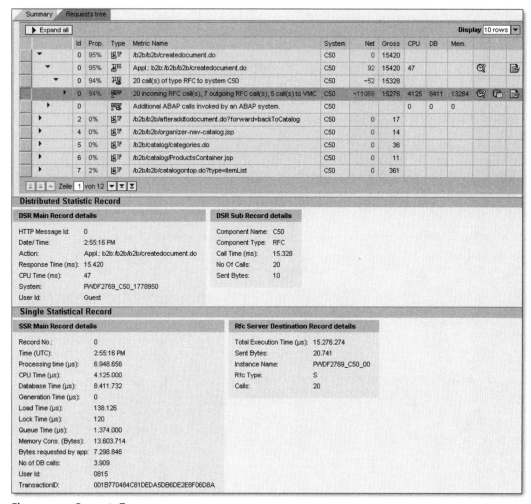) or the SQL trace (by clicking). You can also open the application log. The respective Java tools are provided for Java transaction steps.

The ABAP trace can be displayed directly in SMD. It is also possible to open Transaction ST12 (Section 3.3.13, Single Transaction Analysis (Transaction ST12)) in SAP Web GUI by clicking the button in the JUMP IN column (see Figure 3.51). In the DETAILS tab, you can open Transaction SE30 (Section 3.3.12, ABAP Trace (Transaction SE30)) in the Web GUI using the DISPLAY ABAP-TRACE IN MANAGED SYSTEM link.

Of course, you can also open the ABAP trace in the regular SAP GUI. For this purpose, you must open the corresponding trace file in the local system. This trace file can be identified and read using the TRANSACTION ID in the DETAILS tab or via the time stamp. Figure 3.51 shows the ABAP trace in SMD and in the SAP GUI in Transaction ST12.

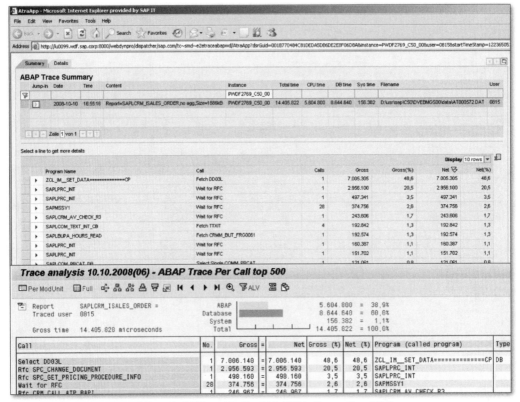

Figure 3.51 ABAP Trace in SMD and in the SAP GUI in Transaction ST12

The SQL trace can also be displayed in SMD. In the DETAILS tab, you can also display the SQL trace in the Web GUI. There you find the time stamps, which are required for a manual opening in Transaction ST05 in the local system. Figure 3.52 shows the SQL trace in SMD and in the SAP GUI.

The last two sections describe the tools that can be used for the analysis of performance problems after a program was executed.

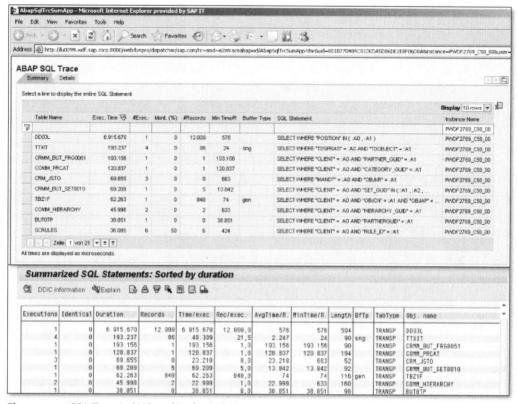

Figure 3.52 SQL Trace in SMD and in the SAP GUI

3.3.15 Single Record Statistics (Transaction STAD)

Statistical records are written for each transaction in SAP NetWeaver Application Server ABAP. This is implemented by default and doesn't need to be activated. The statistical records contain basic metrics, which can be used for the performance analysis.

Transaction STAD is useful already for sizing because some important metrics, such as response time, used CPU time, memory use, and database time provide important values for sizing.

Within the scope of the performance analysis, this transaction is also used for the *post runtime analysis*. This means that the most critical metrics can still be analyzed when the program is exited.

Let's first discuss the technical background of the single record statistics and then the selection and analysis itself. Here, the focus is on the options of special interest for the ABAP developers.

Technical Background

The SAP kernel collects metrics during the execution of a program. Some of these can be viewed in the details of the process monitor (Transaction SM50) at runtime (see Section 3.3.3, Process Analysis (Transactions SM50/SM66) — Status of a Program). The collected data is aggregated in a statistical record at the end of a transaction step. A statistical record is also created in case of a program termination. Initially, this is done in the main memory; the data is written asynchronously into the statistics file.

By default, there are 48 files that each contain an hour of statistical data. So, you can analyze the last 48 hours. Using the `stat/max_files` parameter, you can configure up to 99 of such files — hence you can carry out a performance analysis for the last 99 hours. This way, on Monday morning, you can analyze data from last Friday, for example, which is not possible with the standard setting.

> **Note: Aggregation and Historization of STAD Data**
>
> A job that runs at hourly intervals by default imports the statistical single records from the files and aggregates them. The aggregated data is written to the SWNCMONI table. Transaction ST03 is the analysis transaction for the aggregated data. This book doesn't detail Transaction ST03; instead, it discusses the most critical details of data basis for this transaction.

There are technical statistical records generated for each transaction step in the SAP system and application statistics created by specific applications.

The technical statistical records summarize all data per transaction step. For dialog transactions, all steps, such as the call of a screen, the selection of a button, and so on, are separate transaction steps respectively. These can be combined in a business transaction for the evaluation. A batch program also represents a technical transaction step, even if the program runs for many hours. In this case, the data is aggregated for the entire program because the work process remains occupied for the duration of the program.

In the SAP standard, the application statistics are written by some applications, but they can also be written by custom developments. The process is described at the end of this section.

Selection

When you call Transaction STAD, the system displays a selection screen as shown in Figure 3.53.

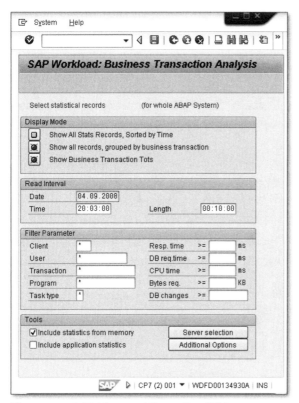

Figure 3.53 Initial Screen of Transaction STAD

The screen is split into four areas.

1. DISPLAY MODE
   Here, you can specify how the data should be formatted. The chronological list of records is activated by default. But you can also select a grouping with or without summary records display for each transaction.

2. READ INTERVAL
   Here, you specify the date and time you want to analyze the single records statistics. Additionally, you must enter an interval (LENGTH). The analyzed time window can be larger than the interval specified by READ TIME because the system analyzes complete transactions if possible. Because the business transaction analysis is very time consuming, keep the interval to be analyzed as short as possible.

3. FILTER PARAMETER
   Here, you can set different filters to find the desired statistical records. You can filter according to client, user, transaction, program, process type, response, database, CPU time, read dataset, and number of database changes.

4. TOOLS

In the tools area, you can use the INCLUDE STATISTICS FROM MEMORY option to evaluate the statistical records still located in the memory that have not been written to the file yet. The INCLUDE APPLICATION STATISTICS option evaluates the application statistics. Using the SERVER SELECTION button, you can specify the server from which you want to read the data. By means of the ADDITIONAL OPTIONS button, you determine the wait time for the RFC calls during the selection.

Evaluation

You start the selection using ⏎ or the OK (ENTER) button (✅). You obtain a list of all statistical records that correspond to your selection. Figure 3.55 shows such an evaluation, which contains application statistics.

The following information in Table 3.15 is available by default.

Column	Description
TIME	System time during recording
SERVER	Server and system name
TRANSACTION	Name of the transaction
PROGRAM	Name of the program
T	Type (D — Dialog, B — Batch, ...)
SCR	Dynpro number
WP	Work process number
USER	User name
RESPONSE TIME	Response time in ms
TIME IN WP	Time in which the program was in the work process
WAIT TIME	Wait time in the dispatcher queue
CPU TIME	CPU time
DB REQ TIME	Database time
LOAD GEN TIME	Time required for loading and generating
VMC ELAPSED TIME MS	Time used in the Virtual Machine Controller
MEMORY	Memory requirement of the program
KBYTES TRANSFERRED	Volume of transferred data

Table 3.15 Table 3.15 Information of the Statistical Records

At this point, the overview of a transaction step is given again (see Figure 3.54), which shows the time components of the single records statistics.

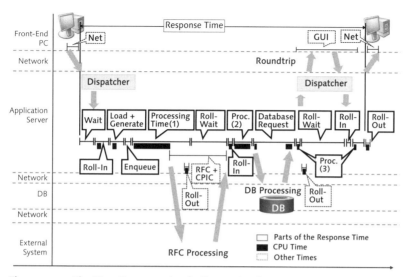

Figure 3.54 The Time Components of a Transaction Step

The following section discusses the values that are most important from a developer's point of view.

The list illustrated in Figure 3.55 already shows important values, such as CPU and database time. If you click the SEL. FIELDS button, the system displays further values.

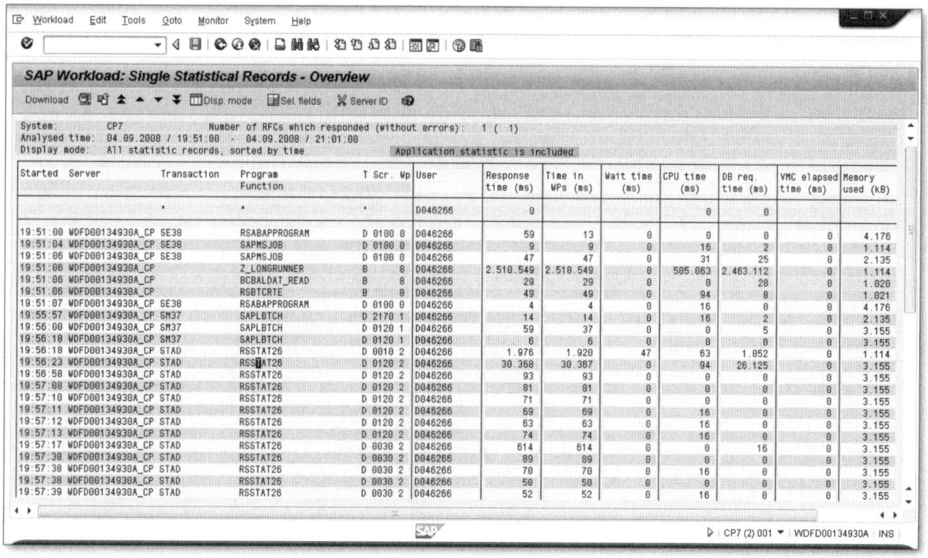

Figure 3.55 List of Statistical Records

If you selected the grouping by transaction, the list appears slightly different (not displayed here). Then, the individual statistic records are displayed grouped by transactions, and the system displays a totals row if requested (SHOW BUSINESS TRANSACTION TOTS). The FCODE column indicates the executed function code for each record.

If you double-click a statistical record in these lists, you obtain all details as shown in Figure 3.56.

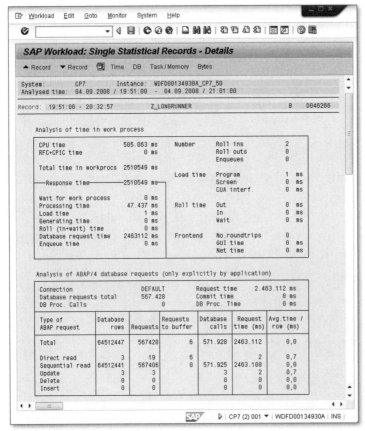

Figure 3.56 Detail Screen of a Statistical Record

The left half of the upper area contains the most essential information.

The CPU TIME is the CPU time used by the process. It is *measured* by the SAP kernel. It usually involves the processing time of ABAP statements, such as accesses to internal tables (see Chapter 7) or accesses to tables in the SAP table buffer (see Section 6.4 in Chapter 6). However, CPU time also occurs for all other times described in the following. The CPU time is the time that was actually used in the CPU, that is, the wait time for the CPU is not part of the CPU TIME; this wait time for the CPU is assigned to the PROCESSING TIME.

The following times are *measured* by the SAP kernel.

► The RFC+CPIC TIME is the time required for the communication via RFC and CPIC.

► The RESPONSE TIME is the time between the receipt of a request and the provision of the results data. This time doesn't include network times.

► LOAD TIME and GENERATING TIME are times required for loading and generating programs.

► ROLL (IN + WAIT) TIME includes the time for roll-in of the user context and the wait time that occurs in RFC calls, for example.

► DATABASE REQUEST TIME is the time used for database requests.

► ENQUEUE TIME is the time required for lock requests.

The PROCESSING TIME is calculated based on the following formula:

Response time – (load time + generation time + roll (in + wait) time + database request time + enqueue time)

Consequently, the PROCESSING TIME contains all times that are not recorded by the other components.

Frequently, the PROCESSING TIME isn't more than 30% above the CPU time. If the PROCESSING TIME is higher than the CPU TIME, this can have different reasons. One reason can be a CPU bottleneck, but it could also be a synchronous update for which the time of the update is added to the PROCESSING TIME. Other reasons could be enqueue calls with the _WAIT option (see Section 4.2.2 in Chapter 4) or one or multiple RFC calls. The wait time for the RFC is added to the PROCESSING TIME within the first 500 ms if there is no roll-out. In these cases, further analysis would have to be implemented by the system administrators.

In the right-hand area under FRONTEND, you obtain information about the round-trips to the GUI and the time required in the GUI.

For more information, see SAP Note 8963.

Tip

This time allocation contains valuable information for the performance analysis. Long after a program is complete, you can still determine what the time was used for. Prior to a performance analysis using traces, always view the statistical record if available because it provides valuable notes about which tool is best suited to analyze the largest time components in more detail (for example, Transaction ST05 for high database times or Transactions SE30/ST12 for high CPU times).

In addition to the discussed values, the statistical record contains further parameters, which provide even more detailed information on the implementation of the traces or make a trace completely unnecessary.

For database accesses, you are provided with another block (ANALYSIS OF ABAP/4 DATABASE REQUESTS), which is located directly below the first block in the details of a statistical record. It contains information on the database accesses. This block is shown in the top left area of Figure 3.57. This block contains the REQUEST TIME, which corresponds to the DATABASE REQUEST TIME. In the following, you can find detailed information for each access type (DIRECT READ, SEQUENTIAL READ, UPDATE, DELETE, INSERT). These are values that are aggregated at the application server level in Transaction ST10 (see Section 3.3.6, Transaction ST10 — Table Call Statistics).

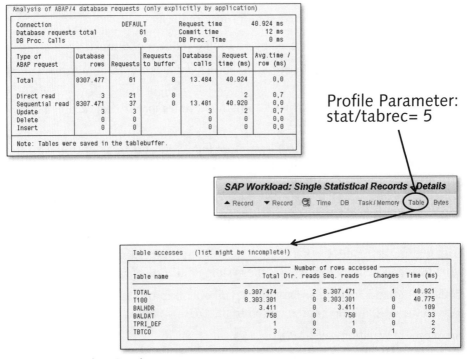

Profile Parameter: stat/tabrec= 5

Figure 3.57 Database Details

Among other things, you can view the number of read rows and the time required for it.

There are SAP profile parameters that allow for an even more precise analysis of the database accesses. By means of the `stat/tabrec` parameter, you can determine that further access statistics need to be collected for a specific number of tables. If this parameter is activated, for example, with the value "5," access statistics are written for the five tables for which the system requires the most access time. Because this evaluation results in an additional overhead and requires spaces in the files, this parameter is not activated by default. But it can be dynamically changed in Transaction ST03 via COLLECTOR AND PERFORMANCE DATABASE • STATISTICAL RECORDS AND FILES • ONLINE PARAMETERS • DIALOG STEP STATISTICS.

You can dynamically change and activate the parameter in the table that is then displayed. The change is temporary until the system is restarted. Then the value set in the profile parameters is valid again.

After the activation, you obtain access statistics for the longest tables, which used the most time. This is shown in Figure 3.57: For each table, the system shows the number of read and changed data records. In production systems, the parameter should not be activated permanently, but you can usually set it for a specific time for analysis purposes.

There are also access statistics for RFC calls. Five subrecords are written for RFC calls by default. This is specified in the `stat/rfcrec = 5` SAP profile parameter, which you can also change dynamically.

If you select the RFC option, you obtain an overview of the RFC calls within this transaction. This overview indicates whether it involves client or server records. Client records are outgoing calls from the program to others; server records are incoming calls. You can view the number of connections (targets of the RFC requests) and the number of calls. For the five longest records (depending on `stat/rfcrec`), you receive further information if you click on the respective number.

For the illustrated values, the RFC connections are the totals.

For the RFC calls, you can see the values per call for the five most expensive calls. In Figure 3.58, the `RFC_READ_TABLE` function module was called for the `Z_D8M` connection, for example. It took 211 seconds, of which 182 seconds account for the time for receiving the data because a large dataset of 1.8 MB was sent (in compressed form).

The following information in Table 3.16 is available in the subrecords.

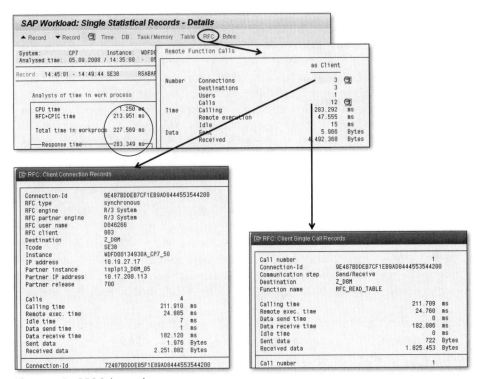

Figure 3.58 RFC Subrecords

Column	Description
DESTINATION	RFC connection (can be checked in Transaction SM59)
FUNCTION NAME	Name of the function module that was called in the remote system
CALLING TIME	The calling time measured in the SAP gateway (outbound time stamp — inbound time stamp). This time can contain the network time, compression time, connection setup time, and so on.
REMOTE EXEC. TIME	The pure execution time is measured and returned by the server in the client record.
DATA SEND TIME	Time required to send the data
DATA RECEIVE TIME	Time required to receive the data
SEND DATA	Dataset sent
RECEIVED DATA	Dataset received

Table 3.16 Information of the RFC Subrecords

Based on the RFC subrecords, you can implement a good preliminary check, provided that the runtime for RFC calls is used. In many cases, an RFC trace is no longer necessary then. The target system contains the RFC server record, which in turn includes a time allocation in ABAP time, database time, and so on. You can then select the appropriate tool for an in-depth analysis.

Application Statistics

The *application statistics* can be written using the PF_ASTAT_OPEN and PF_ASTAT_ CLOSE function modules. By means of these modules, the SAP kernel is instructed to write the coding that runs between these two calls in a separate statistical record. This involves the application statistics because "interesting" code sections can be measured separately within applications or within a transaction step. Note that the function module is not released and therefore is subject to the usual guidelines for function modules not released.

Figure 3.55 shows such an application statistical record (BALDAT_READ). It is highlighted in color in the given display that the application statistics was also selected during the selection (Figure 3.53).

3.3.16 Dump Analysis (Transaction ST22)

If a program terminates during runtime, the dump frequently contains some interesting information, which is referred to now for the sake of completeness.

In the system environment area, you can find information on the memory consumption. A high memory consumption is frequently caused by large internal tables, which can result in performance problems in case of inefficient accesses. Figure 3.59 shows an example of a dump with the system environment. At the time of termination, approximately 9.4 MB of memory was consumed for the program.

Below the source text excerpt, you can find some system variables that can provide further information on the termination point. Some of the important fields are listed in the following.

Field	Description
SY-TABIX	Table index. Contains the index of the last called table row of the index tables (standard or sorted tables).
SY-INDEX	Loop index. Contains the number of the row that was last processed in the loop (for instance, DO).
SY-DBCNT	Database counter. Contains the number of the last process data records of the last SQL command.

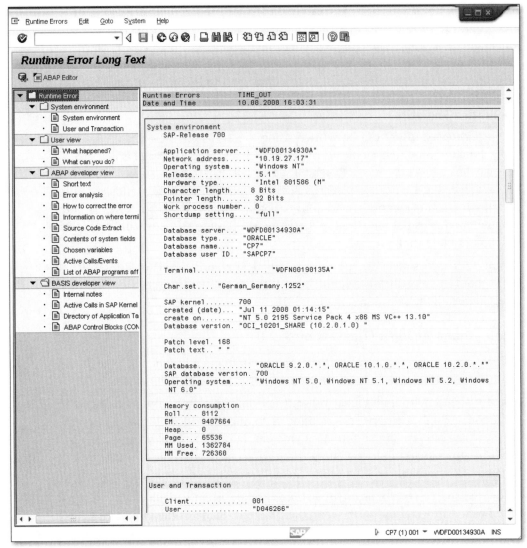

Figure 3.59 ABAP Dump — System Environment

With these values, you can gather some information from the dump. The example of Figure 3.60 shows, based on the SY-TABIX, that the program was terminated in the 177th loop pass. SY-DBCNT is at 383, that is, the last executed SELECT statement read 383 data records.

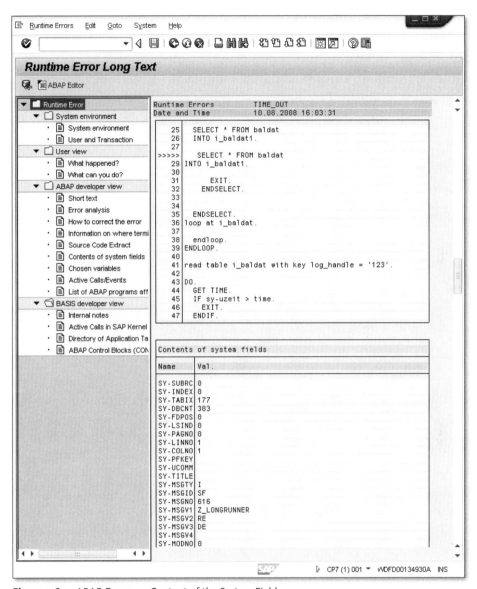

Figure 3.60 ABAP Dump — Content of the System Fields

Finally, you can see a list of selected variables. It also contains notes on the internal tables. The header information for the internal tables contains some interesting fields.

Field	Description
FILL	Number of rows in the internal tables
LENG	Length of a row in bytes

Based on these values, you can calculate the size of an internal table at the time of termination. For example, the I_BALDAT table in Figure 3.61 had a size of 537 KB (FILL (990) × LENG (556)).

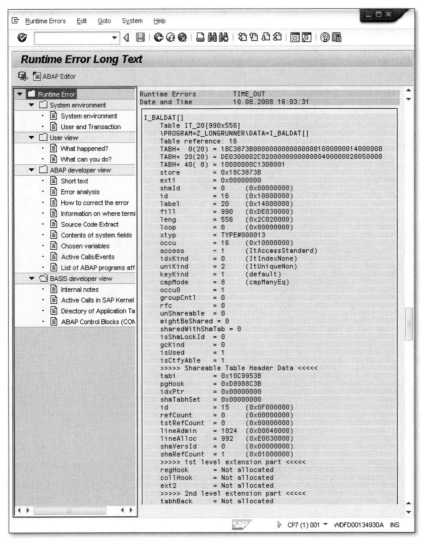

Figure 3.61 ABAP Dump — Selected Variables

3.4 Tips for the Performance Analysis

After learning about the most important tools and their use and information content, the following sections provide some general recommendations about working with the tools.

3.4.1 Consistency Checks

Compare the measured times of the various tools with each other to ensure the consistency of the measurement.

For example, check whether the response time of Transaction STAD corresponds to the runtime of Transactions SE30 or ST12. In Transaction ST05, you can determine a runtime (between the first and the last SQL statement) based on the difference of the last and the first time stamp in the extended trace list.

The database time of Transaction STAD should correspond to the total of the DURATION in the statement summary in Transaction ST05 (SQL trace).

The measurement data from the various tools should originate from different test runs because these tools can influence each other for the measurement values. For example, the CPU time in Transaction STAD for a low measurement accuracy (see Section 3.3.12, ABAP Trace (Transaction SE30)) or with many measuring points in Transaction SE30 can be considerably higher than for a run that was not traced with Transaction SE30.

3.4.2 Time-Based Analysis

Start with the analysis of the biggest "time wasters." For example, if you identify identical selects in the SQL trace, which only occupy 0.8% of the total runtime of an application, you can simply ignore them. Obviously, there are bigger "time wasters."

3.4.3 Prevention

For the largest time consumers (regardless of which tool), first consider how you can prevent them before thinking about the optimization. Prevention is still the best optimization.

Sometimes, it can occur that certain code sections of an application don't need to be performed for the concrete application case. None of the presented tools can identify whether a statement was necessary. You can only perform this analysis if you know the application.

In the ABAP trace, you can check the hit list for modularization units that were called unnecessarily sorted by gross and net time in descending order. In case of a high number of executions, you can check whether all executions were really necessary for the statement or modularization unit.

In the SQL trace, the identical selects and accesses to buffered tables constitute potential candidates for prevention. They can be prevented by buffering or changing the access to buffered tables (see Section 6.4 in Chapter 6). The EXECUTIONS, RECORDS, and RECORDS/EXEC. as well as the table names are further values that you should take into account in the statement summary. Detailed knowledge of the application enables you to identify possible unnecessary accesses.

3.4.4 Optimization

After you've answered the question about preventing the largest time consumers, start with the optimization. Avoid the optimization of statements or program parts that don't need to be executed and consequently are executed "faster" instead of not at all.

3.4.5 Runtime Behavior of Mass Data

If the program should process mass data, it is important that it is parallelizable and scales linear to the number of data records to be processed as far as possible. For this purpose, refer to Sections 4.2 in Chapter 4 (Parallel Processing) and 7.4.10 in Chapter 7 (Nested Loops and Non-Linear Runtime Behavior).

3.5 Summary

After you've learned about the most critical options of the available tools, the following once again summarizes the tools with a usage proposal.

If a performance problem existed, that is, the program no longer runs, check whether the single records statistics (STAD, Section 3.3.15, Single Record Statistics (Transaction STAD)) is still available. This way, you gain a good overview of how the times were used. Based on these times, you can decide which tool is suitable for a more detailed analysis. To subsequently analyze the application in more detail, the performance problem must be reproducible and the application must be restarted.

In case of high database times (DATABASE REQUEST TIME), continue with the performance trace (SQL trace, see Section 3.3.8, Performance Trace — SQL Trace (Transaction ST05)) to identify the database accesses responsible for the runtime. Based on the SQL trace, you can specify execution plans and call positions of the most expensive SQL statements. This way, you can usually identify the position to be optimized directly.

High CPU times (CPU Time) should be analyzed with the ABAP trace (Transaction SE 30 — Section 3.3.12, ABAP Trace (Transaction SE30); Transaction ST12 — Section 3.3.13, Single Transaction Analysis (Transaction ST12)) to find out the ABAP statements responsible for the runtime. Possibly, you may require a performance trace (table buffer trace, see Section 3.3.11, Performance Trace — Table Buffer Trace (Transaction ST05); or RFC trace, see Section 3.3.9, Performance Trace — RFC Trace (Transaction ST05)).

If you identify high enqueue times, use the performance trace (enqueue trace, see Section 3.3.10, Performance Trace — Enqueue Trace (Transaction ST05)).

In case of high RFC+CPIC times, the performance trace (RFC trace, see Section 3.3.9, Performance Trace — RFC Trace (Transaction ST05)) provides detailed information on the further analysis.

If the application is terminated after a long runtime, you can use the dump (Section 3.3.16, Dump Analysis (Transaction ST22)) to gather information for the performance analysis.

For a *currently existing* performance problem, that is, the program is still active, start with the process analysis (Transaction SM50/SM66, Section 3.3.3, Process Analysis (Transactions SM50/SM66) — Status of a Program). You must continually refresh the screen to find out what the running process is *currently* doing. Based on this information, you can schedule the next steps with the suitable tools.

If the process runs and is mainly occupied with database accesses, you can start a trace for the running process using the performance trace (SQL trace, see Section 3.3.8, Performance Trace — SQL Trace (Transaction ST05)).

If you don't see any action and the process is running, this most likely is an ABAP processing, and you can create a trace in the parallel session (Transaction SE30) or for the running work process (Transaction ST12) using an ABAP trace (ABAP Trace, Transaction SE30 — Section 3.3.12; Single Transaction Analysis, Transaction ST12 — Section 3.3.13).

If the process is on hold, you can create a performance trace (Section 3.3.10, Performance Trace — Enqueue Trace (Transaction ST05)) for the ENQ wait reason and a performance trace (Section 3.3.9, Performance Trace — RFC Trace (Transaction ST05)) for the RFC wait reason.

Remember to check the single records statistics (Transaction STAD, Section 3.3.15, Single Record Statistics (Transaction STAD)) at the end of the program. Possibly, the part monitored in the process monitor is only a small portion of the total time. An example: A program spent most of the time for the data selections; the process monitoring was started when they were completed and when ABAP statements were executed on internal table, which only account for a small portion of the total runtime. After you check the single records statistics, you can get an overview of the total time and how it is distributed.

It is essential for applications that need to process mass data that they can work with packages and that they can be parallelized. This chapter describes the most important principles for packaging and parallel processing.

4   Parallel Processing

Applications that need to process mass data should be able to process data in packages and in parallel, so they can be flexibly adapted to the given hardware resources and utilize these resources appropriately. You should have considered the aspects of parallel processing during the design phase of the application. The following sections address the most critical aspects to bear in mind for packaging and parallel processing.

4.1   Packaging

In contrast to individual processing where the objects (data records) are processed separately, package processing enables you to process multiple objects (data records) together in a package. Another extreme case would be a processing where all objects are processed in one large package. However, this doesn't make sense for larger data volumes. Figure 4.1 outlines the difference between single record processing, package processing, and complete processing (for an unlimited package size or a package size that is larger than the data volume to be processed).

Package processing saves time, because it enables more efficient processing. For example, you can use an *array interfaces* (see Sections 5.7, in Chapter 5, and 7.4, in Chapter 7) for the database or the processing of internal tables and SAP locks for enqueue service can also be processed with an array interface (see Section 9.6 in Chapter 9).

Define the package size dynamically if you use package processing. You can adapt your program to different requirements (for example, available memory or different database settings) without modifying the source code to determine which setting is best suited for your program. The package size depends on the complexity of the objects. Define it in such a way that the processing of a single package doesn't last too long, particularly if asynchronous RFC calls (see Section 4.2.3, Parallel Processing Technologies) are used.

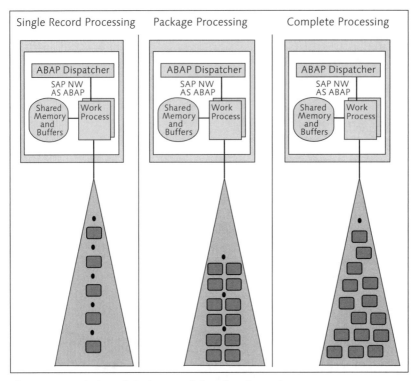

Figure 4.1 Single Record, Package, and Complete Processing

At this point it should be mentioned that the error handling of package processing is much more difficult to program than common error handling. If the processing of a package fails, this often results in additional (programming) effort that shouldn't be underestimated, because you have to determine the status of the objects in the package and perform appropriate error handling for objects that couldn't be processed.

The following listings provide examples of the single record accesses and bundled accesses to the database and internal tables.

Single record accesses:

```
LOOP AT itab.
SELECT SINGLE FROM dbtab
WHERE feld = itab-feld.
* Processing ...
```

```
ENDLOOP.

LOOP AT itab.
CALL FUNCTION
'DBTAB_SELECT_SINGLE'
EXPORTING feld = itab-feld
IMPORTING dbtab = itab.
* Processing ...
ENDLOOP.

APPEND wa TO itab.

INSERT wa INTO TABLE itab.
```

Bundled accesses:

```
SELECT * FROM dbtab
FOR ALL ENTRIES IN itab "Package size
WHERE feld = itab-feld.
* Processing ...
ENDSELECT.

SELECT * FROM dbtab
INTO TABLE itab
WHERE feld in s_opt
PACKAGE SIZE p_size. "Package size
* Processing...
ENDSELECT.

APPEND LINES OF itab1 TO itab2.

INSERT LINES OF itab1 INTO TABLE itab2.
```

4.2 Parallel Processing

Whenever larger data volumes have to be processed, it is important that an application can be parallelized.

In this context, particularly retroactive changes from non-parallel processing to parallel processing can be rather time consuming.

However, only parallelize already optimized programs. The following section describes the options for parallelizing programs, the aspects that you must consider when designing an application that can be parallelized, and how you can optimize programs.

> **Note**
>
> This section focuses on the parallel processing of the application layer, that is, in the ABAP programs. It doesn't consider the options for parallel processing at database level, because they depend on the database used. In the SAP environment, you require the options for parallel processing of the database mainly for the SAP Business Information Warehouse (SAP BW) within SAP NetWeaver Business Intelligence and to enable the system administration to perform administration tasks.

4.2.1 Background

A program that is not parallelized cannot use multiple CPUs at the same time, because a work process in SAP NetWeaver AS ABAP and a database process linked to the work process (see Figure 4.2) can only use one CPU or CPU core each. If you don't take special steps to implement parallel processing, your program cannot use multiple CPUs in the system and therefore processes the complete work queue sequentially—as shown in Figure 4.2.

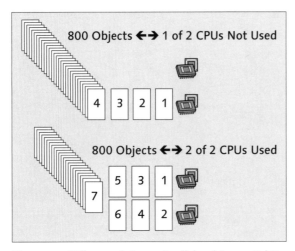

Figure 4.2 Difference Between Parallel and Sequential Processing

You can increase the processed quantity within a specific time unit, the *throughput*, considerably if an application runs in parallel.

To parallelize a program, it must be possible to divide the program into packages according to a parallel processing criterion. This parallel processing criterion is usually a business object (customer ID, account number, and so on), which is divided into areas that are then processed in parallel. Of course, this must also be technically possible. The next section discusses the technical aspects in more detail.

4.2.2 Challenges and Solution Approaches for Parallelized Programs

You meet the following challenges when using parallelized applications:

- Synchronization times
- Locks (database locks and SAP enqueues)
- Deadlocks
- Package sizes
- Distribution of the packages across several processes
- Canceled packages
- Even utilization of the hardware

Synchronization Times

When you parallelize a program, you need to consider the following aspects:

Which parts of the program can run in parallel, that is, as independently of one another as possible? Which parts might be allowed to run only once? Do you have to combine the results of the parallel processes? The next example describes a real situation that occurred in a customer project.

> **Example**
>
> A program that has run sequentially so far is supposed to run in parallel. The program deletes the whole content of a target table (A) and then selects data from one or more tables (B, C) and uses the data for calculations. Afterward, the program writes the calculation result to the target table (A) and adds a statistical record that combines the results of the calculations to a statistical table (D).
>
> In the case of parallel processing, the complete deletion of table A may take place only once, of course. Otherwise, in the case of a parallel execution of the processes, a delayed subprocess might delete the data that another subprocess has already written to this table.
>
> Consequently, either the complete deletion of the tables must be executed only once or the subprocesses delete only data from table A that they will write to the table again, if such a distinction can be implemented. You can implement the selection from tables B and C, the calculation, and the write process to the results table (A) in parallel processes if the data can be restricted according to the parallel processing criterion (for example, customer ID, order number, and so on) without overlaps. Of course, the program cannot determine and write the statistical record for the statistical table until all subprocesses are completed. In this context, this can be performed only once at the end of the processing.
>
> Figure 4.3 shows a schematic diagram of these alternatives. For reasons of clarity, the figure doesn't map time considerations (the programs that are parallelized twice should be shortened accordingly).

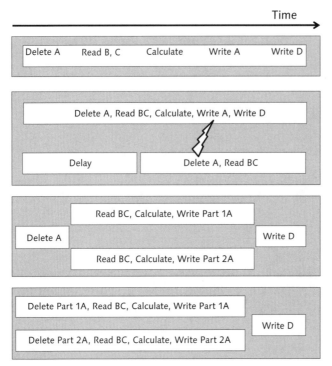

Figure 4.3 Synchronization Times

Locks

Processes can block each other by means of locks and thus considerably decrease the throughput of the parallel processing. This section deals with locks at the SAP level (SAP enqueues) and locks at the database level.

Locks at SAP level are explicitly set by the developer (CALL FUNCTION 'ENQUEUE_...'). If the object that the developer wants to lock is already locked, the system returns a response in the form of the corresponding return value (FOREIGN_LOCK). In this case, the application must respond accordingly, for example, with a termination and an appropriate error message or by waiting and trying to set the lock at a later point in time. The locks are released by calling the dequeue module (CALL FUNCTION 'DEQUEUE_...').

With regard to performance, waiting for a lock but also the termination can result in unnecessary loads on the system. While the application is waiting, it sends lock requests at regular intervals. However, in the case of a termination, already completed work may have to be rolled back and performed again later on. The following provides a brief example of a queue for setting a lock. The WAIT parameter defines that the lock request is repeated after a short wait time in the case of a collision—that is, when the record that is to be locked is already locked. In this case, the work process is not released and remains occupied for the repetitions during the entire process. If the lock couldn't be set successfully in these attempts, the lock request is closed with the FOREIGN_LOCK exception (= the record is locked otherwise).

> **Background**
>
> You can use the enque/delay_max, enque/delay_max_refine, and enque/delay_jitter parameters to control how long the system waits if _WAIT is specified. If a lock request is rejected, the application tries at most five times (default setting for enque/delay_max), about once a second (default setting for enque/delay_max_refine), to set the lock. The lock is requested only "approximately" each second to avoid that requests of parallel processes are made at exactly the same time. The exact time between the attempts varies randomly in a range of +/– 400 ms (default setting for enque/delay_jitter). The lock requests are made in a time interval of 0.6 to 1.4 seconds. You should not change the enque/delay_max parameter.

To adapt the wait times according to your requirements, don't change the system-wide parameters. If desired, you can allow for different wait times through loops. If the lock request is integrated in a loop (see example below) that is not exited until the lock request is successful, the program waits until the lock request is successful. The wait time can therefore become infinite. Consequently, an endless number of lock requests may be required.

```
DO.
 CALL FUNCTION 'ENQUEUE_OBJECT1'
 EXPORTING var1 = itab-field1
 _WAIT = 'X'
...
 IF SY-SUBRC = 0.
*Lock set, exit loop
   EXIT.
 ENDIF.
ENDDO.
```

You can define how long you want to wait for a lock with a similar loop design (e.g., DO 3 TIMES ... ENDDO). In this example, the system would try to set the lock three subsequent times for five seconds (15 enqueue requests). Additionally, you can also integrate WAIT UP TO n SECONDS in order to implement an additional wait time (in which no requests are sent) between the five attempts. However, enqueue requests should never be executed in loops without _WAIT parameter or specifically defined wait times (WAIT UP TO...). Repeated requests in loops to the enqueue server without wait time can easily cause an overload on the enqueue service and have negative effects on the overall system performance.

Database locks are implicitly set when change accesses to the database are used (*Data Manipulation Language*, DML, for example, SELECT FOR UPDATE, UPDATE, DELETE, and so on). If the object that is supposed to be locked is already locked, the process waits until the lock is released without returning the control to your application. You can release the locks with a COMMIT or ROLLBACK. To minimize the probability for such blocks, the locks should be as short as possible (but as long as necessary). For database locks, all inserts should be executed prior to the updates in order to keep the lock times for the updates as short as possible. This is particularly critical for tables that are supposed to be updated by multiple processes in parallel.

> **Tip**
>
> In general, updates should be executed at the end of the processing or as late as possible. Once you start updating, you enter the critical path, which may result in blocks.

Deadlocks

A *deadlock* occurs when processes lock each other. For example, if the data records 1, 11, 3, 12, 16 and the data records 16, 2, 10, 5, 3 of two processes are processed in the given sequence, the locks are set as illustrated in Figure 4.4.

Accordingly, process 1 wants to lock the 16th record that is already locked by process 2. Process 2 wants to lock the third record that is already locked by process 1. Processing can thus not be continued, because the two processes wait for each other. The database releases a deadlock by terminating one of the two processes with the corresponding error message (deadlock) and rolls back its previous work.

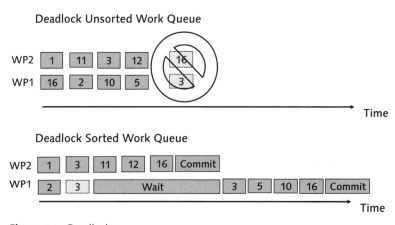

Figure 4.4 Deadlocks

You can avoid deadlocks by previously sorting the data according to its key. As you can see in the lower part of Figure 4.4, the second process then has to wait after the second data record to set the lock for the third data record, because this is already locked by the first process, but the process is not terminated, and the second process can continue as soon as the first process releases the locks.

Background: Further Reasons for Database Deadlocks

Locks between two database processes may also occur at database level, if *lock escalations* occur due to multiple locks.

For Oracle, you maintain the locks in the database block yourself. If the space available for locks is occupied by processes, it is possible that this block is locked for further processes with additional lock requests, although in comparison to the previous processes they want to lock a completely different key than the processes that hold the existing locks. Other databases usually contain a special memory area where locks for data records are stored. To ensure that no single process occupies this memory, all locks of a process are combined in a table lock for a table if a specific limit is exceeded (for example, if a process occupies more than 10% of the available entries). The table is locked for other processes with lock requests of other key values for that table. In this case, the database administration must resolve the problem, for example, by increasing the lock areas. For this reason, the package size should not be too large.

Furthermore, deadlocks can also occur between database locks and SAP enqueues or solely between SAP enqueues.

Example: Deadlock between Database Lock and SAP Enqueue

Process 1 sets database lock X.

Process 2 sets SAP enqueue Y.

Process 1 wants SAP enqueue Y.

Process 2 wants database lock X.

The system doesn't recognize such deadlocks or deadlock between SAP enqueues automatically. How you can release such deadlocks depends on the programming of the application, that is, whether and how long it waits for setting the SAP enqueue or how it behaves in the case of a negative response of the enqueue service.

Package Sizes

The goal of parallel processing is to distribute the packages across several processes. The processes that were started in parallel should begin at the same time and end at the same time. This is important to obtain optimal throughput by always keeping the system load at an equally high level. If three of four parallel processes are completed after 30 minutes and the fourth process has a runtime of two hours, the throughput is not optimal. As the hardware is not completely utilized for 1.5 hours, you could obtain better throughput by distributing the work more efficiently. This is illustrated in Figure 4.5.

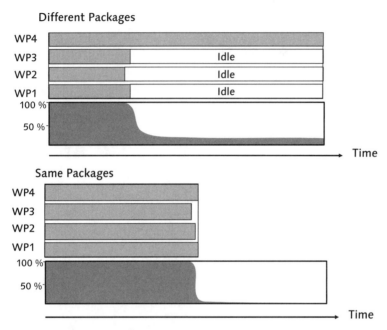

Figure 4.5 Same and Different Packages and System Load in Parallel Processing

Different packages are particularly critical if they occur in an entire chain of sequentially running programs. In this case, the hardware resources are not utilized optimally for large periods of time. This is illustrated in Figure 4.6.

It is therefore essential that the packages have almost the same size, if it is possible. However, this is not always possible, for example, when you create packages by order numbers. If 4,000 orders have to be processed in total, and you create four processes with 1,000 order numbers each, it is possible that there may be large orders that contain significantly more items. If one package includes several of these larger orders while another package only contains small orders with three to five items, the package with the large orders probably takes more time than the other packages.

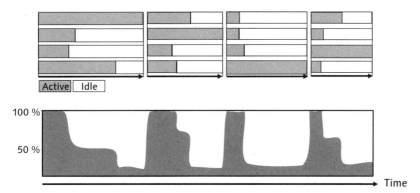

Figure 4.6 Parallel Processing and System Load in Process Chains (Different Packages)

An option to distribute the data more evenly is to combine the data in more packages that contain fewer orders. This can be implemented manually, for example, with intervals in variants, or by means of a program that distributes the data and then launches the processes. If you want to achieve a parallel processing of 4, you could create 16 packages with 250 orders each, for example.

Distribution of the Packages Across Several Processes

If you assign these packages statically to the processes, that is, packages 1 to 4 to the first process, packages 5 to 8 to the second process, and so on, it is possible that this doesn't lead to an improvement, because you've already permanently assigned one-quarter of the work queue to each process. Figure 4.7 illustrates this.

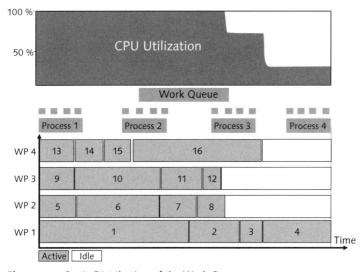

Figure 4.7 Static Distribution of the Work Queue

In contrast, if you distribute the packages dynamically, that is, assign one package to a process and another after the first package has been processed, the result could be as shown in Figure 4.8. However, this requires a kind of "driver program" that assumes the task of dynamically restarting the packages. This reduces the total time but still results in idle time. This is because a large package (16) was triggered at the end.

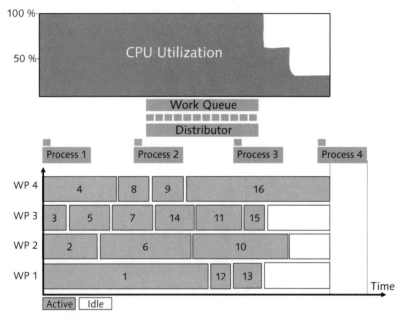

Figure 4.8 Dynamic Distribution of the Work Queue

An option for reducing the time even more is to analyze the packages in a preparation run to identify the packages with the large order and trigger long running packages first. However, this preparation run can be very complex and time-consuming. Figure 4.9 illustrates this.

Canceled Packages

If the system cancels packages during the processing, the state of the overall processing and the state of the packages need to be defined. Can you simply restart and repeat the canceled packages? Do you have to carry out specific clean-up tasks if a package is canceled? You must clarify these and similar issues and include them in the program.

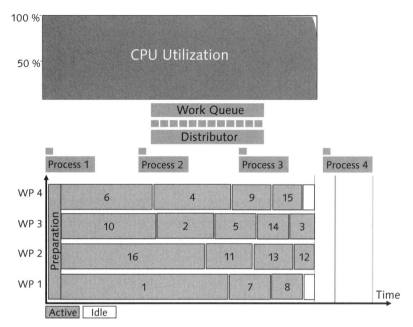

Figure 4.9 Preparation and Dynamic Distribution of the Work Queue

For the example described in the context of the synchronization times, the system would not be allowed to write the statistical record if a package was canceled, because the record would be incorrect. The complete process had to be terminated.

For canceled packages, you must check whether everything needs to be repeated or whether the process can be restarted. In this case, partial results have to be reusable.

For the example described in the context of the synchronization times, the complete process had to be repeated, because no partial results were persisted.

Even Utilization of the Hardware

When distributing the packages, ensure that the hardware is equally utilized. If you use multiple application servers, distribute the parallel processes equally across these servers to achieve optimal throughput and avoid overloading the servers. The options that are available for this purpose are described in Section 4.2.3, Parallel Processing Technologies.

Make sure that you don't place an overload on the hardware. There is no general rule of which degree of parallelization leads to the optimal throughput. The only way to find this out is to run various tests with different degrees of parallelization. Here, first implement a test with one process for each available CPU, then with 1.5 processes for each CPU, then with two processes for each CPU, and so on. This enables you to determine up to which degree the throughput increases and to determine when it finally ceases to increase. The maximum possible degree of parallelism depends on the hardware and on logical bottlenecks, such as locks and deadlocks. The more parallel processes are started, the higher the risk of logical bottlenecks.

CPUs as well as the database may cause bottlenecks. For the database, the I/O throughput often is the limiting factor, that is, the number of I/O requests that can be executed in a specific period of time.

If your application uses packages, you can usually prevent memory bottlenecks (for example, by reducing the package size) and increase the parallel processing factor until either the CPU capacity, the main memory, or the I/O capacity of your system is fully utilized.

If your application should run in parallel to dialog processing, don't schedule all system resources. In this case, it is particularly important that the parallelized application can be controlled and that you can define how many processes are started and where they are started to further ensure dialog processing is not affected. The next section discusses the corresponding options in more detail.

4.2.3 Parallel Processing Technologies

There are basically two options to implement parallel processing for your programs: batch jobs and asynchronous RFCs (Remote Function Calls). Both options are explained below.

Parallel Processing with Batch Jobs

You can use batch jobs to parallelize your program by scheduling the program in the background multiple times and assigning different variants to the individual batch jobs. In these variants, the packages are clearly separated from each other, so each batch job processes a certain range of customer IDs, for example. This enables a static distribution as illustrated in Figure 4.7, because you assign a static work queue to each batch job in advance. As long as you can distribute the work queue in such a way that the runtimes of the batch jobs don't differ considerably, you can relatively easily enable static parallel processing.

You can still determine for each batch job where it should be executed, that is, distribute your batch jobs across several servers by assigning either a specific server or, as of SAP Release 6.20, a server group containing multiple servers to each batch job. The system administration defines these server groups in Transaction SM61. If you don't make any assignments here, the SAP system executes the batch job on any server with available resources at the desired start time.

If more dynamics are required, for example, if several packages with different runtimes should be restarted as soon as the first packages are completed, it is more difficult to implement this with batch jobs. With ABAP, you may use the *batch job API* to create batch jobs, but then the batch job no longer returns a callback when it is completed.

To determine when a batch job is complete, you must query, for example, table TBTCO (job state overview table) or work with events. In a loop, bear in mind that the queries on table TBTCO always need to be executed with some wait time between the queries (for example, ten seconds) to avoid unnecessary high load on the database.

For all these jobs, you must develop a main program that assumes these job handling tasks. The batch job API, its most important function modules, JOB_OPEN, JOB_SUBMIT, and JOB_CLOSE, as well as the events have a very good online documentation (Programming with the Background Processing System).

Generally, parallel processing with batch jobs is instead suited for long processes that can be well divided into static packages. Otherwise, you must develop the appropriate main program that performs the dynamic tasks (distribution, restart, status checks, and so on).

Parallel Processing with Asynchronous RFCs

You trigger asynchronous RFC modules with the Starting New Task keyword. In this context, one also speaks of parallel RFCs, but we continue to use the *asynchronous RFC* concept in the following. For asynchronous RFCs, the calling program can continue processing immediately after the RFC call and doesn't have to wait until the RFC module is completed. If the system starts multiple asynchronous RFC modules, they run in parallel. RFC modules always run in dialog mode. That means the "distributor" as illustrated in Figures 4.8 and 4.9 can run either in dialog mode or in the batch job. However, RFC modules that are triggered by the distributor always run based on dialog processes. They are therefore subject to the limitation of the maximum runtime for dialog processes (rdisp/max_wprun_time system parameter).

When an asynchronous RFC call is complete, it can call back to the calling program if it is called with the corresponding option (PERFORMING form_name ON END

OF TASK). Within this form routine, you can then retrieve the results of the asynchronous RFC module using RECEIVE RESULTS FROM ....

> **Caution: PERFORMING ... ON END OF TASK**
>
> If you trigger an asynchronous RFC with the PERFORMING ... ON END OF TASK option, you must retrieve the results with RECEIVE RESULTS FROM. Then, the connection is closed and the context of the RFC is cleared. If you don't retrieve the results, the context is retained and may cause memory problems over time.

Asynchronous RFC modules enable you to easily implement a dynamic distribution. For this purpose, you can assign the RFC modules to an RFC server group by means of DESTINATION IN GROUP. This group is created by the system administration in Transaction RZ12 and contains one or more servers. The system then dynamically distributes the work processes that were started against this group across the servers contained therein. Due to the fact that the asynchronous modules call back, you can also easily implement the restart of multiple packages. This way RFC groups usually distribute the load very evenly across the servers.

The following example illustrates the essential issues of parallel processing with asynchronous RFCs. You can also have a look at the SPTA_PARA_TEST_1 program, which uses this technology for parallel processing and has a good documentation. The online help also provides an example and further notes if you search for the keyword IMPLEMENTING PARALLEL PROCESSING.

```
Report Z_ASYNCHRONER RFC.
....
SELECT * FROM dbtab INTO itab WHERE ....
DESCRIBE TABLE itab LINES zeilen.
......
WHILE tab_idx <= zeilen.
tab_idx = tab_idx + 1.
READ TABLE ITAB INDEX tab_idx.
CALL FUNCTION 'Z_ASYNC_FUNCTION'
        STARTING NEW TASK 'ABC'
        DESTINATION IN GROUP 'A'
        PERFORMING get_results ON END OF TASK
        IMPORTING ...
        EXPORTING ...
        EXCEPTIONS
        COMMUNICATION_FAILURE = 1
        SYSTEM_FAILURE = 2
        RESOURCE_FAILURE = 3.
....
```

```
NUM_PROC = NUM_PROC + 1.
.....
   IF NUM_PROC >= MAX_NUM_PROC.
       WAIT UNTIL NUM_PROC < MAX_NUM_PROC.
   ENDIF.
   ....
ENDWHILE.
.....
*(END OF PROGRAM)
FORM get_results USING taskname.
  NUM_PROC = NUM_PROC - 1.
  ...
  RECEIVE RESULTS FROM FUNCTION 'Z_ASYNC_FUNCTION'  ... .
ENDFORM.
```

This example first imports the work queue to the internal table, `itab`. Then, it reads the first/next data record of the internal table, `itab`, and triggers an asynchronous RFC module for this data record, which should execute the `get_results` form routine as soon as it is completed. If the desired degree of parallelization is achieved with processes triggered in parallel (`MAX_NUM_PROC`), the program waits until a process that was triggered in parallel has been completed (`WAIT UNTIL ...`). If a parallel process is complete, its results (`RECEIVE RESULTS FROM`) are retrieved and the number of running processes (`NUM_PROC`) are reduced by 1. This interrupts the wait state (`NUM_PROC < MAX_NUM_PROC`) and the next data record is read from the internal table, `itab`, and triggered asynchronously. This process is executed until all rows of the internal table, `itab`, have been processed (`WHILE`).

The last example used program-internal counters to control the degree of parallelization in order to avoid overloading the system. Another option for controlling the RFC load is to send the RFCs to an RFC group that has been configured with the corresponding resource limits. In this case, you can start asynchronous RFCs against the group until the system throws the corresponding exception (`RESOURCE_FAILURE`). This indicates that the resource limits of the RFC group have been reached. Once the first asynchronous process is completed and calls back, you can trigger new asynchronous RFCs against the group until the resource limit of the group is reached again. Then, wait until one of the triggered processes returns, and so on. You can control this process with a restart flag, which is set as soon as an asynchronous RFC is returns. This could look as follows:

```
Report Z_ASYNCHRONER_RFC.
....
SELECT * FROM dbtab INTO itab WHERE ... .
DESCRIBE TABLE itab LINES zeilen.
```

```
.....
WHILE tab_idx <= zeilen.
tab_idx = tab_idx + 1.
READ TABLE ITAB INDEX tab_idx.
CALL FUNCTION 'Z_ASYNC_FUNCTION'
        STARTING NEW TASK 'ABC'
        DESTINATION IN GROUP 'A'
        PERFORMING get_results ON END OF TASK
        IMPORTING ...
        EXPORTING ...
        EXCEPTIONS
        COMMUNICATION_FAILURE = 1
        SYSTEM_FAILURE = 2
        RESOURCE_FAILURE = 3.
   IF SY-SUBRC = 3.
        restart = ' '.
        WAIT UNTIL restart = 'X'.
   ENDIF.
   ....
ENDWHILE.
.....
*(END OF PROGRAM)
FORM get_results USING taskname.
RECEIVE RESULTS FROM FUNCTION 'Z_ASYNC_FUNCTION'  ... .
restart = 'X'.
ENDFORM.
```

The system administration is responsible for configuring the RFC groups. Numerous profile parameters are available for the distribution of the resources in RFC groups during the processing of asynchronous RFCs. The following section provides a brief overview of these parameters. A detailed description is available in the online documentation and in SAP Note 74141.

Background: Resource Parameters for RFC Groups

▶ rdisp/rfc_check
   Controls the precision of the resource checks.

▶ rdisp/rfc_use_quotas
   Activates the usage of the quotas for the resource determination.

▶ rdisp/rfc_max_queue
   Specifies the maximum number of waiting processes in the queue.

▶ rdisp/rfc_max_login
   Defines the percentage of the maximum number of possible RFC logins.

- rdisp/rfc_max_own_login
  Defines the percentage of the maximum number of possible RFC logins for *one* user.
- rdisp/rfc_min_wait_dia_wp
  Specifies how many dialog work processes are reserved for the dialog mode.
- rdisp/rfc_max_own_used_wp
  Defines the number of dialog work processes that a user is allowed to occupy simultaneously.
- rdisp/rfc_max_comm_entries
  Defines the percentage of the communication entries the user is allowed to occupy.
- rdisp/rfc_max_wait_time
  Specifies the maximum wait time in seconds that the system must wait after a load check.

The rdisp/rfc* parameters apply to queued RFCs (qRFC) and asynchronous RFCs with an RFC group but not to all other RFC types, such as synchronous RFCs or asynchronous RFCs without a group.

4.2.4 Summary

This section provided a summary of the most critical questions related to parallel processing.

What are the parallel processing criteria from both a technical and a business perspective (for example, customer ID, material number, and so on)?

Which locks are set by the application? How long are the locks set? Which objects can be locked by several processes? The locks should be set at the end of the processing as long as necessary but as short as possible.

Which package size is best suited for the application? Too small packages result in overheads, too large packages may lead to an uneven distribution, lock problems, and memory problems.

Is the central "distributor" provided with sufficient log messages, so you can analyze how many (and which) packages were started where and when and analyze their runtimes? This makes it easier to analyze performance problems.

Database accesses affect the performance of an individual application but also the performance of the entire SAP system. This chapter describes efficient database accesses.

5   Data Processing with SQL

The database is a central resource in the SAP system and keeps all data of the system persistent. All processes in the SAP system that execute database accesses consequently compete for the resources of the hosts on which the database runs. A process that places load on this resource may therefore also affect the performance of the other processes and thus of the entire SAP system.

Let's first take a look at the software architecture of a database system and the technical background for the execution of SQL statements in SAP NetWeaver AS ABAP and the database. Afterward, this chapter turns to the options of writing efficient SQL statements with ABAP.

Where possible, this chapter provides examples of good and poor coding. These examples are marked by [+] and [−] icons in the margin.

5.1   The Architecture of a Database

For analyzing and tuning SQL statements, it is helpful or even mandatory to understand the architecture of database systems, particularly if you want to understand how expensive and time-consuming SQL statements affect the entire system. SQL statements that have high resource consumption with regard to I/O, memory, CPU, network, runtime, and so on are referred to as *expensive*.

Of course, the databases supported by SAP distinguish themselves from one another. This applies to the architecture but also to the details of the access options and the physical storage of the data. Nevertheless, the architecture contains basic structures that are universally valid. The only exception is the DB2 for iSeries (AS/400) database, because it is a part of the operating system. At the end of each section, the exceptions are described briefly.

Every SAP work process is connected to one (or more) database process(es) or thread(s). Some databases are implemented with threads; however, this is isn't critical for further considerations. Consequently, the following sections only refer to *database processes*. This connection is implemented either via a TCP/IP connection (Transmission Control Protocol/Internet Protocol) through the network if the SAP work process and the database process don't run on the same server or via an IPC connection (Inter Process Communication) if the SAP work process and the database process run on the same host (in some cases, TCP/IP is used here, too). All data that is read or written by the application needs to be transferred to the SAP NetWeaver AS via this connection.

> **Note**
>
> For DB2 for iSeries, the SAP work processes of the central instance access the database files directly. Some database processes only exist for SAP work processes of application servers that don't run on the same host.

In addition, there are also database service processes that are triggered by the normal database processes to perform particular tasks (for example, changing logging or data files).

> **Background: Terminology Definition**
>
> Strictly speaking, the concept *database* refers to the data files. Database instance refers to the processes and main memory structures. The database management system finally refers to the actual software, that is, the executable programs.
>
> To improve readability, this chapter also uses the database concept to refer to the database instance. If the text refers to the data files, this is clarified.

All database processes have shared access to a part of the main memory. This part is divided into different areas within the database. In addition to the internal administration data of the database (for example, the *Data Dictionary*), logging information is also stored here before it is written to the log files. The two most important areas are certainly the so-called *SQL cache* (also referred to as *cursor cache*) and the *data cache* (also referred to as *buffer pool*). Furthermore, there is also thread-local or process-local memory that is not shared and is designed for specific tasks, such as sorting data.

> **Note**
>
> In DB2 for iSeries, the main memory is divided into machine memory and base memory. Both can be used to store data.

In the SQL cache, the SQL statements are provided with placeholders for the parameters of the WHERE condition and their execution plans (see Section 5.4, Access Strategies) in an executable form to ensure that the database can access the same statement when it is executed again, so the database doesn't have to generate a new execution plan for every new execution of the SQL statement. Generating an execution plan is also referred to as *parsing* or *compiling* (or *preparing*).

Depending on the database, these concepts differ considerably. Strictly speaking, this task includes a syntax check, an authorization check at the database level, and the implementation of an execution plan that is then stored together with the SQL statement for reuse. Parsing or compiling consumes CPU resources.

Note

DB2 for iSeries stores the execution plan in the SQL package itself. The new versions of the database store the plan in an SQL cache.

The data cache is the largest part of the database main memory. It buffers data from the data files. After receiving an SQL query, the corresponding database process first queries this cache for the required data. This takes CPU resources. If the searched data is not found in the cache, it must be read to the data cache through the physical I/O. The physical I/O is about ten times slower than the access to data in the data cache.

The database manages the data in blocks or pages in which the database files are stored. The size of these blocks or pages may vary from database to database and also within one database. They contain zero, one, or more data records (depending on their size and the distribution of the data records). These blocks (or pages) are also the smallest unit that the database can physically read from the data files.

Background: Block Sizes

The sizes of these blocks range between 2 KB to 64 KB. This may differ depending on the database manufacturer or database version. Some databases also provide multiple block sizes for different tables or table areas. In this case, different data caches (again with different block sizes) are required to manage these blocks in the main memory.

For the IBM databases, DB2 for z/OS and DB2 for LUW, it may be necessary to use different block sizes if considerably large tables need to be stored, because in some (older) versions the number of blocks (pages) per tablespace/container is limited. In some DB2 versions, a block size of 4 KB may be mandatory for index tablespaces. For DB2 for AS/400, the block size is always 4 KB.

Oracle allows for different block sizes; however, always use 8 KB blocks for SAP systems. Microsoft SQL Server (MS SQL Server) and SAP MaxDB only permit a block size of 8 KB. In general, always adhere to the block sizes defined for the installation or to the recommendations of the installation guide.

If an application wants to read only one record, the database needs to physically import the complete block (or page). From the point of view of the database, this is a physical I/O, although the data don't necessarily have to be read from the physical hard disk but can be buffered in additional caches of the operating or storage subsystem. However, it may be possible that a data record is distributed across more than one block. In this case, all blocks that include this data record must be imported. The database processes run on the operating system of the database server. Depending on its configuration, this operating system may also include data blocks in its own cache (the so-called *filesystem cache*). This behavior is normally not desired in order to avoid double caching on the same hardware. Usually, the data files are managed by the operating system; however, for *raw devices*, they can also be addressed by the database — by bypassing the operating system layer for the file administration. These files are generally stored on the storage system, which is connected to the database server and, in turn, has a cache in which the data can be stored. This storage system includes the hard disks on which the data is physically stored in blocks.

Figure 5.1 provides an overview of this architecture.

Regarding the previously described architecture, the following performance bottlenecks are possible:

▶ The connection between the database and the SAP NetWeaver AS
▶ The available CPUs
▶ The available main memory
▶ The connection between the database and the storage system
▶ The performance of the storage system

There are further database bottlenecks, such as database locks (see Section 4.2.2 in Chapter 4) or configuration settings. These settings are database specific and are in the focus of the database administration — they are not further discussed here.

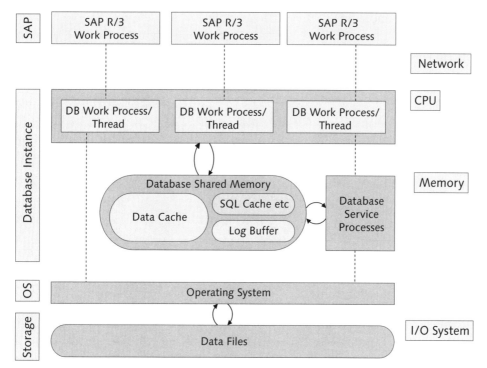

Figure 5.1 Schematic Diagram of the Most Critical Components of a Database System

5.2 Execution of SQL

This section describes how you can perform database accesses in the database. This background knowledge helps you understand the topics related to efficient SQL programming, which are discussed in the following sections.

5.2.1 Execution in SAP NetWeaver AS ABAP

The DBI (*Database Interface*) is part of every SAP work process. If the statement is written in Open SQL, the DBI formats it for the database as long as it is not a statement that only accesses tables that are buffered on the application server (see Section 6.4 in Chapter 6). In this context, it is translated into the respective SQL dialect of the underlying database. For pool and cluster tables (see Section 5.9.2, Pool and Cluster Tables), the DBI is also responsible for implementing the SQL statement for the pool or cluster that refers to the pool or cluster table. In addition, the DBI translates FOR ALL ENTRIES statements and range conditions or SELECT

OPTION statements into a native SQL statement, which the database can understand and replaces the values in the WHERE condition with placeholders. The values
are separately transferred to the database as bind variables (also called parameter
markers). For example, the following statement in ABAP

```
select *
from table
where key1 = '003'
and key2 = 'C'
```

is translated into:

```
select *
from table
where key1 = '003'
and key2 = 'C'
```

These placeholders differ for each database. Separated from the values, the statement with the placeholders is transferred to the database. For DB2 and Oracle,
these placeholders are used for compiling and the concrete values are not inserted
until the statement is executed. In the case of MS SQL Server, the first set of transferred values is evaluated for the compiling process. Subsequent values are not
evaluated. For RECOMPILE, the set of values transferred at this moment in time is
used for compiling again. In the case of SAP MaxDB, the transferred values are
always included in the decision for an execution plan.

The placeholders reduce the number of different SQL statements that the database
must manage. For this purpose, the following three statements are combined in
one statement in the SQL cache, for example:

```
select *
from table
where key1 = '003'
and key2 = 'C'

select *
from table
where key1 = '002'
and key2 = 'O'

select *
from table
where key1 = '001'
and key2 = ' '
```

The statement with the placeholders looks as follows:

```
select *
from table
where key1 = ?
and key2 = ?
```

In most cases, the combination of SQL statements is a good thing, because this reduces the parsing or compiling work for the database. However, in exceptional cases, this exact replacing of the values with placeholders may lead to performance problems for DB2 and Oracle. Sections 5.4, Access Strategies, and 5.9, Special Cases and Exceptions, discuss these problems in detail.

If the statement was written in native SQL (EXEC SQL or ADBC (ABAP Database Connectivity), see Section 5.8, Used API. It is transferred to the database without modifications.

5.2.2 Execution in the Database

Once the database receives an SQL statement, the system searches for the statement in the SQL cache (or SQL package) after it has been checked against syntax and authorizations (at the database level). If the system cannot find the statement, it has to generate an execution plan.

> **Note**
>
> SAP MaxDB always generates an execution plan.

Basically, the execution plan is a small program that defines how the data is supposed to be read for this SQL statement. Section 5.4, Access Strategies, deals with execution plans in more detail. If the SQL statement was found, the execution plan is available. The generation of the execution plan (parsing or compiling) is CPU-intensive. The placeholders in the SQL statements reduce the number of parsing operations significantly. After parsing, the placeholders are replaced by concrete values, and the system executes the SQL statement. The following sections explain the differences for read and write accesses.

Read Accesses

The database uses the internal administration information to determine which blocks (pages) need to be read. These blocks are first queried in the data cache. If the required data blocks are found here, the data records that correspond to the WHERE condition (the resulting set) is returned to the SAP work process. If the required data blocks (or parts of them) are not found in the data cache, the blocks that have not been found need to be read into the data cache first. This process takes place synchronously, that is, the SAP work process (or the user) must wait until the action is completed. Usually, the data cache is always involved when blocks (pages) are read and transferred to the application. There are a few exceptions where data can be directly read; however, these are not required for the basic understanding. The database processes try to store the database blocks (pages) that are frequently used (or have been used recently) in the data cache and displace blocks (pages) that were read less frequently (or haven't been read for some time). Whether a block (or page) is stored in the cache consequently depends on the LRU (*Least Recently Used*) and LFU (*Least Frequently Used*) algorithms. It depends on the database which strategy is used.

If a process imports a lot of blocks, it is possible that this displaces other blocks. In this case, these blocks need to be reimported by other applications, because they are no longer located in the cache. A tuning measure has thus the goal to write SQL statements in such a way that they need to read as less blocks as possible. Sections 5.4, Access Strategies, and 5.5, Resulting Set, describe these options in greater detail.

Write Accesses

In case of write database accesses, the system first checks whether the blocks that have to be modified are located in the data cache. If not, they must be read into the data cache (as described in the context of the read accesses) before they can be modified. As modifying database statements can usually be rolled back (ROLLBACK), the modifications must not only be written but also the information with which the modifications are supposed to be rolled back must be written. This information is also stored in blocks that occupy space in the data cache. Additionally, logging information (a kind of log function for modifications) must also be written. This is necessary so that — in case of a crash — the modifications that have already been confirmed with a COMMIT statement can be repeated at a later stage when the database needs to be restored. With regard to the data security, this logging information is the most critical information and is thus written synchronously to the log files of the database by the service processes when a COMMIT is executed. Depending on the database used, this memory area has different names (in MS SQL Server, it is called *transaction log*, in DB2 for AS/400 it is called *journal*). If COMMIT has been executed, modifying database statements must wait until the logging information has been written from the buffer to the files and confirmed. The process of writing the modifications of the data blocks to the files is synchronous, because the modifications can be reproduced anytime with the help of the logging information.

The next sections introduce optimization options for SQL statements in ABAP. The background information of the architecture and execution in the database lay the foundation for better understanding these measures.

5.3   Efficient SQL: Basic Principles

The performance of SQL statements is basically influenced by the following four factors:

1. The access strategy and the browsed data volume

2. The resulting set

3. The execution frequency

4. The used Application Programming Interface (API)

The access strategy and the resulting set have the greatest impact on the performance of an SQL statement. The execution frequency often takes over a minor role but can nevertheless lead to measurable differences in performance. The used API plays an even more minor role but needs to be mentioned here for the sake of completeness. The following sections deal with these issues in more detail. Of course, the existing hardware of the database is also important: The number and speed of the CPUs, the available space of main memory, and the performance of the hard disks influence the SQL performance significantly. However, because the hardware is beyond the control of the ABAP developer, this chapter only discusses the optimization of the SQL statements in the source code.

5.4   Access Strategies

If possible, this section describes the topics independently of a particular database or database version. Otherwise, this chapter alone could take up half the book. In some contexts, however, it may be necessary to refer to different databases, but this is restricted to the required minimum.

You're introduced to the various options of how a database can access data. Afterward, the following sections address typical problems that can be caused by inappropriate access paths and describe the options for analyzing and resolving these problems. Finally, statements with appropriate access paths are differentiated from statements with inappropriate access paths.

5.4.1   Logical Structures

Before the different access paths can be discussed, you have to take a look how the data is stored in the logical structures (tables and indexes) for the various databases.

At this point, the first differences become obvious. While the DB2 and Oracle databases in the SAP environment store the data unsorted in so-called *heap tables* and create the corresponding primary index that ensures the uniqueness and sorting, the SAP MaxDB and MS SQL Server databases create the tables uniquely and sorted in index format. In the context of the access paths that are discussed in this chapter, this difference will be mentioned once more. Figures 5.2 and 5.3 illustrate these differences. All databases have in common that there can be additional indexes that point to data in the table.

The differences are not described any further at this point. This would go too much into detail of the database specifications, particularly because some databases also allow for exceptions. For example, MS SQL Server enables you to create the data in unsorted tables and a uniquely sorted primary index, and Oracle enables you to create the data in an index-organized table. However, these are exceptions. As long as you haven't defined anything else and created and activated a table in the SAP Data Dictionary (DDIC), the behavior is as shown in Figures 5.2 and 5.3.

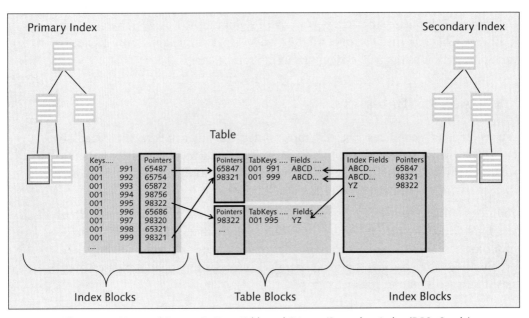

Figure 5.2 Unsorted Storage in Heap Table and Primary/Secondary Index (DB2, Oracle)

Indexes usually have the following levels:

- ▶ Root level
- ▶ Branch level(s)
- ▶ Leaf level

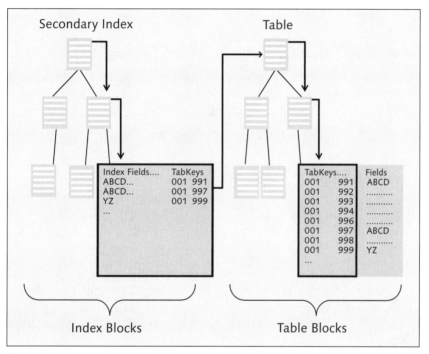

Figure 5.3 Sorted Storage in Index-Organized Tables (Clustered Index for MS SQL Server) and Secondary Index (MS SQL Server and SAP MaxDB)

There's always only one single root block. If the index is sufficiently small and all entries fit on this block, the root block is also the leaf block. If there are more entries than fit on the root block, the root block points to the next level, which may be either the branch block level or the leaf block level. Beyond that, there may be additional levels, that is, a branch block points to other branch blocks at a lower level or to blocks at the leaf block level. The leaf blocks are connected to each other by linked lists. This enables you to navigate in both directions within the leaf blocks without having to return to the branch block level. The number of levels depends on the block and index size. Because every block can only store a certain number of pointers to individual blocks of the next level, larger indexes require multiple levels. Figure 5.4 maps an index with three levels.

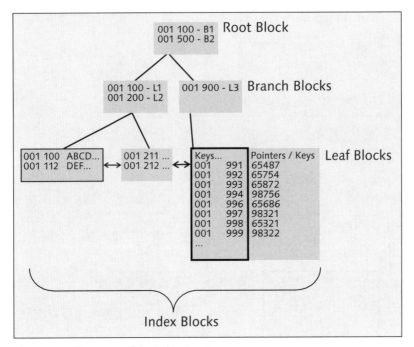

Figure 5.4 Illustration of the Index Structure

The primary index ensures the uniqueness of data records in the table. You can also create secondary indexes as unique and thus define the uniqueness of rows. In addition to ensuring the uniqueness, indexes are also search helps. This is the main task of secondary indexes and is explained in the following section before the individual access paths are described.

5.4.2 Indexes as Search Helps

The best way to explain how indexes function as search helps is to use an analogy. An index-oriented table as it is created by MS SQL Server and SAP MaxDB corresponds to a telephone directory as you know it. The data segment (street and telephone number) together with the key fields (city, last name, first name) is stored in the same structure (telephone directory). Strictly speaking, the street is also a part of the key. However, for this example, the city, last name, and first name fields are sufficient to clearly identify a data record, that is, the street is a normal data field. In the case of heap tables (DB2, Oracle), you have to imagine two directories with the sorted key fields (city, last name, first name) in the index part and a pointer to the data part (street and telephone number) in the other directory (table structure). The data part (second telephone directory) is not sorted by the key fields (city, last name, first name) and contains the complete data record (city, last name, first name, street, and telephone number). The pointer usually consists of the file number, block number, and row number in the block. With regard to the telephone directory, this would include the directory number, the page, and the row on the page. This information lets you find the data for the key (street and telephone number) in the data part (second telephone directory) very quickly.

Secondary indexes now contain specific fields of the data record in a different sort sequence. In the example of the telephone directory, there may be an additional directory that contains the city and street key fields and is sorted according to these criteria. This combination is not unique; the number of entries in this directory would correspond to the number of telephone numbers per city and street. To find the telephone number by means of these entries, another reference is necessary. In the case of heap tables, this is a pointer that consists of the file number, block number, and row number in the block (directory number, page number, row on the first page for the telephone directory). For index-organized tables, in contrast, there is no such pointer. They include the complete key of the primary index (city, last name, first name), which enables you to quickly find data in the index-organized table (main telephone directory). In the case of index-organized tables in Oracle, the first instance is already a pointer, the *logical row ID*. The complete primary key is used only if you cannot find the required data by means of this ID.

An additional and now unique secondary index is an index of the telephone number to find the related name and address (inverted search). Because every telephone number is assigned only once, this index contains solely unique entries. This corresponds to another structure, which is sorted by telephone numbers. In the case of telephone directories, this is a telephone directory sorted by telephone numbers and contains an entry for each telephone number and, for heap tables, a pointer to the data or, for index-organized tables, the primary key.

The following sections use this example to reproduce some search queries to determine the possible access paths.

Index Unique Scan

Find a telephone number by city, last name, and first name.

Here, you can use the primary index, which contains the city, last name, and first name fields. The search criterion is unique; the system returns a data record (a unique telephone number). This is called an *index unique scan*; the primary index is read from the root block level, to the branch block level, to the leaf block level. That is, if only a branch block level exists, the system reads three blocks. In the case of the index-organized tables, the data is then available. If heap tables are used, the system needs to read an additional data block via the pointer to retrieve the telephone number from the data part. In this example, the system merely reads three (index-organized tables) or four (heap tables) blocks. This only applies if the index has three levels (root, branch, and leaf level) and the data record isn't distributed across multiple blocks.

Find an address by telephone number.

This is another example for an index unique scan. You can use the unique secondary index of the telephone number here. For heap tables, the process corresponds to the process of the first example. The only difference is that the system uses the unique secondary index instead of the primary index. If the secondary index has no more than three levels and the data record is located in one block, the system needs to read four blocks at most. For index-organized tables, the system reads the three blocks of the secondary index (if it includes three levels) and determines the key for the index-organized table (city, last name, first name). This key is then used to access the data (street) via the root, branch, and leaf blocks. If the primary index has three levels, too, the system reads six blocks in total. If only city, last name, and first name were queried instead of the entire address (city, last name, first name, and street), it would be sufficient to read the secondary index because it contains the fields of the primary key (city, last name, and first name) in addition to the telephone number. This *index only* access would thus require only three blocks (index with three levels). For heap tables, four blocks would still have to be read, because the secondary index doesn't stores the fields of the primary index but a pointer to the data part.

Index Range Scan

In the last example, you created a non-unique secondary index with the city and street fields. A common index range scan uses such an index. The corresponding search query is as follows:

Find all telephone numbers in a specific street of a city.

In this example, the system browses a range of the index. It navigates to the corresponding street in the corresponding city via the root, branch, and leaf blocks. Here, it also reads the data part (telephone number) for each entry. At leaf level, it navigates from leaf block to leaf block via the linked lists. The system doesn't return to the branch level. It reads the leaf blocks until the searched street in the leaf block changes and no longer corresponds to the query. It depends on the following factors how many blocks are read:

▶ The organization of the table (heap or index-organized table)

▶ The clustering factor of the index compared to the table

The following examples illustrate these two aspects.

Let's assume the following: There are only ten telephone numbers for a street in a city. They have been inserted one after the other and are consequently located directly one after the other in two table blocks. In the index, the data also spans two leaf blocks. These numbers were chosen at random in order to explain this process. The number of the entries in the leaf and table blocks depends on the block size and is usually considerably higher. The following accesses would be necessary for heap tables:

▶ Root, branch, and leaf block to determine the first appropriate index entry (three blocks).

▶ All entries of this leaf block are stored in a table block that has to be read (fourth block).

▶ Reading the next leaf block (fifth block).

▶ All entries of this leaf block are again stored in a(nother) table block (sixth block).

For a secondary index of an index-organized table, the process is as follows:

▶ Root, branch, and leaf block to determine the first appropriate index entry (three blocks).

▶ All entries of this leaf block are stored in a table block that must be read via the primary key. This read operation is implemented for each entry separately (+ 5 × 3 blocks = 18 blocks).

▶ Reading the next leaf block (19th block).

▶ All entries of this leaf block are again stored in a(nother) table block (+ 5 × 3 blocks = 34 blocks).

For an index-organized table with the city and street key, the index range scan would look as follows:

▶ Root, branch, and leaf block to determine the first appropriate index entry (three blocks).

- ▶ All entries of this table block are read.
- ▶ Reading the next leaf block (fourth block).
- ▶ All entries of this table block are read.

That is, there would be less I/O than for the heap table where two structures must be read.

The next example illustrates the access for the case that the data in the table isn't well sorted compared to the index. This can apply to all indexes of heap tables or to secondary indexes of index-organized tables. Let's assume that respectively two telephone numbers of the searched city were inserted one after the other; other data records were inserted between them and deleted again. Consequently, the data records are located in three table blocks: the data records 1 and 2 in the first, 3 and 4 in the second, 5 and 6 in the first, 7 and 8 in the second, and 9 and 10 in the third table block. Leaf blocks store sorted data, so the ten entries are still stored in two leaf blocks. This would result in the following for a heap table:

- ▶ Root, branch, and leaf block to determine the first appropriate index entry (three blocks).
- ▶ All entries of this leaf block are stored in two table blocks: records 1 and 2 in one table block (+ 1 block), records 3 and 4 in another table block (+ 1 block), and record 5 again in the first table block, which has to be reread because a different table block has been read in the meantime — the second table block for records 3 and 4 (+ 1 block). So far, six blocks have been read.
- ▶ Reading the next leaf block (seventh block).
- ▶ All entries of this leaf block are again stored in two table blocks. Record 6 is stored in the first table block (+ 1 block); for records 7 and 8 the second table block has to be read again because a different table block has been read in the meantime — the first for record 6 (+ 1 block). For records 9 and 10, the third table block must be read (+ 1 block) — in total, ten blocks were read.

For access via the secondary index of an index-organized table, the process would be the same: However, the access of the table data would require the reading of 15 blocks each instead of only one block — in total, 34 blocks to be read.

Index-organized tables also have specific benefits—whenever ranges of related data (for example, customer number range) are read and sorting is done via this data. Compared to heap tables, this involves less I/O and the related range can be read sequentially. For heap tables, for example, if a range is read via the primary key, a poor sorting of the table compared to the index may involve much more I/O due to repeated reading of the same blocks than for index-organized tables (in index format), because the reading already takes place in an efficient and sorted manner.

Furthermore, index-organized tables let you use a *covering index more often*, because secondary indexes of index-organized tables also contain the fields of the primary index. For example, if only fields from the secondary and primary index are required, an index-organized table may be advantageous, because only one structure needs to be read. Therefore, if the query is "all last names of a specific street of a specific city," for example, you benefit from an index-organized table, because only the index needs to be read (contains the last name as a part of the primary key). In the case of heap tables, by contrast, the system still has to navigate to the table blocks from the index.

Consequently, the aforementioned examples don't indicate advantages or disadvantages of index-organized tables.

At this point, the physical storage of the data is not further discussed, particularly because you as the developer cannot influence it. This example merely illustrates how quickly the size of the data volume to be read can increase for index range scans. The more leaf blocks must be read, and the poorer the table blocks are sorted compared to these leaf blocks, the more blocks must be read in total. However, as a developer, you can influence how many leaf blocks are read — with the access path (Section 5.4, Access Strategies), the resulting set (Section 5.5, Resulting Set), and the index design (Section 5.6, Index Design). Let's assume for the previous example that you can also specify the house number as a search criterion in addition to the city and the street. Instead of ten data records, the system would return four data records. If these four records are stored in one leaf block instead of two, considerably less I/O is involved if the sorting of the table is the same compared to the index, for example, equally poor as in the second example. For the heap table, six instead of ten blocks would be read and for the access via the secondary table of the index-organized table 18 instead of 34.

Index Full Scan

An *index full scan* is performed if there is no appropriate index for the search and the selected data is located in one index. In our telephone directory example, the following search query could trigger an index full scan:

Show all cities that have a street called "Boardwalk."

Because a specific telephone directory sorted by city and street (secondary index) is given, you could use it for this search. The first field of the index (city) is missing in the search query (WHERE condition). Therefore, the search range cannot be restricted, and all data records need to be browsed. Because this directory is smaller than the main telephone directory (which contains more data), the search query could be processed more quickly, because less pages have to be browsed.

The index full scan doesn't lead to access differences for heap tables or index-organized tables, because the entire blocks of the respective index must be processed. Every index block is read once, and the appropriate data records are filtered out. The only difference is that — despite the same block sizes — index-organized tables may contain fewer entries in one index block than heap tables, because the used pointer (complete primary key) occupies more space than the pointer of heap tables. Secondary indexes of index-organized tables are consequently larger than secondary indexes of heap tables. The index full scan scans the individual leaf blocks of an index separately via the linked lists. It thus returns the read data in sorted order. Nevertheless, you *always* need to specify ORDER BY in ABAP programs if the database requires sorted data, because the data could also be read via another access path, which can no longer ensure the sort sequence. Alternatively, you can also use the SORT statement for sorting in ABAP programs (Section 5.9, Special Cases and Exceptions).

Some databases also support an *index fast full scan*, which is also called *read ahead* by some of these databases. The execution plan, however, shows the index fast full scan on Oracle but doesn't indicate a read ahead on other databases. The execution plan still refers to the index full scan on these databases. If the blocks are physically stored on the hard disk one after another, some databases can optimize the scan process in such a way that the blocks don't have to be read separately, but multiple blocks can be read at once. As a result, the sort sequence of the index cannot be ensured if the index blocks are not read via the linked lists but in larger related ranges that cannot ensure sorting.

The index fast full scan is very similar to the full table scan. The only difference is that an index fast full scan requires reading of the index blocks only. This usually includes fewer blocks than for the full table scan.

Full Table Scan

A *full table scan* has to be performed if there is no appropriate index for the search (that is, the selected columns are not stored at the beginning of an index). In our telephone directory example, the following search query could trigger a full table scan:

> Show the telephone numbers of the persons with a specific first name that live in a specific street.

Even if the result is small, for example, there's only one data record that meets these conditions, the system must browse the entire telephone directory, which is sorted by city, last name, and first name, because the existing indexes — one index for the city and the street and one index for the telephone number — cannot be used for this query. The system also has to browse the entire table if no data record meets the WHERE condition. For heap tables, the full table scan scans all table blocks. It must also scan all leaf blocks in the index for index-organized tables. Each block is read once. The larger the size of the table (the more blocks it utilizes for the data storage), the longer the process. However, full table scans enable the databases to scan multiple blocks in one pass instead of one block after the other. If an application requires all data records (or a large part) of a table, the full table scan is the most efficient way to access the data. For example: The telephone directory lists a city that represents 40% of the entries. There's an index for the city and the street. If you used this index for searching for this city, the system would have to read half of the index blocks of this index. It has to access the table data (telephone number) for each entry in a leaf block of this index. Half of the table blocks needs to be scanned as well. This corresponds to a large index range scan where a large range of the index leaf blocks must be read. If the sort sequence is not optimal, the system must read the table blocks again and again (whenever a different table block has been read in the meantime). So more blocks than for the full table scan had to be read in total. Moreover, an index range scan reads the blocks separately, one after the other. A full table scan wouldn't read index leaf blocks and would read each table block only once. Like for the index fast full scan, some databases can also scan multiple blocks in one pass, which additionally increases the access speed.

> **Background: Performance of Different I/O Types**
>
> The databases usually distinguish between the *single block I/O* (also referred to as *random I/O*) and the *multiblock I/O* (also referred to as *sequential I/O*). While index unique scans, index range scans, and index full scans basically scan single blocks (random I/O), the index fast full scan and full table scan can scan several related blocks in one pass (sequential I/O).
>
> In the case of random I/O, a seek is implemented for each block. A seek includes rotating the hard disk and repositioning the read head. The seek time is a significantly larger portion of the time required for the entire I/O than the actual read time of the block (transfer time).
>
> For the sequential I/O, multiple sequential blocks are transferred after a seek.

For current hard disks with 15,000 rpm, the average seek time, which is divided into the average rotation time (approximately 2 milliseconds) and the average positioning time of the write/read heads (approximately 3 to 4 milliseconds), can be approximately 6 milliseconds.

You may have to add wait times until an I/O query is actually processed. Finally, you have to add the transfer time for transferring the page (one millisecond at the most). Compared to the other times, this time can be neglected. An average physical I/O consequently requires 8 to 10 milliseconds.

Compare: An I/O query that can be processed in the cache (of the storage area network or filesystem), in contrast, requires merely one millisecond. However, the filesystem cache shouldn't be activated for databases to avoid double caching on the same hardware.

Because the sequential I/O usually performs fewer seeks for a specific number of blocks, the time required for each block is less than for the random I/O, which usually performs one seek for each block. Full table scans or index fast full scans can generally perform more sequential I/O than index range scans or index unique scans, which usually perform random I/O operations. Full table scans or index fast full scans are therefore considered more efficient with regard to the I/O speed.

Caution: Don't confuse these descriptions with Oracle concepts where the *DB File sequential read* refers to the single block I/O (random I/O) and the *DB file scattered read* to the sequential reading of multiple related blocks (multiblock I/O or sequential I/O).

If you want to analyze I/O times on your database system using database monitors (Transaction ST04), a physical I/O on the database side doesn't necessarily have to be a physical I/O on a hard disk but may originate from other cache layers, such as the filesystem cache (which should be deactivated, however), the cache of the Storage Area Network (SAN), or the cache of the hard disks. The times for such a "physical I/O" on the database side also include accesses to these caches and are thus usually considerably shorter. Database monitors therefore often specify 1 to 5 milliseconds for a physical I/O if fast storage systems are used. As described above, the time required for a *real* physical I/O is also longer for modern hard disks.

Changes

Before summarizing this section in the following, one critical aspect has to be mentioned. Indexes can accelerate the process of searching for data but also decelerate the changing of data. If someone moves and the city, street, and telephone number change, this change has to be implemented in the table data and/or in the primary index but also in the index for the city and street and in the index for the telephone number. Instead of one directory, three directories had to be maintained for this change. This involves three times more effort and time. Section 5.6, Index Design, addresses this aspect again. At this point, however, indexes don't only have benefits but may also have a negative effect on the performance, because indexes always need to be changed synchronously if changes have to be implemented. Additional disadvantages of indexes are the increased space requirements on the hard disks and in the main memory, and for most databases, the possibility of wrong decisions on the optimizer side if there are a lot of indexes that contain the same fields.

Summary of the Search Strategies for a Table

All databases can perform the index unique scan, index range scan, and full table scan search strategies. Some of the database also allows for further optimized search strategies, such as the index skip scan (Oracle) or the sorting of addresses of the data records by the physical location to benefit from the sequential read process. However, these search strategies are not discussed in greater detail here.

The next section describes which selection criteria of indexes can be supported and how the database selects a specific access path. Afterward, this chapter introduces the analysis and optimization options in ABAP. It then discusses accesses to several database tables (joins) and finally addresses the possible problems and solutions of the determination of access paths.

5.4.3 Operators

This section describes which selection criteria can be used for indexes and how the various operators can be used for the indexes to minimize the search effort as much as possible.

So far, you only know what happens in the case of conditions for columns with equality conditions (`field = var`). In `WHERE` conditions, you can define conditions with = but also with additional operators, such as not equal (<>), greater (>), greater or equal (>=), less (<), less or equal (<=), between (`BETWEEN`), and like (`LIKE`).

Figure 5.5 shows an index structure that is sorted by last name, first name, and street. Let's have a look at how the different operators behave for these fields.

Example with = condition:

```
... WHERE last name = ? AND first name = ?
```

Both conditions can be mapped to the index and restrict the data blocks to be read to those blocks that meet the conditions.

Example with <> condition:

```
... WHERE last name <> ? AND first name = ?
```

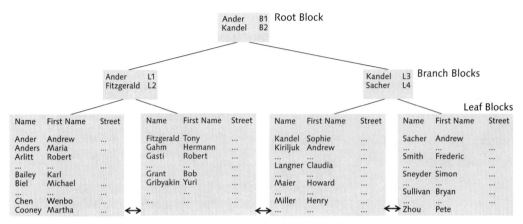

Figure 5.5 Schematic Index Structure with Last Name, First Name, and Street

The <> operator doesn't allow for an efficient index use although the second field is defined with =. *All leaf blocks* must be read. After the system has read the index blocks, it can *filter out* the data records with the conditions. Instead of an index range scan, you could also implement a full table scan or index (fast) full scan; however, in this case, the same number of blocks had to be read. The <> operator consequently doesn't allow for restricting the blocks that are to be read. If you compare this example to the telephone directory, it is apparent why the index cannot be used efficiently: Imagine you had to browse a telephone directory for the telephone numbers of all persons whose last name is not Smith and whose first name is Richard. Because the telephone directory is sorted by last names, you had to browse the entire directory and find the appropriate data records on each page to perform this task. The only section you wouldn't have to browse is the section with the last names "Smith"; however, this hardly decreases the data volume that needs to be processed.

Example with > and < or BETWEEN condition:

```
... WHERE last name > ? AND last name < ? ...
... WHERE last name BETWEEN ? AND ?
```

This query corresponds, for example, to the process of searching for all telephone numbers of the persons whose last names starts with S (>= 'S' AND < 'T'). Here, you can implement a restriction to the searched range, that is, the condition used to determine a start and stop point in the leaf blocks. Then, the range between these points must be scanned (index range scan).

Example with LIKE condition:

```
... WHERE last name LIKE ?
```

A search pattern is used in this context. The usage of the "_" and "%" wildcard characters corresponds to the SQL standard. In other ABAP cases, the "+" and "*" wildcard characters are used for similar logical expressions, particularly if selection tables are used. Such search queries could be: `last name LIKE 'S%'` — all last names that start with S, or `last name LIKE '%s%'` — all last names that contain an s. If the `LIKE` operator contains a placeholder at the beginning, it also doesn't allow for an efficient search process, because it doesn't allow for limiting the blocks that are to be read (just like the `<>` condition). If the `LIKE` operator contains only one placeholder at the end, it has the same behavior as a `BETWEEN` condition and can be used to restrict the leaf pages.

5.4.4 Decision for an Access Path

The *optimizer* decides which access path is used if this decision is not enforced by hints on the application side. From the technical point of view, the optimizer is a component of the database software and is integrated with its kernel. Today, all databases use cost-based optimizers.

Previously, some databases provided rule-based optimization instead of cost-based optimization. This type of optimization is no longer used or only in certain exceptional cases by some databases. The rule-based optimization decides, based on predefined rules, which execution plan is selected. These rules consider the table definition, the column definition, the index definition, and the `WHERE` condition. Because rule-based optimization plays a minor role today, it is not discussed in greater detail here.

The cost-based optimization still uses the table definition, column definition, index definition, and `WHERE` condition but also uses various statistics to create an execution plan. This includes table, column, and index statistics but also system statistics. SAP MaxDB doesn't necessarily require statistics, because it can retrieve this information via evaluations.

Table, column, and index statistics describe the data more precisely. For example, the statistics contain the following values: size of the table in blocks, number of rows of the table, number of unique values of fields, number of unique keys in an index, clustering factor of the index compared to the table, smallest value for each field, and largest value for each field. These statistics differ depending on the database used. However, they generally correspond to the ones mentioned and differ only minimally.

Some databases also use system statistics that describe some parts of the system on which the database runs. This may include values for the speed of the CPUs and I/O system as well as the available main memory for the database.

The optimizer can use these statistics, for example, to perform a full table scan if a table is short according to the statistics, because in this case fewer blocks are usually read than via an access path for an index.

The optimizers can also be affected by the database parameters and the current system load.

The cost-based optimizer defines the access paths by means of these factors. Two aspects have to be mentioned in this context:

▶ Usually, such an optimization achieves a better result, because the optimization is implemented based on the state of the tables, columns, indexes, or system and not according to fixed rules (as in the case of rule-based optimization).

▶ Of course, the optimization on the basis of the statistics on the state depends on how well the statistics describes the state of the reality. For this purpose, the statistics don't have to be up-to-date in the sense of new. Old statistics can also be good if the state which the statistics describe hasn't changed a lot. If statistics have been deliberately "frozen" to describe a specific state, it may also be possible that old statistics are still useful. Sometimes, the statistics for tables with strong variances are "frozen" to define a good state of tested statistics.

5.4.5 Analysis and Optimization in ABAP

Within SAP NetWeaver AS ABAP, you can analyze the access plans with the EXPLAIN PLAN function. You can find this function in Transaction ST05, for example. Transaction ST05 is the so-called performance trace. This transaction lets you record SQL statements, buffer accesses, enqueues, and RFCs in a trace. You can call the EXPLAIN PLAN function from the SQL trace (see Section 3.3.8 in Chapter 3) or enter an SQL statement using the bottommost button in Transaction ST05 (Enter SQL STATEMENT). The statement that you enter mustn't be Open SQL but Native SQL (see Section 5.8, Used API). The system then returns an execution plan, which you can use to analyze how the database accesses the data.

The concrete execution plans greatly depend on the database. Due to lack of space, not all variants can be discussed here. Appendix A documents the different execution plans of the databases in more detail. At this point, only the different concepts for the execution plans are summarized in Tables 5.1, 5.2, and 5.3.

Database	Direct Read (SM50 SAP Concept)
ORACLE	Index unique scan
MSSQL	Clustered index seek (... SEEK: all index fields) for primary indexes or index seek (... SEEK: all index fields)
SAP MAX DB	EQUAL CONDITION FOR KEY COLUMN
DB2 for LUW	IXSCAN (with all key fields)
DB2 for iSeries	Index (key row/scan key positioning for n fields) where n is equal to the number of fields in the index
DB2 for zSeries	Index (with n matching columns of m index columns) where n and m have the same value

Table 5.1 Database-Specific Concepts for the Execution Plans for Direct Read

Database	Sequential Read (SM50 SAP Concept)
ORACLE	Index range scan
MSSQL	Clustered index seek (... SEEK: not all index fields) for primary indexes or index seek (... SEEK: not all index fields, also WHERE... if required)
SAP MAX DB	RANGE CONDITION FOR KEY COLUMN for primary indexes or RANGE CONDITION FOR INDEX for secondary indexes
DB2 for LUW	IXSCAN (with some of the key fields)
DB2 for iSeries	Index (key row/scan key positioning for n fields) where n is less than the number of index fields
DB2 for zSeries	Index (with n matching columns of m index columns) where n < m if the first field in the index is specified with =, otherwise: (... nonmatching index) with further specifications which fields are used

Table 5.2 Database-Specific Concepts for the Execution Plans for Sequential Read and Index Range Scans

Database	Sequential Read (SM50 SAP Concept)
ORACLE	Full table scan
MSSQL	Clustered index scan (without SEEK: with WHERE... if required) for primary indexes or index scan (without SEEK, with WHERE... if required)

Table 5.3 Database-Specific Concepts for the Execution Plans for Sequential Read and Full Table Scans

Database	Sequential Read (SM50 SAP Concept)
SAP MAX DB	TABLE SCAN
DB2 for LUW	TBSCAN
DB2 for iSeries	... using arrival sequence... **or in more recent releases** ... TABLE SCAN on...
DB2 for zSeries	sequential tablespace scan

Table 5.3 Database-Specific Concepts for the Execution Plans for Sequential Read and Full Table Scans (Cont.)

These tables are supposed to facilitate the orientation in the respective execution plans. This section now introduces the general analyses and provides tuning examples. The entire chapter uses the Oracle terminology for the access paths. The SAP concept *direct read* can be used in the work process overview (SM50) for unique accesses but also for the counting of data records (SELECT COUNT) or for accesses to the table buffer. *Direct read* can therefore also refer to a full table scan that is performed to count data records.

In the execution plan, you can find the access method and the used index if required. In addition, it also provides information on the number of the columns of the WHERE condition that you can use for this index for the search or even on the concrete names of these columns.

Use the WHERE condition and used index columns to check whether the database can map the *selective* fields of your WHERE condition to the index. Check additionally whether the selective columns are available *without gaps and ranges*. Fields that are not specified at all or fields that are specified via ranges (BETWEEN, <, >, and so on) should precede the selective columns. To check the selective conditions, you require the concrete values of the variables. You can find them in the SQL trace in Transaction ST05 (see Section 3.3.8 in Chapter 3).

The following example illustrates a case where the selective field is not available without gaps. There is an index for the client, company code, and document number fields, which are unique in this combination. However, the WHERE condition only specifies the following: WHERE MANDT = ? AND belnr = ?. The DBI additionally generates MANDT if CLIENT SPECIFIED is not defined.

The following example illustrates a case where the selective BELNR field is not available without gaps.

Index fields: 1. MANDT, 2. BUKRS, 3. BELNR   [−]

```
SELECT * INTO linevar FROM dbtab
WHERE belnr = varbelnr.
```

The document number (BELNR) is selective and the index is used but only for index range scans. Because the company code (BUKRS) is missing, the leaf blocks are limited based on the clients for the start and stop points only. The system then reads these leaf blocks to filter out the document number. If there's only one client in the system, no limitation is set. Instead, the system reads all leaf blocks of the client to filter out the document number.

In the next example, the company code is added to the WHERE condition:

Index fields: 1. MANDT, 2. BUKRS, 3. BELNR   [+]

```
SELECT * INTO linevar FROM dbtab
WHERE bukrs = varbukrs
AND    belnr = varbelnr.
```

If you add the company code (BUKRS) to the WHERE condition, the selective BELNR field is available without gaps in the index for MANDT, BUKRS, BELNR. The blocks that have to be read are defined using all of the three fields. Because the combination is unique, only one leaf block (including one branch block and one root block for three levels, one table block in the case of heap tables) needs to be read, and the database can use an index unique scan. An essential tuning measure is thus to use used indexes without gaps with = conditions up to the field selected.

The next example illustrates how gaps can occur during the index usage:

Index fields: 1. MANDT, 2. BUKRS, 3. BELNR   [−]

```
SELECT * INTO linevar FROM dbtab CLIENT SPECIFIED
WHERE bukrs = varbukrs
AND    belnr = varbelnr.
```

Here, the CLIENT SPECIFIED addition lets you specify any client. Accordingly, the DBI doesn't generate and add the client to which you're logged on to the WHERE condition. However, this means that the WHERE condition doesn't define any client if the client isn't explicitly specified in the ABAP source code. This leads to an inefficient access plan again. If all created indexes contain the client as the first field in the index, the optimizers run a full table scan or a (fast) full index scan in this case. This is indicated in the execution plans by the defined search strategies, the used indexes, and the fields that are used for the index.

The sample solution would be as follows:

Index fields: 1. MANDT, 2. BUKRS, 3. BELNR

```
SELECT * INTO linevar FROM dbtab CLIENT SPECIFIED
WHERE mandt = '001'
AND    bukrs = varbukrs
AND    belnr = varbelnr.
```

Now, all fields of the index are specified with = again. If possible, don't use the CLIENT SPECIFIED addition at all.

Real-Life Example — Transaction SE30, Tips & Tricks:

In the TIPS & TRICKS under SQL INTERFACE • INDEX AND BUFFER SUPPORT • SELECT WITH INDEX SUPPORT, Transaction SE30 provides an example whose runtime you can measure. Of course, you can also analyze this example with the SQL trace (Transaction ST05).

It has similarly negative effects if an unselective range condition (BETWEEN, <, >, LIKE) precedes the selective field, because this condition doesn't allow for early restrictions of the leaf blocks in the index that have to be read (just like a gap). ABAP applications cannot optimize such situations. In an index, the fields that are accessed with unselective range conditions should thus appear behind the selective fields that are queried with =, if possible. This is an example for the index design (see Section 5.6, Index Design).

Background: Selectivity and Distribution

The previous section introduced you to the *selective conditions*. A selective condition refers to a condition that is used to select a small dataset from a large dataset. Usually, fields such as customer number, document number, and so on are selective if they are queried with =.

However, selective fields are often talked about if there are various different values available for a field, which applies to customer number, document number, and so on. Conversely, a field is unselective if there are only a few different values available for the field. This includes fields such as gender or status fields if there are only a few statuses. There can also be selective conditions for fields that have only a few different values. Let's assume that a table has a status field for which the majority of the data records has the Completed status. Some have the In Process status and the minority the New status. There are three different values. Against this background, you know that

```
WHERE status = 'new'
```

is a selective condition, because it restricts the dataset to a large extent, while

```
WHERE status = 'completed'
```

is an unselective condition that doesn't restrict the dataset.

The problem is now that the default settings of some database optimizers (DB2, Oracle) always assume that the data is equally distributed. Consequently, they evaluate all statuses in the same way and assume that every status returns the same dataset (1/3 respectively). If the dataset is very large, it is possible that they don't evaluate the index as an efficient search help and run a full table scan instead (which is actually more efficient if you really want to read 1/3 of all data).

The solution of the database manufacturers (DB2, Oracle) is to enable you to make such unequal distributions of the data known to the database using a specific type of statistics. However, this option needs to be activated when creating the statistics. SAP MaxDB and MS SQL Server store the distribution information by default (MS SQL Server) or determine it at runtime (SAP MaxDB).

But even if the distribution of the data is known, you still face the problem that the database of the SAP system receives the WHERE condition in the following form:

```
WHERE status = ?
```

To decrease the number of parse operations or compile operations, the system combines queries that only differ in terms of the variables using placeholders for variables. Consequently, the optimizer wouldn't be able to use these statistics to select the index for the New status and run a Full Table Scan for the Completed status, because it doesn't know the content of the variables at the time of the optimization.

For this purpose, you must have the SAP system send the value instead of the variable to the database if this statement is used. You don't have to do so for SAP MaxDB, because it always uses the concrete values for the optimization.

Section 5.9, Special Cases and Exceptions, explains how you can send values instead of variables to the database.

The specification of negative conditions can also lead to an inefficient index usage.

The following example is an example of a negative condition:

Index fields: 1. MANDT, 2. KUNNR, 3. AUART   [−]

```
SELECT * INTO TABLE itab FROM dbtab
WHERE kunnr = varkunnr
AND auart NOT IN ('TA','KL','SO')
```

Here, the index can only be used restrictively for the first two fields (MANDT, KUNNR), because the negative NOT IN condition cannot be mapped restrictively to the index. During the scan process of the data records, the condition can only be used for filtering.

One solution for using the index efficiently is to convert the negative condition into a positive condition, for example, into the following:

[+]   Index fields: 1. MANDT, 2. KUNNR, 3. AUART

```
SELECT * INTO TABLE itab FROM dbtab
WHERE kunnr = varkunnr
AND auart IN ('BV','WV','MV')
```

The positive IN list corresponds to a linked OR. Consequently, the following statement has the same meaning:

```
SELECT * INTO TABLE itab FROM dbtab
WHERE kunnr = varkunnr
AND (auart = 'BV'
OR  auart = 'WV'
OR  auart = 'MV')
```

In this case, the index would be used for all three columns. Of course, this is only possible if the AUART field has only a few order types in total. In the first example with the negative IN list, the optimizer can use merely two columns from the index for the index range scan. Here, it can use three columns, but has to implement this iteratively for every value in the IN list (or for every OR) several times. The benefits of the restriction for the leaf blocks due to the third field usually outweigh the iterative execution. In this example, one large index range scan is slower than three smaller index range scans.

If the positive list (or the number of the OR conditions) becomes too long, it is possible that the third condition is also no longer mapped to the index. This is the case if the effort for the repeated accesses via three fields is more time-consuming than an access via two fields according to the optimizer's assessment. In this case, specify the negative condition instead of omitting it completely, because it actually reduces the data volume that is returned to the application even though it doesn't restrict but filters the leaf blocks that are to be read.

However, always use positive WHERE conditions if possible.

The following example covers range queries. It queries a range of five document numbers:

```
SELECT * INTO TABLE itab FROM dbtab
WHERE bukrs = varbukrs
AND   belnr BETWEEN '0000005001' AND '0000005005'
```

The system usually only transfers placeholders to the database in this example. The database thus receives the following information:

```
WHERE bukrs = ?
AND    belnr BETWEEN ? AND ?
```

Due to the placeholders, the database optimizes to a universal, hard-coded result-ing set (not for MS SQL Server and SAP MaxDB), because it cannot "view" the extent of the range in the document number interval. It assumes that a BETWEEN ? AND ? condition returns 1% of the data records. This may impede efficient index usage. In the second example, the range is replaced by a list:

```
SELECT * INTO TABLE itab FROM dbtab
WHERE bukrs = varbukrs
AND    belnr IN ('0000005001', '0000005002', '0000005003',
'0000005004', '0000005005')
```

The database receives the following WHERE condition:

```
WHERE bukrs = ?
AND    belnr IN ( ? , ? , ? , ? , ? )
```

It then knows that five individual document numbers are searched. If the docu-ment number is unique in the index, a maximum of five data records can be returned, so in some cases, a more efficient access path can be used.

The BETWEEN and LIKE operators usually lead to efficient execution plans; however, in some cases, they may also lead to misjudgments of the optimizer. In this cases, check whether a conversion from BETWEEN or LIKE to IN would achieve a better result. There is no general rule for checking in advance whether such a conversion is useful. This also depends on the extent of the ranges and how close data is physi-cally stored. This example was only included here to mention the aspects of gen-eral cost estimation for BETWEEN and LIKE, which may affect the execution plan.

The fact that the BETWEEN and LIKE operators are evaluated universally by most of the optimizers in cost estimation assumes a more critical role in another context: If a statement contains a lot of LIKE and BETWEEN operators that are linked with an OR, it is possible that the general cost estimation is higher due to the large number of LIKE and BETWEEN operators than the cost estimation for a full table scan.

The following example maps a statement with a lot of LIKE operators that are linked with OR:

```
SELECT * INTO itab FROM dbtab
WHERE bukrs = varbukrs
AND(   belnr LIKE '000001500%' OR belnr LIKE '0000002500%'
OR     belnr LIKE '000003500%' OR belnr LIKE '0000004500%'
OR     belnr LIKE '000005500%' OR belnr LIKE '0000006500%'
OR     belnr LIKE '000007500%' OR belnr LIKE '0000008500%')
```

You could simplify the statement by dividing it into several smaller statements, for example:

```
SELECT * INTO TABLE itab FROM dbtab
WHERE bukrs = varbukrs
AND(   belnr LIKE '000001500*' OR belnr LIKE '0000002500*'
OR     belnr LIKE '000003500*' OR belnr LIKE '0000004500*')

SELECT * APPENDING TABLE itab FROM dbtab
WHERE bukrs = varbukrs
AND(   belnr LIKE '000005500*' OR belnr LIKE '0000006500*'
OR     belnr LIKE '000007500*' OR belnr LIKE '0000008500*')
```

An even more elegant solution is to use a FOR ALL ENTRIES, which is described in more detail in Section 5.7, Execution Frequency.

In this case, more individual statements had to be executed, but they are executed considerably more quickly if efficient index usage is possible instead of a full table scan.

Another option is to enforce an index access via a hint (Section 5.9, Special Cases and Exceptions).

The tips that this section discussed for WHERE conditions apply both to SELECT statements and to DELETE and UPDATE statements.

Summary: Analyzing the Access Path to a Table

To analyze SQL statements via the EXPLAIN PLAN function, you thus compare the WHERE condition of the statement to the fields of the indexes to check whether an efficient access is possible at all. For this purpose, you check how selective the fields in the indexes and the variable values in the WHERE condition are. You also check whether the selective fields can be filled by the WHERE condition without gaps with the equal (=) or IN condition. If this is not the case, check whether the gap can be filled by the program (for example, the company code is missing). Additionally, check whether the selective fields can be accessed without range condition in front of the selective fields via =.

If you cannot access a selective field in the index, which contains an = in the WHERE condition, or only access it via the intermediary range conditions, you should have a look at the index design (Section 5.6, Index Design).

If there are multiple fields with = conditions, the fields that restrict the resulting set (and thus the number of leaf blocks that have to be read) the most should be mapped to one index. To check this, it may be required that you check the assessment of the optimizer manually with Transaction SE16 (Number of Entries) to determine which field has the fewest hits. For this purpose, you can also use Transaction DB05, which is described in Section 3.3.2 in Chapter 3.

Even though this section dealt mostly with the efficient usage of indexes implemented by modifying the WHERE condition, it should still be mentioned that such modifications are sometimes not possible and that a full table scan may be more efficient than the efficient index usage. An index range scan for solely unselective fields (that is, if all or the majority of the data records are supposed to be read) is less efficient than a full table scan, for example (see Full Table Scan in Section 5.4.2, Indexes as Search Helps). In this case, you can optimize the execution by initiating a full table scan. Section 5.9, Special Cases and Exceptions, discusses the possible options if the optimizer doesn't implement this automatically.

Access to Multiple Database Tables — Joins

This section deals with accesses to several tables at database level. Section 5.7, Execution Frequency, covers the ABAP level (nested SELECT statements, FOR ALL ENTRIES). At the database level, you refer to joins and views. The execution of views is identical to the execution of joins. For views, the definition is defined in the database and in the SAP Data Dictionary (reusability in other programs). For joins, the definition is not permanently stored in the database but defined in the SQL statement and consequently in the program.

The performance of a join depends on the same criteria as an SQL statement — read data volume, access path to the corresponding tables, execution frequency, and used API. As already mentioned, the access paths (Section 5.4, Access Strategies) and resulting set (Section 5.5, Resulting Set) are most important here.

The join's performance additionally depends on the following aspects:

- Join method
- Table sequence
- They both depend on each other and are therefore described together in the following.

Most of the current databases support the following join methods:

- Nested loop join
- Sort merge join (also called merge scan join)
- Hash join

Note
DB2 for AS/400 doesn't support the sort merge join method.

There are even more join methods, for example, the star join, but these are mainly critical for the BI environment only. Figure 5.6 provides a schematic overview of these join methods.

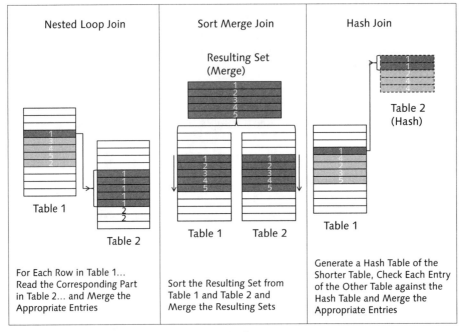

Figure 5.6 Schematic Diagram of the Join Methods

These three join methods are described in detail in the next sections.

The nested loop join is based on the following procedure:

▶ For each record of the first table that corresponds to the WHERE condition for the first table, the following steps are carried out:

  ▶ Read every record that corresponds to the WHERE condition for the second table and the join condition from the second table.

  ▶ Return the matching records.

  ▶ End of the loop for the second table.

▶ End of the loop for the first table.

The first table is also called outer table and the second table inner table. It is easy to see that the second step has to be executed for each hit in the external table. The performance of the nested loop join consequently depends on the complexity of the search process for the inner table (access path) *and* how often this search has to be executed. Of course, it is also important how complex the search process for the outer table is (access path), but it is executed only once. Furthermore, the entire hit list is also relevant for the performance.

The optimizer will select that table as the outer table from which it expects the smallest number of results *and* that table as the inner table that probably provides the most efficient access path. These assessments depend on the statistics.

To optimize the performance of a nested loop join, you must thus consider the following aspects:

- How are the tables, particularly the inner table, accessed?
- How often is the inner access plan executed, that is, does the system start with the table with the shortest hit list?

In real life, the hit lists that were estimated by the optimizers can often vary (see, for example, the "Background: Selectivity and Distribution" box in this section). Section 5.9, Special Cases and Exceptions, and the upcoming Problems section introduce various optimization options.

The sort merge join is based on the following procedure:

- Read table 1 and table 2, and sort the resulting sets according to the join criteria (if the access paths to the two tables don't ensure this sort sequence).
- Read the first record of table 1 that corresponds to the WHERE condition for table 1.
  - Repeat this provided that the join criteria of table 1 are greater than those of table 2.
  - Read the next record of table 2 that corresponds to the WHERE condition for table 2.
  - Provided that the join criteria of table 2 are equal to those of table 1
  - Merge the results, and read the next record of table 2 that corresponds to the WHERE condition for table 2.
  - If the join criteria of table 1 are greater than those of table 2
  - Exit the internal table, and read the next record of table 1.
- Provided that table 1 contains records that correspond to the WHERE condition for table 1.

The performance of the sort merge join mostly depends on the scope of the data volume to be read of the respective tables and on the access paths to these tables or whether the access paths are implemented via an index that already maps or doesn't map the sort sequence of the join criteria. If the index doesn't support the sorting according to the join criterion, the resulting sets need to be sorted accordingly before they can be merged. The performance of the sort merge join additionally depends on whether the sorting can be done in the main memory that has been provided for sorting or whether it has to be implemented on the hard disk. Hard disk accesses are always slower, but hard disks can provide more space than the main memory.

The hash join is based on the following procedure:

► Create a hashed table from the table that probably returns the smaller resulting set
  ► Provided that table 1 contains rows
  ► By reading every row of table 1 that corresponds to the WHERE condition for table 1
  ► By generating a hash value for the join condition
  ► And by adding it to the hashed table.
  ► End of the loop for table 1.
► Then, read the second table, and for every record that corresponds to the WHERE condition for table 2
  ► Generate a hash value for the join condition
  ► Check it against the hashed table
  ► If they match
  ► Merge the record from table 1 and table 2, and return the result.
  ► End of the loop for table 2.

The performance depends on which table is defined as the hashed table and whether it can be completely hashed to the main memory or has to be moved to the hard disks due to lack of space. The access path, that is, how the individual tables are accessed, assumes a critical role as well. This also involves the reliability of the estimation of which table is the shortest table and thus is the table that should be hashed. The "access path" to the internal (hashed) table is efficient, so the number of attempts for the hashed table plays only a minor role.

It depends on the concrete parameterization of the database and on the statistics or cost calculation of the optimizers which join method the optimizer selects. Preferably, a nested loop join is used if a rather small data volume is expected from the entry table. If a larger data volume is expected, a hash join is used. If the space of main memory that is available for the hash joins is too small or the hash joins are deactivated in the database parameters, a sort merge join is also executed in the case of larger expected data volumes.

If more than two tables are joined, you can combine the various join types as desired. For example, if there are three tables, the resulting set of a join uses table 1 and 2 to create a "table" that is then joined with the third table. It can use different join methods for the two joins. However, a join method usually joins only two sets.

The following tips are principally useful for analyzing joins:

▶ Check whether the most selective conditions (the conditions that return the fewest records) are used first in order to reduce the subsequent effort as much as possible. For this purpose, you need the concrete variables of the SQL statements, such as from the SQL trace (Transaction ST05 — see Section 3.3.8 in Chapter 3). Transaction SE16 lets you determine the actual resulting set and check whether the estimation of the optimizer is correct. If it is not correct, check the statistics (see the Problems section). Section 5.9, Special Cases and Exceptions, discusses further optimization options.

▶ Check whether the access paths to the tables are efficient, that is, whether the join and/or WHERE condition can be accessed without gaps and intermediary ranges via index fields and are supported accordingly. This is particularly critical for internal tables, that is, for accesses that are executed frequently (for each row of the external table or hit list).

Problems

If the database optimizer doesn't select the appropriate execution plan, check the parameterization of SAP NetWeaver AS ABAP and the database system first. To do so, you can use the recommendations of the SAP GoingLive Check or SAP Early-Watch Check or the most recent versions of the parameter notes.

In Transaction DB02, you can use the MISSING INDICES function to check whether there are indexes that haven't been created on the database. When indexes are transported, it is possible that an index isn't created on the database if the table to which the index refers is currently locked. In this case, the system imports only the definition of the index to the SAP Data Dictionary (SAP DDIC) and writes a warning into the transport log. The transport is then completed with a warning (sy-subrc = 4). The MISSING INDICES function in Transaction DB02 enables you to compare the indexes defined in SAP DDIC and the indexes that are actually created on the database. If indexes are listed here, they should also be created. If you manually delete an index on the database deliberately, you should also delete its definition in SAP DDIC to ensure a consistent state of the system.

Another problem may be that the statistics for the tables do not correspond to reality and thus lead to inappropriate access paths. In this context, one often speaks of obsolete statistics. Note, however, that the age of the statistics is not relevant but to which degree the statistics map the reality or whether the statistics lead to an efficient access path. Statistics that are older than one year may still be good if the table hasn't changed significantly in the meantime. Similarly, statistics created a few hours ago can be poor, for example, if the table was empty when the statistics was created and has been filled afterward.

Usually, a job that updates the statistics runs in the SAP environment at regular intervals (for example, daily or once a week). The interval for this job is defined by the system administratiors. The job usually updates the statistics of the tables that have changed significantly since the last update run. It may happen that it doesn't catch all tables that require statistics if the extent to which the table has changed is small enough to be neglected for the statistics creation but large enough to lead to an inefficient execution plan.

Accordingly, check for inappropriate access paths whether the statistics still reflect the reality or allow for an efficient execution plan.

5.4.6   Summary

This chapter assumed that only an inappropriate access path is available for the SQL statements, that is, that the data cannot be accessed very efficiently. You can determine this in Transaction ST05 by looking at the time required for each read data record. This does only apply to plain SQL statements but not to SQL statements with aggregate functions. They require more time for each aggregated result data record, because have to read more data records in order to aggregate them. This also holds true for SQL statements that don't return data records. Figure 5.7 shows an example from the statement summary of an inappropriate access path of Transaction ST05. The average time required per data record (Avg. Time /R) and the minimum time per data record (Min Time /R) are about 161 milliseconds. In total, eight data records were read in 1,291 milliseconds. The high times per data record indicate an inappropriate access path.

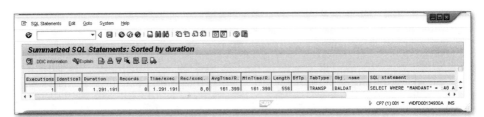

Figure 5.7   Example of an Inappropriate Access Path

All examples in Section 5.4, Access Strategies, describe statements characterized by problems regarding the access path. These statements are also known as statements with inappropriate access paths. In contrast, statements that use an efficient or optimum execution plan are statements with an appropriate access path. You can optimize them by modifying the program logic (complete avoidance, reduction of the resulting set (Section 5.5, Resulting Set)) and reducing the execution frequency (Section 5.7, Execution Frequency). For SQL statements with an inappropriate access path, there are numerous optimization options, which were described in this chapter. If the discussed options are not sufficient, you can also optimize the statements by creating a new index. Section 5.6, Index Design, explains when and particularly how to create indexes.

5.5   Resulting Set

This section describes how you can restrict the resulting set of an SQL query. It examines this process from a logical perspective and then discusses the physical structures where necessary.

In general, an application should only read the data that it actually requires for processing. If you stick to this basic rule, you can already avoid some performance problems by reading less data and thus performing less I/O. Moreover, less data is transferred to the application server — consequently, less memory is required in the application server and the load on the network is reduced. After all, prevention is still the best optimization.

You can reduce the resulting set in two dimensions — you can limit the number of columns and the number of rows that the database returns to the application, as illustrated in Figure 5.8. Here, the range of the data to be read is restricted to the gray fields.

Less data is read by to the application in both cases, when limiting the columns and when limiting the rows. The data is transferred via packages between the database and the application server. This means that a limitation of the columns and rows can only be noticed if the data volume exceeds the limit of the package. The package size depends on the respective database platform and on whether it is a Unicode system or not. Common package sizes are between 8 KB and 128 KB and are always a multiple of 8 KB (network package size).

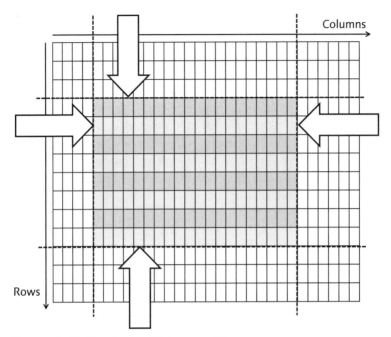

Figure 5.8 Limiting the Read Columns and Rows

The following provides some examples of how the limitation of rows and columns affects the number of the packages that have to be transferred between the database and the application server. Each package comprises both user data and administration data that also require space. At this point, the administration data is not considered to keep the examples simple. The examples should illustrate the concept and the effects of reduced data volume.

Example

A table has 50,000 data records, each with a size of 64 bytes.

▶ All columns of a record are read.
The set to be read (64 bytes) is smaller than a package (32 KB). A partially filled package (32 KB) is transferred from the database to the application server.

▶ Half of the columns (32 bytes) of a record is read.
The set to be read (32 bytes) is smaller than a package (32 KB). A partially filled package (32 KB) is transferred from the database to the application server.

▶ All columns (64 bytes) of 2,000 data records are read.
The set to be read (128 KB) is larger than a package (32 KB). Four completely filled packages (32 KB each) are transferred from the database to the application server.

- ▸ Half of the columns (32 bytes) of 2,000 data records is imported.
  The set to be read (64 KB) is larger than a package (32 KB). Two completely filled packages (32 KB each) are transferred from the database to the application server.
- ▸ All columns (64 bytes) of 50,000 data records are imported.
  The set to be read (3,125 KB) is larger than a package (32 KB). 100 completely filled packages (32 KB each) are transferred from the database to the application server.
- ▸ 2/3 of all columns (43 bytes) of 50,000 data records are imported.
  The set to be read (2,100 KB) is larger than a package (32 KB). 68 completely filled packages (32 KB each) are transferred from the database to the application server.

These package transfers, also called FETCH, have a negative effect on the connection, which can be a network connection between the database and the application server.

On the database side, the I/O is performed in blocks or pages. For the database, it is only critical across how many different blocks the data to be read is distributed. To identify and read a data record, more than one block is usually read. In addition, it is also important how the data is physically stored and which strategy is used to access the data. This was already described in Section 5.4, Access Strategies. In this context, it is crucial that fewer blocks can be imported, for example, if all queried columns are located in one index (*covering index*). For heap tables, for example, the system then no longer has to read the corresponding table block. The decisive factor for the performance at the database level is the number of blocks that have to be processed. If only one record should be read and this record is located in a block together with other records, the database must always import the complete block, regardless of the number of fields that must be read. Afterward, the required fields for the data record are extracted from the block. However, it is also possible that a data record spans several blocks. Limiting the columns can also reduce the number of blocks to be read here.

Consequently, the number of blocks that need to be processed is the decisive factor at the database level. The I/O system must import these blocks into the data cache. At this point, other blocks may be displaced from the data cache and will need to be reimported at a later stage. The less blocks an SQL statement processes at database level, the better for this specific application, which requires less time for importing the data, and the better for other applications whose blocks may continue to be stored in the data cache, because they are not displaced.

The following sections provide brief examples of how you can reduce the resulting set.

5.5.1 Reducing the Columns

All columns of the `dbtab` database table are imported into the internal table, `itab_like_dbtab`:

```
SELECT * FROM dbtab
INTO TABLE itab_like_dbtab
WHERE ...
```

To reduce the data volume, only specify the columns that the program actually needs. The next two examples show a reduced field list.

The fields 1 to 3 of the `dbtab` database table are read into the internal table, `itab_with_more_fields`: The internal table can have additional fields. The fields are read to the identically named fields of the internal table:

[+]
```
SELECT field1 field2 field3 FROM dbtabelle
INTO CORRESPONDING FIELDS OF TABLE itab_with_more_fields
WHERE ...
```

The fields 1 to 3 of the `dbtab` database table are read into the internal table, `itab_struct_f1_f2_f3`: A row of the internal table has exactly the same structure (`feld1`, `feld2`, `feld3`) as the field list.

[+]
```
SELECT field1 field2 field3 FROM dbtabelle
INTO TABLE itab_struct_f1_f2_f3
WHERE ...
```

> **Real-Life Example — Transaction SE30, Tips & Tricks**
>
> In the TIPS & TRICKS under SQL INTERFACE • SELECT WITH SELECT LIST, Transaction SE30 provides an example whose runtime you can measure. Of course, you can also analyze this example with the SQL trace (Transaction ST05).

These examples illustrate how you can use field lists to reduce the number of columns that need to be transferred. The more columns you can limit by defining a field list compared to the SELECT * statement and the more data records the resulting set includes, the better the effect.

The INTO CORRESPONDING FIELDS OF addition copies the identically named fields into the target structure and should only be used when it is really necessary, for example, because you use a structure that already contains other fields, because the name comparison means some effort for the application server. Compared to the other times, this usually involves little effort but may also imply relatively great effort in case of very fast accesses to buffered tables (see Section 6.4 in Chapter 6).

The SQL trace (Transaction ST05) defines how many data records have been transferred from the database to the application server and in how many packages these data records have been transferred. Section 3.3.8 in Chapter 3 discussed the SQL trace in greater detail; here, only the relevant areas in the SQL trace are critical. Figure 5.9 shows the SQL trace of two SQL statements for table DD01l, which transfer 5,397 data records each.

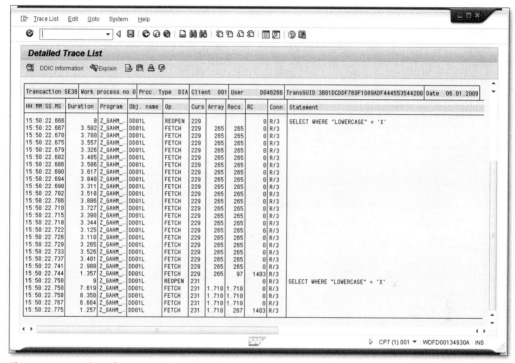

Figure 5.9 Number of Data Records and Packages

The RECORDS column displays the number of data records in a package and the ARRAY column displays how many records fit into a package. The first SELECT statement transfers 20 completely filled packages with 265 data records each and one partially filled package that provides space for 265 data records but contains 97 data records only. (97 data records are the "remainders" of the 5,397 data records of which already 20 times 265 = 5,300 data records were transferred.) This SELECT statement read all columns (SELECT *) of the table.

The second SELECT statement transfers four packages, of which three contain 1,710 data records each (= 5,130 data records) and one package the remaining 267 data records (5,397 – 5,130). This statement read only two columns of the table.

This example nicely illustrates how reducing the columns affects the data volume transferred. Reducing the rows leads to a reduced number of transferred packages (FETCH rows) in the SQL trace. Figure 5.9 shows an example with an Oracle database. For DB6 and MS SQL Server, the transferred packages can be aggregated to trace rows or split up in the SQL trace. Therefore, the number of the transferred packages may differ from the number of the FETCH rows for these platforms. You can thus not use the SQL trace to determine the package size in these cases. For DB6, please contact the database or system administrator to determine the package sizes, because the package size is usually configured there. For MS SQL Server, the packages have sizes of 8 KB or 40 KB (depending on the type of the cursor), regardless of the definition in Transaction ST05.

Generally, always limit the columns to the actually required columns, particularly if this avoids a transfer of not required columns that are considerably long, so-called LOB fields (Large Object). Such fields are created as a string in SAP DDIC, for example, and may contain complete XML documents.

5.5.2 Reducing the Rows

All columns of the dbtab database table are read to the wa_like_dbtab work area. The more rows in the database table, the longer the process.

```
[–]   SELECT * FROM dbtab
      INTO wa_like_dbtab.
      MOVE wa_like_dbtab TO ...
      ...
      ENDSELECT.
```

You should always restrict the data volume with a WHERE condition, especially if the table's volume increases. Shorter tables, such as customizing tables, whose volume doesn't continuously increase or tables that must be processed completely are exceptions, because they are critical for the business process. Usually, a database table should be read via selective accesses, and only the rows that are actually required should be read. Often, such a selection or filtering cannot be implemented until the read process has been completed as illustrated in the following example with a check condition within a SELECT/ENDSELECT loop.

```
[–]   SELECT * FROM dbtab
      INTO wa_like_dbtab.
      Check wa_like_dbtab-field1 = ...
      *Processing...
      ENDSELECT.
```

Such a filtering can also be implemented with an IF statement as in the next example:

```
SELECT … FROM dbtab
INTO wa_like_dbtab.
IF wa_like_dbtab-field1 = ...
*Processing...
ENDIF.
ENDSELECT.
```

[−]

Filtering is sometimes not as obvious as shown in these examples, and the filtering is implemented later on and not directly after the SELECT command.

If a subsequent filtering is used, data rows are read unnecessarily. To avoid this, you have to additionally specify all selection conditions in the SELECT statement as WHERE conditions, so the filtering can take place at database level and only the rows that are actually required are read. In the following example, the filters for field1 and field2 are directly specified in the WHERE condition:

```
SELECT * FROM dbtab
INTO wa_like_dbtab.
WHERE feld1 = cond1
AND feld2 = cond2...
*Processing...
ENDSELECT.
```

[+]

> **Real-Life Example — Transaction SE30, Tips & Tricks**
>
> In the TIPS & TRICKS under SQL INTERFACE • SELECT... WHERE VS. SELECT + CHECK, Transaction SE30 provides an example whose runtime you can measure. Of course, you can also analyze this example with the SQL trace (Transaction ST05).

5.5.3 Reading a Defined Number of Rows

Unnecessary data transfer can also be less obvious, for example, if only a defined number of rows should be read:

```
SELECT * FROM dbtab
INTO wa_like_dbtab.
WHERE field1 = cond1
AND field2 = cond2...
IF sy-dbcnt = 150.
*Termination of processing
    EXIT.
ELSE.
*Processing...
```

[−]

```
ENDIF.
ENDSELECT.
```

In this example, 150 records are expected during the read from the `dbtab` database table. Your application then provides the required 150 records, but more records may be transferred from the database to the application server. Because the termination criterion is not anchored in the SQL statement and therefore not transferred to the database, the `SELECT` loop returns data packages until the loop is terminated. For example, if such a package (32 KB or 64 KB) that is transferred between the database and the application server can include 113 records, the system first transfers a completely filled package with 113 data records to the DBI (Database Interface) of the application server. Here, the data records are separately transferred to the ABAP program. Because the 150 data records haven't been reached yet, the loop requests a second package and transfers it. The data records from the second package are again separately transferred to the ABAP program. Only then is the termination condition set at the 150th record (the 37th record in the second package). The remaining 76 records of the package have already been transferred from the database to the application server and are no longer provided by the DBI. These unnecessarily read records can be physically located in different blocks than the 150 required data records in the database. This would require additional I/O on the database. You can avoid this if you define the number of the required records already in the SQL statement, as shown in the following example:

[+]
```
SELECT * FROM dbtab
INTO wa_like_dbtab.
WHERE field1 = cond1
AND field2 = cond2...
UP TO 150 ROWS.
*Processing...
ENDIF.
ENDSELECT.
```

In this example, too, 150 data records are transferred to the ABAP program. However, this time, a full package (113 records) and an incompletely filled package (37 records) are transferred from the database to the DBI in the application server. From there, the data records are separately transferred to the ABAP program. The DBI translates the `UP TO n ROWS` condition for the respective database, so the database must only read the blocks that contain the required 150 data records.

Figure 5.10 maps the difference between the mentioned variants in the SQL trace.

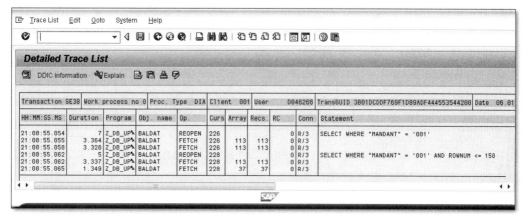

Figure 5.10 Effects of the UP TO n ROWS Condition

The first SELECT statement reads two packages with 113 records each, while the second statement reads one package with 113 and one package with 37 records. The Statement column displays the AND ROWNUM <= :A1 addition. This is the translation of UP TO n ROWS for the Oracle database platform.

The difference becomes more obvious if only one record from the database is required. If you don't use SELECT SINGLE or SELECT ... UP TO 1 ROWS..., the system reads and transfers as many data records as fit into the first package to the application server, while only one data record is read and transferred in one package if SELECT SINGLE or SELECT ... UP TO 1 ROWS... is defined.

For the WHERE conditions, it is also critical that the number of rows (selectivity) is kept as constant as possible over time. If you read the transaction tables (for example, BKPF, BSEG, COBK, COEP, LIPK, MKPF, VBAK, VBAP), you must ensure that the number of selected data records remains constant over time and doesn't significantly increase as the tables. Options for stabilizing the selected data records are, for example, time restrictions on fields with a date or restrictions to specific statuses in status fields. Furthermore, an index should be created for these fields.

5.5.4 Aggregating

You can find other examples of unnecessary data transfer when summarizing or counting data or determining minimum, maximum, and average values. In the first example, the data records that meet a specific condition are read and summarized in the ABAP program:

```
SELECT field2 FROM dbtab
INTO wa_like_field2.
WHERE field1 = cond1
```

[−]

```
AND field2 = cond2... .
...
sum = sum + wa_like_field2.
...
ENDSELECT.
```

The program merely requires the sum of feld2 of the data records that meet the WHERE condition. For this purpose, the system reads and transfers all data records that meet the condition. You can avoid the transfer using so-called aggregate functions. The SELECT statement would then look as follows:

[+]
```
SELECT sum(feld2) FROM dbtab
INTO wa_like_f.
WHERE field1 = cond1
AND field2 = cond2... .
```

Here, the system reads all data records that meet the WHERE condition at database level and summarizes them at database level. The result is then transferred to the application server.

The aggregate functions comprise the following functions:

- ▶ Count (count)
- ▶ Summarize (sum)
- ▶ Minimum value (min)
- ▶ Maximum value (max)
- ▶ Average value (avg)

You can use these functions together with or without grouping (group by) to use the respective function for a specific group or for all data records. These aggregate functions imply more effort for the database than statements that don't use aggregate functions: After the data has been read, the aggregate function must be deployed for the resulting set. Depending on the constellation, it might be necessary to sort the resulting set first. The use of aggregate functions requires more time at the database level than the mere reading. However, this time difference is usually compensated during the data transfer if the data volume that needs to be transferred with aggregate function is considerably smaller than the data volume without aggregate function.

If you want to further restrict the aggregated data, you can reduce the data volume that needs to be transferred even more. Let's assume you want to obtain a list of all customers that have more than ten purchase orders. The corresponding SELECT statement could look as follows:

```
SELECT kunnr count(aufnr) FROM dbtab_auftraege          [–]
INTO ( wa-kunnr, wa-sum_auftr ).
WHERE field1 = cond1
AND field2 = cond2...
GROUP BY kunnr.
IF wa-sum_auftr >10
*Processing
ENDIF.
ENDSELECT.
```

Here, all customer numbers are transferred. The customer numbers that have more than ten purchase orders are then filtered out at the application server level. You can avoid this using the following statement:

```
SELECT kunnr count(aufnr) FROM dbtab_auftraege          [+]
INTO ( wa-kunnr, wa-count_auftr ).
WHERE field1 = cond1
AND field2 = cond2...
GROUP BY kunnr
HAVING count(aufnr) > 10.
*Processing
ENDSELECT.
```

Now, the system transfers only the customer numbers that have more than ten purchase orders. In both cases, the system reads the same number of data records (and thus data blocks) at the database level to determine the result. The additional restriction means more effort for the database. However, this is compensated if the data volume that is to be transferred is reduced.

Real-Life Example — Transaction SE30, Tips & Tricks

In the TIPS & TRICKS under SQL INTERFACE • SELECT AGGREGATES, Transaction SE30 provides an example whose runtime you can measure. Of course, you can also analyze this example with the SQL trace (Transaction ST05).

5.5.5 Existence Checks

Another example of avoiding unnecessary data transfers is the existence check. If you want to determine whether a table contains data records for a particular condition, you often find the following statement:

```
SELECT count(*) FROM dbtab                              [–]
INTO wa_counter.
WHERE field1 = cond1
AND field2 = cond2... .
IF wa_counter > 0 ...
```

Here, the database has to count all data records of the table that meet the WHERE condition. For the program, however, it is not the number that is important but the information whether there is a data record that meets the WHERE condition or not. You can meet this requirement more efficiently:

```
SELECT * FROM dbtab
INTO wa_fields.
WHERE field1 = cond1
AND field2 = cond2...
UP TO 1 ROWS.
IF sy-subrc = 0 ...
```

This ensures right from the start that only one record is read and transferred if the selection has been successful. If there are no appropriate records, no record is transferred to the application server. You can check the success or failure of the SELECT statement by means of the sy-subrc return code. The variant where only the first field of the record is queried instead of all fields of the record is even more efficient:

[+]
```
SELECT field1 FROM dbtab
INTO wa_feldliste.
WHERE field1 = cond1
AND field2 = cond2...
UP TO 1 ROWS.
IF sy-subrc = 0 ...
```

As the data of a data record may be distributed across several blocks or the access path requires reading several blocks (see Section 5.6, Index Design), you can further restrict the number of the blocks that need to be read at database level by specifying the first field — particularly if only the index and not the table has to be read additionally.

Real-Life Example — Transaction SE30, Tips & Tricks

In the TIPS & TRICKS under SQL INTERFACE • TEST EXISTENCE, Transaction SE30 provides an example whose runtime you can measure. Of course, you can also analyze this example with the SQL trace (Transaction ST05).

5.5.6 Updates

The last example for reducing the data volume transferred involves data updates. A field of a data record in the wa_vvbap variable is updated. The system then transfers the update to the database. In this case, all fields are transferred for the update and overwrite the old fields, regardless of whether they have been updated or not:

```
wa_vvbap-zmeng = var_meng.
UPDATE zvbap FROM wa_vvbap.
```

[–]

To only transfer the updated field, UPDATE would look as follows:

```
wa_vvbap-zmeng = var_meng.
UPDATE zvbap
SET zmeng = var_meng
WHERE vbeln = wa_vvbap-vbeln.
```

[+]

Here, only the actually updated field is transferred to the database for the update and only this field is updated. All other fields retain their old values, because they weren't changed.

> **Real-Life Example — Transaction SE30, Tips & Tricks**
>
> In the TIPS & TRICKS under SQL INTERFACE • COLUMN UPDATE, Transaction SE30 provides an example whose runtime you can measure. Of course, you can also analyze this example with the SQL trace (Transaction ST05).

5.5.7 Summary

SQL statements that can only be optimized via the resulting set are also known as statements with appropriate access paths. In this context, it was assumed that only an appropriate access path is available for the SQL statements, that is, that the data is accessed in the most efficient way. You can determine this in Transaction ST05 by looking at the time required for each read data record. This does only apply to plain SQL statements but not to SQL statements with aggregate functions, because they must read more data records. To aggregate them, they require more time for each aggregated result data record than for statements without aggregate function. This holds also true for SQL statements that don't return data records. Figure 5.11 shows an example from the statement summary of an appropriate access path of Transaction ST05. The average time required per data record (AVG. TIME /R) and the minimum time per data record (MIN TIME /R) are about 39 milliseconds. In total, 940 data records were read in 36 milliseconds. The low times per data record indicate an appropriate access path.

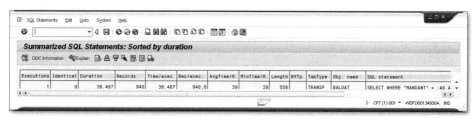

Figure 5.11 Example of an Appropriate Access Path

When creating SQL statements, always ensure that only the actually required data is transferred. You can further optimize SQL statements with an appropriate access path only by reducing the resulting set or limiting (or even avoiding) the execution.

5.6   Index Design

The fact that there are usually no absolute truths and recommendations for the performance topic also holds true for the index design topic. This section therefore focuses most on the basic principles of the index design topics to enable you to identify the necessary criteria based on your general conditions, so you can make a decision. Wherever possible, concrete recommendations are given.

Before you create an index, answer the question for which SQL statements should be used. This question can be approached from different perspectives:

- Perspective of the application development
- Perspective of the system administration

The two perspectives have certain differences, which are described in the following:

From the point of view of the application development, the SQL statements of a specific program or transaction are of interest. This usually involves reducing the response time of long-running SQL statements in the program for which users have to wait or that must be completed within a defined period of time due to overnight processing. Compared to others, these statements can be relatively fast. For example, if an action in a dialog program executes an SQL statement with a runtime of three seconds, this may be too long for a user who has to wait. So if this transaction is rarely used, it wouldn't be identified as expensive within the overall system if there are a lot of statements executed more often and/or run longer. From the point of view of the application development, this is still a problematic SQL statement, which needs to be optimized.

From the point of view of the system administration, the SQL statements that consume the most resources are of particular interest. For example, there may be statements that account for a significant part of the overall database load. Of course, it is possible that they come from programs whose runtime plays only a minor role, for example, because the program creates a report at night and the runtime isn't of interest for the user department, because the program is finished the next morning. From the point of view of the system administration, this SQL statement consumes resources and affects the system performance (and consequently other applications that run at the same time). Remember, for example, the displacement in the data cache as described at the beginning of this chapter.

After you have identified an SQL statement that you want to optimize, answer the following questions:

Is the program or SQL statement (still) used at all?

This question may sound funny or you may assume that it is a matter of course that only programs or SQL statements are running that are actually required. However, if you take a closer look, you may determine that the SQL statement or the whole program is no longer required. For example, it is often the case that programs that ran in the nightly background processing created an evaluation list that no one needed the next day. You can simply deschedule these programs. Of course, you can only determine whether a statement or a whole program is no longer required if you have knowledge of the application and the business background. Don't create an index for such statement but simply delete the statement or program.

Is the SQL statement or program frequently used?

If the SQL statement or program is rarely used, it depends on the circumstances whether you should create an index or not. If the response time of the SQL statement desperately needs to be improved, optimize the statement. In contrast, if it is *only* a resource consumer whose response time isn't that critical, it mainly depends on which programs run *in parallel* to this statement. If the program runs — due to its high resource consumptions (for example, used I/O or CPU capacity or block displacement in the cache) — in parallel to other programs whose response time assumes a central role, also optimize the statement. If the program runs in periods of low loads during which no essential programs are affected, you don't necessarily have to optimize the statement.

If the statement is often used and/or definitely needs to be optimized, analyze whether the SQL statement cannot be changed via a code modification as described in Section 5.4, Access Strategies, so it uses an existing index (in a better way). This may prevent you from creating a new index.

If you cannot adapt the SQL statement to use an existing index, you can also check whether you can modify the existing index to better support the statement. However, closely monitor these modifications of the index, because a modification of the index design may have positive as well as negative effects on other SQL statements. The least risky approach is to add an additional field at the end of an index.

Only create a new index if the measures mentioned previously cannot be implemented. Creating a new index may also affect other SQL statements or programs — positively or negatively. This is because the optimizer can now potentially select the new index for other SQL statements even though this may lead to an inefficient execution plan. You must therefore also monitor the effects that a new index has on other SQL statements.

But how are new indexes structured? Before discussing the general conditions, here are some rules and comments that you may often hear or read in the context of indexes:

▶ You shouldn't create more than five indexes for each table.

▶ An index should not contain more than five columns.

▶ The columns should be sorted by selectivity.

These "rules" are mentioned here, because such general rules of thumb should be handled with care. As often, it all depends on the concrete case. For example, the question whether the planned sixth index for a table isn't too much arises frequently. To answer this question, look at the concrete conditions. Strictly adhering to the general rule *No more than five indexes* is as useless as completely ignoring the mentioned rules. It all depends on the general conditions. These are described in the following.

5.6.1 Read or Write Processing?

Usually, the following rule applies to the number of indexes of the table: as less as possible but as many as necessary. Besides the additional space requirements both on the hard disk and in the main memory, every additional index on the database involves the following administration effort for Data Manipulation Language (DML) statements (statements such as INSERT, UPDATE, DELETE):

▶ INSERT and DELETE statements *always* have to maintain *all* existing indexes for any inserted or deleted data record.

▶ UPDATE statements have to maintain all indexes that contain *fields that are supposed to be updated.*

Background: UPDATE SET... vs. UPDATE dbtab FROM...

At this point, the UPDATE SET should be mentioned once again, which was discussed in the context of reducing the columns to be transferred. In contrast to UPDATE dbtab FROM wa, UPDATE SET... only transfers the fields specified with the SET condition. Consequently, only the indexes that contain the specified fields need to be maintained. The UPDATE dbtab FROM WA statement transfers all fields for UPDATE to the database. Therefore, all indexes must be maintained. Even though the old value and the new value of a field are identical, the maintenance is carried out at database level.

Because the indexes are stored sorted by their fields, this has the following consequences: If a table is sequentially populated, for example, based on a constantly increasing document number, you can usually also find this sorting by document number within the table blocks. If subsequent processing again includes deletion and further insertion processes, the space that particularly obsolete entries occupied before the deletions is reused for new entries. Physical sorting cannot be ensured in the long run. However, adjacent document numbers are usually physically stored in the same or in adjacent blocks. A range of document numbers, such as 50.000.100 to 50.000.200, could be stored in two adjacent blocks. An index for the document number must be sorted by document number, while other indexes (for example for customer ID, item number) are sorted according to the corresponding fields. Consequently, the document number range in these indexes is distributed across multiple blocks. If INSERT or DELETE is used, the system must read all of these blocks to insert a new record or delete an existing record. If it cannot find these blocks in the data cache, 10 ms may be required for each block. If now, for example, 100 documents should be deleted, the worst case may be that one block has to be read for each document for each existing index (except for the one sorted in the same way as the table). If these blocks are not buffered in the cache, for our example with five indexes, you have to calculate as follows: two table blocks, two index blocks for the index that is sorted in accordance with the table plus 4 * 100 index blocks for the other indexes. If all blocks require a physical I/O, this would result in a response time of 4,040 ms (= 4 seconds) for the index maintenance costs. Probably, such an extreme example doesn't exist in real life, because some blocks may be buffered in the cache and the distribution across different blocks doesn't have to be an extreme case. Nevertheless, this example illustrates the maintenance effort that basically results from the additional I/O for the index pages.

UPDATE may require removing the respective index entry in a block and inserting it elsewhere. UPDATE only maintains the indexes that contain the field that needs to be updated. However, it is possible that two identical blocks have to be read for each row to move the index entry to the new position, because the index needs to be sorted. For this purpose, the system must also read the corresponding blocks at the higher level to implement the changes in the branch blocks.

For both INSERT and UPDATE (if field content is extended), it is possible that a block is too full and needs to be split up. To do so, the existing content of one block is distributed across two new blocks. This process also involves additional I/O, because the second block is read. For this purpose, the system must also read the corresponding blocks at the higher level to implement the changes in the branch blocks.

Now that you're more familiar with the possibly incurring maintenance costs, for the index design, the following question arises with regard to the performance: Are the write programs or read programs time-critical? As long as the write programs don't cause performance problems, you can create additional indexes from the view of the maintenance costs. If the programs that write data to these tables are time-critical, consider how many indexes you actually require.

For example, read or write processing is time-critical in BI systems if the system has to load (write) larger data volumes and must then evaluate (read) this data. In such a scenario, it may be helpful to delete the indexes before loading the data and recreate them before evaluating the data. This enables you to optimally support both scenarios. Of course, this is only possible, because read processing is handled at a different time than write processing. However, the recreation of the indexes also requires time that should be compensated by a quicker processing of the data load programs. Otherwise, deleting the indexes doesn't make sense here. In general, you should use this procedure for Data Warehouse applications or administration tasks where the system has to write and evaluate large data volumes.

For OLTP systems that process relatively small datasets, it is rather uncommon to delete and recreate indexes. In this case, if the performance of the read and of the write programs is critical, find a compromise to keep the write performance and the read performance of the most important programs at a satisfactory level. Never delete unique indexes during running operations due to consistency reasons.

5.6.2 How is Data Accessed?

The second question that you should consider for the index design is which fields are *usually* used to access the data. In this context, take into account the access paths that are particularly frequently used and don't consider special exceptions at first. In addition to the individual fields, this question also addresses the field combinations. For field combinations, it is often recommended to position the most selective fields in the field sequence to the left in the index. This recommendation is generally true. However, let's have a look at an example from the telephone directory. A general query to a telephone directory is to display a telephone number for a city, last name, and first name, such as:

```
SELECT telephone_number
FROM telephone directory
WHERE city = ? AND last name =? AND first name =?
```

Sorted by selectivity, the index would be sorted by first name, last name, and city, because the first name usually has more different values than the last name. This, in turn, has more different values than the city. An index with these fields would support the WHERE condition of the query mentioned above.

Other queries, for example, a list of all persons with a specific last name from a specific city or a list of all persons from a specific city, as illustrated in the next two examples, cannot use the previously created index.

```
SELECT telephone_number
FROM telephone_directory
WHERE city = ? AND last name = ?

SELECT telephone number
FROM telephone_directory
WHERE city = ?
```

Because the WHERE condition doesn't contain the first field in the index (the first name), there's a gap in the index. Because the index is sorted by the first name, the system must read the entire index. You would have to create new indexes to optimally support these queries, for example, an additional index for the last name and city fields and another index for city.

Now, an appropriate index for the WHERE condition is available for each query. DML statements then incur higher maintenance costs because of these three indexes, as described earlier.

If you look at these three queries together, *one* index for city, last name, and first name is sufficient for all three statements. There would be less maintenance work for the database and space requirements for *one* index. With regard to the space requirements, this includes the occupied space on the hard disks but also the space for index pages in the data cache. Three different indexes usually occupy more space in the data cache than one index.

Therefore, select the field sequence not only based on the selectivity but also on the highest possible support with = conditions for your frequently executed queries. Basically, insert fields that are queried with range conditions (BETWEEN, LIKE, <, >) *after* the columns that are queried with =.

Consequently, the way how you access the data, for example, which fields and which field combinations are accessed using = and for which fields range conditions are used, should be mapped to the indexes in such a way that as few indexes as possible have to be created.

Background: CLIENT as the First Field in Secondary Indexes?

A frequently asked question is whether the CLIENT field should be included in second-ary indexes as the first field or not. As a matter of fact, there is no general answer to that question.

It depends on numerous conditions whether you can omit the field — for example, on the number of live clients in the system, that is, whether the client is selective.

Another question is whether the client is also selected in the queries. In this case, it should be included in the indexes to avoid additional table block accesses.

Adding clients, however, also increases the size of the indexes. This also affects the space that the database requires and consequently the backup and restore runtimes. Of course, the indexes then also require more space in the cache.

In general, even though the CLIENT field is not required, its existence in the index hardly has a negative effect on the performance. The CLIENT field (if it isn't programmed with `CLIENT SPECIFIED`) is always generated in the `WHERE` condition. Because it is useful to have selective fields and/or fields that are specified with = in the leading index columns, the CLIENT field does not do any harm at the beginning of an index. Older database versions even required the client in the first position of the index if a range condition (`BETWEEN, <, >, LIKE`) was specified in the second position, because, if the index didn't contain the client, the database version didn't use the index if a range condition was specified for the first index column.

At this point, there are rare exceptions where the execution plan was modified and the performance improved when the client field was not included as the first field in the index.

For individual, especially time-critical, SQL statements, it may be necessary to design the indexes in such a way that all required fields can be read from the index and the table doesn't have to be read in addition. However, only create such specific indexes in exceptional cases for especially critical SQL statements. Whenever possible, first optimize the statement, for example, in such a way that fields are read only from a particular index. This is known as a *covering index*.

5.6.3 Summary

The goal of your index design is to support *all frequently executed* SQL statements (and the critical resource consumers) with *good* indexes (not necessarily the best possible ones, because this significantly increases the number of required indexes). "Good indexes" means that the *essential* restriction of the data should be implemented as early as possible by the index: The index should prevent the system from scanning too many index or table blocks to filter out the relevant data. This is achieved by ensuring that the *selective conditions* are provided in the index fields and that they can be accessed without gaps via = conditions for the other fields.

5.7 Execution Frequency

You cannot further accelerate an SQL statement with an appropriate access path that only reads the data required. You can only further improve the performance if the complete statement is executed less often, for example, by changing the processing from single record processing to set processing.

To do so, use the various array interfaces provided by Open SQL. One example is the classic `SELECT/ENDSELECT` loop:

```
SELECT * INTO linevar
FROM dbtab
WHERE ... .
*Processing of the individual records

ENDSELECT.
```

Here, the Database Interface (DBI) already implements an optimization. The system doesn't read the individual records from the database but accesses the data in the database in packages and multiple data records are transferred from the database in `FETCH` operations. The data is then buffered in the DBI and separately returned to the ABAP program until all data records have been processed. Afterward, the next package is retrieved from the database. This is the array interface, which is always used by the DBI. Only if you use `SELECT SINGLE` or `SELECT ... UP TO 1 ROWS` does the DBI read only one data record from the database.

For the `SELECT` statement, use the ABAP array interface with the `INTO TABLE` keyword. Here, the DBI transfers the data, which has already been transferred in packages, to your program and copies it into an internal table that you can subsequently process with a loop:

```
SELECT * INTO TABLE itab
FROM dbtab
WHERE ... .
LOOP AT itab.
*Processing of the individual records from the internal table
ENDLOOP.
```

If the data volume that is to be read is very large, the import to an internal table can result in (too) high main memory requirements on the application server. To avoid this, use the following variant:

```
SELECT * INTO TABLE itab
PACKAGE SIZE n
FROM dbtab
WHERE ... .
```

```
 LOOP AT itab.
*Processing of the individual records from the internal table
 ENDLOOP.
ENDSELECT.
```

Here, the `PACKAGE SIZE n` addition defines the number of data records that should be transferred in the package. These data records must then be processed using the loop *within* the `SELECT/ENDSELECT` loop. This variant also uses both array interfaces. Always ensure that the `SELECT` arrays do not become too large to reduce the memory consumption on the application server. For this purpose, keep in mind the width of the required fields of the `SELECT` list.

Figure 5.12 illustrates the differences between `SELECT/ENDSELECT` where *only* the array interface of the DBI is used and `SELECT ... INTO TABLE` that uses both the DBI array interface and the ABAP array interface.

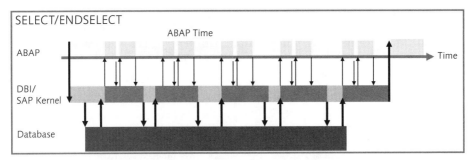

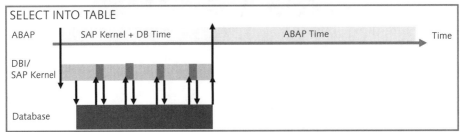

Figure 5.12 Comparison of SELECT/ENDSELECT and ABAP Array Interface

The runtime differences for these variants are not that big, because the DBI already accesses the data in an optimized way via the array interface. Nevertheless, using the ABAP array interface saves CPU time on the application server, because the data records are not transferred separately between the DBI and the ABAP program but in packages. For the database, both variants have the same behavior; because the dataset remains the same, both variants require the same number of `FETCH` statements.

If data is required from multiple tables, for example, order header data and the corresponding items of the orders, the system often uses nested loops to reduce the access to multiple tables.

The next example deals with SELECT SINGLE or SELECT... UP TO 1 ROWS. This involves *real* single record processing — between the ABAP program and the DBI as well as between the DBI and the database. Here, SELECT SINGLE or SELECT ... UP TO 1 ROWS is executed in ABAP in a loop. The loop can be a loop statement or any other type of loop. It may also be a SELECT/ENDSELECT loop, in this case, nested SELECT statements, which are explained in the following in more detail. Usually, the WHERE condition is filled from the loop. A common example is the following:

```
LOOP AT itab.
SELECT SINGLE * INTO linevar FROM dbtab
WHERE field = itab-field.
APPEND linevar TO new_itab.
ENDLOOP
```

For each row in the itab, a single SELECT statement is triggered against the database. Each package transfers only one data record. So, for each single record, the necessary communication effort, which basically includes opening the database cursor and the transfer of the data package, is carried out for database queries. This exact communication effort is the potential for savings.

If multiple records are read from the database at once, the communication effort occurs less often. The cursor is opened once, and the effort for transferring the packages occurs, as previously, for each package. However, there are now more records in one package, that is, less packages are transferred. Consequently, less communication effort is involved.

Background: Call Position of the SQL Statement and Call Stack

SELECT statements in loops are not always as apparent as in the example above. The call hierarchy may also be very complex: For example, a PERFORM statement is executed in a loop. This statement, in turn, calls a function module in which a SELECT statement is executed. This SELECT statement is also in a loop but cannot be identified that easily, especially because it may consist of two different program objects, an executable program and a function module. In the SQL trace, you can navigate to the call position (in the function module) and don't see the call stack called via the function module. Currently, you can trace this via the ABAP trace transactions only (Transaction SE30/ST12), which are described in Chapter 3. Future versions of Transaction ST05 will provide the option to also record the call stack (see Chapter 10).

Another possible problem of SELECT statements in loops can be identical accesses to the same data records. Let's assume there's an internal table that contains the order headers. The customer ID is one field of the order header. This customer ID lets you access the customer master table in the loop via the internal table with the order headers to determine the address data of the customer. If a customer has multiple orders, the system reads the same customer address several times from the database without any further checks. You can analyze in detail the various identical accesses to the data records using Transaction ST05 (see Section 3.3.8 in Chapter 3), based on the basic list, under TRACE LIST • DISPLAY IDENTICAL SELECTS. It displays how often the combination was queried for every field combination that has been frequently queried from the database. The IDENTICAL column in the statement summary (aggregate trace by SQL statement) displays the percentage of identical values for each statement with the same structure. You can only avoid identical SELECT statements on the database by buffering the data. Chapter 6 describes the buffering options in detail.

The problem of the increased communication effort also arises for nested SELECT/ ENDSELECT loops. The external statement of the SELECT statement is executed in an optimized way via the array interface of the DBI; the inner statement, however, may not execute efficient array FETCHES via the DBI. If there is only one or a few records in the inner table for each record of the outer tables, the resulting set in the package is defined by the outer table. As a result, one query for one or a few data records to the database may be required for the inner SELECT statement. The problem of the increased communication effort (opening the cursor, transferring the packages) consequently arises for the inner table. The same may apply to identical access if the WHERE condition for the inner table doesn't change for the individual rows of the outer table (for example, customer IDs in order header table). Only accept nested SELECT loops if the hit list for the internal table is short in order to reduce the effort for accessing the inner table(s) as much as possible.

Strictly speaking, the nested SELECT statements in ABAP are a join between two database tables. For nested SELECT statements, you as the developer define the sequence in which the tables should be accessed. This doesn't have to be a disadvantage but is hard-coded in the program, so the database optimizer cannot dynamically change this for different basic conditions.

There are various options to optimize SELECT statements in loops or nested SELECT/ ENDSELECT loops. The most important options include:

- View
- Join
- FOR ALL ENTRIES statement

5.7.1 View

Views are accessed in the same way as SELECT statements:

```
SELECT * INTO linevar
FROM dbview
WHERE ...
*... Processing...
ENDSELCT.
```

Create the dbview in Transaction SE11. You must make the following specifications when creating a view:

1. The tables and fields with which the tables should be linked (join condition)

2. The fields from the tables that can be selected

If desired, you can define further restrictions (WHERE condition, selection conditions) when defining the view in Transaction SE11. Transaction ST05 doesn't indicate these selection conditions when views are accessed. They are provided in Transaction SE11. The performance of views behaves in the same way as the performance of joins. The optimizer uses statistics to determine the best access path when the view is accessed. This access path defines which table is read first before the other tables are accessed and which indexes are used to access the tables or whether full table scans are used. Consequently, the performance analysis and the tuning are similar to those of joins as well.

Views may have the following disadvantages:

For hierarchically linked tables, redundancies may occur for the transferred fields of the leading tables. For example, the data for the order header are generated n times (once for each order item) to the resulting set and transferred to the application server. If n is very large and there are a lot of columns of the leading tables or/and the columns are very wide, this may have a negative effect on the performance. This also holds true for joins.

The advantages of views are as follows:

▶ Compared to nested SELECT statements, they can transfer less data if nested SELECT statements transferred all fields, because the fields contained in both tables are transferred only once.

▶ The access sequence for the tables is not hard-coded in the program (as are the nested SELECT statements) but selected in a flexible way by the database by means of statistics. The optimization may also have the wrong result (as is also the case for joins), that is, it is possible that the database optimizer selects the wrong table as the entry table. However, usually, these problems can be solved at the database level (see, for example, Section 5.9, Special Cases and Exceptions) without accessing the tables separately as for nested SELECT statements.

▸ In total, the system sends less queries to the database than for nested SELECT statements, because the access to a view is *one* query, while the nested SELECT statement accesses the inner table for each row of the outer table once. This reduction of the number of queries to the database reduces the communication effort and has a positive effect on the performance.

> **Real-Life Example — Transaction SE30, Tips & Tricks**
>
> In the TIPS & TRICKS under SQL INTERFACE • SELECT OVER MORE THAN ONE TABLE • SELECT WITH VIEW, Transaction SE30 provides an example whose runtime you can measure. Of course, you can also analyze this example with the SQL trace (Transaction ST05).

5.7.2 Join

Joins in the ABAP source code have the same advantages and disadvantages as defined views on the database.

Another advantage of joins is that they can be used in a more flexible way compared to views. Joins in ABAP let you implement *left outer joins*. They also often return a result record for the data records in the leading table for which the joined table doesn't provide the corresponding records based on the join criterion. For the fields of the joined table, they simply return initial values for non-existing fields. The potential resulting set can be larger for left outer joins. It is also possible that the optimizer selects a different execution plan than for the "normal" join referred to as *inner join* (and is also used for the view and ABAP join without the LEFT OUTER specification). Here are two examples for joins in ABAP:

```
SELECT * INTO linevar
FROM dbtab1
INNER JOIN dbtab2 ON dbtab1~field1 = dbtab2~field2
WHERE ...
*... Processing...
ENDSELECT.

SELECT * INTO linevar
FROM dbtab1
LEFT OUTER JOIN dbtab2 ON dbtab1~field1 = dbtab2~field2
WHERE ...
*... Processing...
ENDSELECT.
```

5.7.3 FOR ALL ENTRIES

The usage of the FOR ALL ENTRIES ABAP language element is an elegant option to bundle SELECT statements in loops to further reduce the number of queries and the communication effort with the database.

Colloquially, this is also called a join of an internal table with a database table. The following provides two examples for FOR ALL ENTRIES:

```
SELECT * FROM dbtab
FOR ALL ENTRIES IN itab
WHERE field1 = itab-field1.
*... Processing...
ENDSELECT.
SELECT * FROM dbtab
FOR ALL ENTRIES IN itab
WHERE field1 = itab-field1
AND field2 = itab-field2.
*... Processing...
ENDSELECT.
```

Here, the conditions of the internal table itab (for example, itab-field1), are generated for each row of itab from the database interface to SQL statements. This is implemented in blocks whose size you can define via SAP profile parameters. The goal here is to generate a specific SQL statement neither for each row of itab (compared to the SELECT statement in the loop, this wouldn't be advantageous) nor for the entire itab table (this statement could easily become too large). It depends on the parameterization of the SAP system, the version of the SAP kernel, and the used database (version) in which sizes and with which SQL database command is implemented. There are various options to generate *a specific number* of conditions from itab against the database in *one* statement. This can be implemented via UNION SELECT statements or OR or IN conditions or specific methods only supported by a particular database. The default settings of the SAP system have been defined on the basis of the best experiences in terms of method and size. The DBI, for example, can translate the ABAP Open SQL statements mentioned above as follows:

```
SELECT * FROM dbtab
WHERE feld1 IN (itab-field1(1) itab-field1(2), itab-field1(3)...)
```

```
SELECT * FROM dbtab
WHERE (field1 = itab-field1(1)
AND field2 = itab-field2(1))
OR (field1 = itab-field1(2)
AND field2 = itab-field2(2))
OR (field1 = itab-field1(3)
AND field2 = itab-field2(3))
OR (field1 = itab-field1(4)
AND field2 = itab-field2(4))
OR (field1 = itab-field1(5)
AND field2 = itab-field2(5))

SELECT * FROM dbtab
WHERE (field1 = itab-field1(1)
AND field2 = itab-field2(1))
UNION ALL
SELECT * FROM dbtab
WHERE field1 = itab-field1(2)
AND field2 = itab-field2(2)
UNION ALL
SELECT * FROM dbtab
WHERE field1 = itab-field1(3)
AND field2 = itab-field2(3)
UNION ALL
SELECT * FROM dbtab
WHERE field1 = itab-field1(4)
AND field2 = itab-field2(4)
UNION ALL
SELECT * FROM dbtab
WHERE field1 = itab-field1(5)
AND field2 = itab-field2(5)
```

The numbers in brackets indicate the respective row of itab. This is only one example how you can implement the FOR ALL ENTRIES statement. The system administratiors are responsible for the correct parameterization and should ensure the appropriate settings for the respective combination from SAP and database release using SAP notes or recommendations from the SAP EarlyWatch Check. SAP Note 48230 and the related or referenced SAP notes provide a good overview of this topic.

As long as there are no performance problems, the method in which the FOR ALL ENTRIES statement (FAE) is implemented plays only a minor role for you as the ABAP developer. In case of performance problems with FAE statements, have the SAP system administrators check the correct configuration of the SAP system, because performance problems with FAE statements can usually be solved with the appropriate parameterization, except for two cases, which are described in the following section.

Before the performance-critical aspect in ABAP of the FAE statement is discussed, the restrictions of the FAE should be mentioned:

▶ You can sort FAE SELECT statements only by the primary key (solely ORDER BY PRIMARY KEY is allowed).

▶ Aggregate functions (GROUP BY, COUNT, SUM, ...) are not permitted for FAE.

▶ Not-equal-to (<>) or negative conditions (NOT) are not permitted for FAE.

▶ You aren't allowed to use more than one internal table for FAE.

In terms of the performance, consider the following two aspects for FAE:

▶ For FAE queries, don't use complex range tables in addition to avoid that the system generates complex SQL statements. Otherwise, there's the risk that the database optimizer makes the wrong decision, so the appropriate indexes cannot be used due to the complex WHERE condition.

▶ The internal table used for the FAE statement must not be empty. If the internal table is empty, the system ignores the entire WHERE condition and reads the complete table (or the complete current client). Before you perform an FAE statement, always check whether the internal table is filled (IF itab[] IS NOT INITIAL).

> **Background: FOR ALL ENTRIES with an Empty Internal Table**
>
> Even though you consider FOR ALL ENTRIES a join between the internal table and the database table, it doesn't behave as a join on the database. If one of the tables included in the join is empty in the case of a database join (inner join), this would lead to an empty resulting set. This doesn't apply to FAE statements. Why?
>
> The FOR ALL ENTRIES statement was originally designed as OR of all conditions. It was introduced to substitute long range tables or IN lists that sometimes had had problems with the maximum size of statements permitted. If individual conditions are removed from multiple OR or IN conditions, the resulting set increases steadily. If the last OR or IN condition is removed or an empty range table is used, the resulting set includes all data records. In this context, FAE behaves as a range table or a long OR or IN list.

This section finally deals with modifying database queries (DML) in loops. In the case of modifying database queries, such as INSERT, UPDATE, or DELETE statements, the array interface for these queries is more critical than for the SELECT array interface. If these statements are executed for each record in loops, the system also transfers the ABAP Open SQL statements separately to the database in the case of single record processing. In contrast to SELECT/ENDSELECT statements, the DBI doesn't have its own array interface.

For INSERT, UPDATE, and DELETE statements, the following array interfaces are available:

INSERT ... FROM TABLE
UPDATE ... FROM TABLE
DELETE ... FROM TABLE

The data that should be inserted, updated, or deleted is included in an internal table, which is transferred to the database as a whole. This approach is generally more efficient than executing the corresponding statement for each individual data record. Errors (for example, if a data record couldn't be inserted, updated, or deleted) lead to additional programming effort, because the ABAP program doesn't notify you which of the records caused the problem in the transferred internal table but only indicates that there was a problem (sy-subrc <> 0). You must then handle this error, for example, roll back all modifications or determine which records caused the problem. This can also result in additional database load. Not all databases support these array interfaces. In this case, they're converted into single executions. This also applies to modifying array commands for database views.

> **Real-Life Example — Transaction SE30, Tips & Tricks**
>
> In the TIPS & TRICKS under SQL INTERFACE • ARRAY OPERATIONS, Transaction SE30 provides various examples whose runtime you can measure. Of course, you can also analyze these examples with the SQL trace (Transaction ST05).

You cannot perform MODIFY with an array interface. The MODIFY ... FROM TABLE command exists, but it is implemented as single commands by the database interface. If possible, don't use MODIFY at all. At least, if the number of data records that should be inserted is too large. MODIFY first executes an UPDATE *against the database*. If the transferred record does not exist, it executes an INSERT. If MODIFY concerns mostly new data records that need to be inserted, the system tries to run an UPDATE prior to any INSERT. The UPDATE fails and doesn't implement any modifications but is still an additional query to the database. To reduce such queries, avoid the MODIFY.

Particularly in conjunction with the COMMIT statement, the performance for modifying array operations can be considerably improved. In this context, the behavior for DML queries with array interface may change on the database. The system logs all modifications carried out in the database in such a way that they can be rolled back in the case of a ROLLBACK. Accordingly, all so-called *before images* (what did the data record look like before the modification) are stored in a specific memory area to enable the system to restore the old state in the case of a ROLLBACK. When the modifications are committed, the system releases the memory areas for the logged before images for overwriting. If numerous modifications are implemented, for example, for an array interface, without running a COMMIT, it is possible that the memory area that logs the before images grows significantly or even overflows and the transaction is terminated. In addition to the before images, the database also manages locks for the modified data records that have to be stored until the COMMIT or ROLLBACK is executed. In some databases, this area may also overflow. If multiple data records should be modified, it doesn't make sense to confirm these modifications at the end (COMMIT) but implement package processing. However, in this case, the programming effort increases — if specific packages are terminated for other reasons, the application has to be programmed in such a way that it can be resumed.

In general, COMMIT is a statement that ensures the transactional security and consequently avoids data inconsistencies.

With ensuring the transactional security, you can also use the COMMIT to increase the performance, for example, if not every data record is committed individually but a larger package of data records. This results in less queries to the database but also in a reduced database load, because each COMMIT causes internal administration effort for the database, which occurs less often in this case. By reducing the number of COMMIT statements, you can increase the performance for large datasets.

For this purpose, some programs implement a parameter, which lets you define a so-called COMMIT width. It specifies after how many data records a COMMIT should be executed. Then, you can determine the optimum setting in various test runs. For such an approach, you still have to remember the transactional security. For the reasons mentioned previously, also ensure that the number of the modifications without COMMIT doesn't become too large to avoid overflows of the memory areas in the database.

5.8   Used API

It should depend mostly on the tasks and not on performance differences which API is used for database queries. This holds basically true, because the differences between the various variants are in the microsecond range. Nevertheless, these differences exist. Consequently, the following also briefly describes the different APIs.

You can distinguish between the following database queries in ABAP:

▶ **Portable queries**
Portable queries are written in Open SQL, have a restricted language scope, and can run on *all* databases that SAP supports.

▶ **Native queries**
Native queries are written in Native SQL, let you use the SQL language scope of the database platform on which the ABAP stack runs, and can *only* run on this database if specific features are used.

Both variants can either be static (definition of fields, tables, and conditions at design time) or dynamic (definition of fields, tables, and conditions at runtime).

5.8.1 Static Open SQL

In static Open SQL, you can only use tables that have been created in the SAP Data Dictionary. Compared to the SQL standard, Open SQL additionally provides commands defined by SAP but doesn't support database manufacturer-specific commands.

Open SQL is optimally integrated with ABAP; for example, it allows for some performance-relevant options not supported by Native SQL. These include ranges (`WHERE field IN sel_op`), `FOR ALL ENTRIES`, array operations, and the usage of the table buffer (see Section 6.4 in Chapter 6).

5.8.2 Dynamic Open SQL

Dynamic Open SQL provides the same benefits as static Open SQL — the difference is that you can define the fields, tables, `WHERE` conditions, and so on dynamically with variables. Because they must be evaluated at runtime, dynamic Open SQL is somewhat slower. However, you can neglect this difference, because it is in the microseconds range. For the performance of SQL queries, the read dataset, the access path, and the execution frequency are much more important.

5.8.3 Static Native SQL

In the case of Native SQL, the database queries are written in the SQL dialect of the database used. This lets you use the entire language scope of the respective database. If you use specific language constructs outside the SQL standard that only apply to the database used, your program is not portable. In this case, the SQL syntax is wrong for other database systems. All queries are transferred to the database without modifications — the SAP table buffer is not used. The ABAP array interface cannot be used. However, in the case of read access, the array interface of the SAP database interface is used. Tables that are not defined in the SAP Data Dictionary, such as dictionary tables, at database level or tables that are integrated externally can be used.

Dynamic Native SQL

Dynamic Native SQL is implemented in ABAP via the so-called *ABAP Database Connectivity* (ADBC). It is an object-oriented class wrapping for dynamic Native SQL. ADBC behaves in the same way as EXEC SQL. However, it additionally allows for array operations. Due to the object-oriented wrapping and the evaluation of the dynamic components, ADBC is slower than Native SQL.

5.8.4 Summary

Only use Native SQL if you want to access tables that are not available in the SAP Data Dictionary and if you want to use SQL commands not supported in the Open SQL language scope.

For Open SQL and Native SQL, only use dynamic accesses if this is absolutely necessary, that is, if fields, tables, and/or conditions are not known until runtime.

5.9 Special Cases and Exceptions

This section discusses some of the special cases and exceptions.

5.9.1 Sorting

If sorted data is required, the question arises whether the data is should be sorted by the database or by the SAP kernel.

The database sorts the data using the ORDER BY addition. This addition is the only way to implement sorting at database level. Without this addition, sorting cannot be ensured. The data records are sorted if a sorted index is used as the access path. However, it cannot be ensured that this access path is always selected. Therefore, if you want to sort at the database level, always specify the ORDER BY addition. Databases can implement the sorting based on an index by reading the data records in the index sequence. This is only possible if the desired sorting corresponds to the field sequence in the index. For example, the index is structured via the last name and first name fields and the data should be sorted first by the last name and then by the first name. Sorting data via an index doesn't involve much effort, because the data can be retrieved from the index in the required sort sequence by reading the individual rows sequentially.

If you want to have the data sorted another way but no appropriate index is available, the system first has to read the data and then sort it. This can be done in the main memory. If the data volume is quite large, the data is written to a temporary hard disk area for sorting. This requires additional I/O, because the system first has to write the data and then reimport it in the sorted order.

In the application server, the SAP kernel can sort the data using the SORT ABAP statement. In this case, it reads the unsorted data from the database into an internal table (Chapter 7 describes internal tables in more detail). This internal table can then be sorted using the SORT command. Just as for the database, the sorting takes place in a specific area in the main memory. For larger datasets, it can also be implemented on the file system.

Because the database is a central resource and you should decrease the load on the database as much as possible, carry out sorting operations that cannot be supported by an index on the SAP application server. The load is placed on the application layer that features a better scaling.

5.9.2 Pool and Cluster Tables

So far, you've only dealt with transparent tables. These transparent tables are defined in the SAP Data Dictionary and have a corresponding table on the database each. They can also have one or several secondary indexes. The majority of the tables in SAP systems are transparent tables.

SAP systems also provide so-called pool and cluster tables (don't confuse them with so-called cluster tables of some databases!). SAP pool and cluster tables are assigned to physical table pools or table clusters. These are "common" database tables (that is, heap or index-organized tables).

Physical table pools and table clusters combine several logical Data Dictionary tables. Accordingly, there's no direct relationship between logical pool or cluster tables that have been defined in the SAP Data Dictionary and the database.

Pool tables exist for historical reasons: Previously, because the maximum permitted number of tables was restricted but additional tables were required, multiple short tables (pool tables) were combined in table pools. Here, each data record in a logical pool table corresponds to a data record in a physical table on the database. The table name is part of the primary key and is supplemented by the VARKEY field that contains the combined part of the key of the logical pool table. Further fields store the length of the data record and the data record itself as a compressed binary string. Due to this fact, you cannot create secondary indexes, because some fields of the logical pool table against the database are only a part of a binary data stream.

Cluster tables summarize logically related data of several tables. Here, the intersection of the primary key fields of the logical cluster tables supplemented by a unique counter is the primary key of the database table. This way, various records of several tables are combined in one logical data record. An additional field stores the data records of the logical cluster tables. You cannot create additional secondary indexes here either.

Figure 5.13 illustrates the pool and cluster tables.

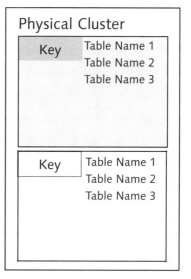

Figure 5.13 Schematic Diagram of the Pool and Cluster Tables

Pool and cluster tables provide the following advantages:

▶ Due to the compression, the data can be stored more efficiently.
▶ Less I/O is required to read more data records.

However, pool and cluster tables also have disadvantages:

▶ Secondary indexes are not feasible.
▶ Too many data may be transferred if only subsets are required.
▶ Modifications are implemented with MODIFY (UPDATE, and then INSERT).

When you access pool and cluster tables, ensure that the complete key of the table in which the data is combined is specified, if possible. You can trace this in Transaction ST05 via the EXPLAIN PLAN function. The DELIVERY AND MAINTENANCE tab in Transaction SE11 displays in which table pool or table cluster the logical pool or cluster table is stored. Transaction SE12, in turn, displays their definitions. Here, you can obtain the primary key of the underlying table pool or table cluster.

5.9.3 Hints and Adapting Statistics

Hints are notes for the database interface or the database that define how an SQL statement should be translated or executed.

You initiate hints with the %_HINTS keyword at the end of the SQL statement in Open SQL. This is followed by the type of the database to which the hint refers and the text of the hint. In Native SQL, the hint must be specified in the respective database syntax.

Hints for the DBI are not transferred to the database and can thus be written with a general applicability (one hint for all supported databases). They define how to convert a specific statement. Despite their general applicability, these hints need to be considered in the context of the database used, because not all hints are useful on all platforms.

The most important hints for the DBI are statements that provide variables in the WHERE condition with concrete values and not with placeholders during parsing. For this purpose, two hints are available:

▶ &SUBSTITUTE LITERALS&

▶ &SUBSTITUTE VALUES&

The first hint substitutes concrete values for literals and constants; the second hint additionally replaces the variable values. As of SAP Release 4.5, some databases automatically implement such substitutions for complex statements. In the context of the access paths, you learned that the creation of specific statistics in combination with the transfer of the concrete WHERE condition may lead to a better execution plan in the case of unequal data distributions. These hints are provided exactly for such cases.

Consider several aspects when using these hints. If you use values instead of the placeholders, a higher number of different SQL statements need to be parsed or compiled and managed. If a lot of different statements are involved, this may cause performance problems, if the statement cache displaces data due to the many different SQL statements and thus constantly has to parse and manage new SQL statements. Consequently, you have to be particularly careful when substituting variable values (&SUBSTITUTE VALUES&) in SELECT statements that are often executed with different values (in loop designs).

Other hints for the DBI define how the FOR ALL ENTRIES ABAP statement is handled and whether individual statements need to be translated again. SAP Notes 129385 and 48230 provide further information on these aspects. However, you usually don't have to use these hints. For these FAE statements, the optimum setting is already predefined for the respective database platform. In any case, an experienced SAP consultant should always analyze and carefully check whether such hints should be used.

The system transfers hints for the database usually without modifications from the DBI to the database. Therefore, the hints must be written in the syntax of the corresponding database. There are major differences for the individual databases. Not only do they concern the writing but also the functional scope of the hints. At this point, not all options can be described in detail. The following section mentions only some of these options and particularly refers to the basic conditions and consequences when using database hints.

A hint is always specific for a particular database. Accordingly, if you specify a hint, this hint is executed by a specific database or database release only. Moreover, it also often depends on the system configuration and the datasets. If you specify a hint, the hint is only evaluated on the defined database platform and the program has to be tested again if the database is upgraded or any other changes are made to the database system.

Some databases allow for hints for defining commands to the optimizer on how an SQL statement needs to be performed. This enables you, for example, to manipulate the access path in such a way that a full table scan, an index, or even a specific index should be used. Because indexes may have different names than in the SAP Data Dictionary (especially if the system had been installed on older releases and was upgraded), some databases also let you specify the SAP index name. Furthermore, you can define join methods and sequences for tables in joins using hints. However, if multiple tables are involved, these tasks can quickly result in extremely complex hints.

In general, specifying a hint for execution plans should be the last way to solve a performance problem. There are several reasons for that. On the one hand, the hint only applies to a specific database platform and, on the other hand, the statement's execution is specified although there might be better alternatives in the future because of modified datasets or more efficient execution plans due to a new database release. Therefore, hints involve considerable test and maintenance work.

To conclude the hint topic, the following table provides numerous SAP notes that deal with the usage of database hints:

Platform	SAP Note
Database hints—general	129385
DB2 for zSeries	162034, 724614
DB2for iSeries	485420
DB2 for LUW	150037
MS SQL Server	133381
Oracle	130480
SAP MaxDB	652096

To manipulate execution plans, you can modify the statistics on some databases (Oracle and DB2). For Oracle, you can refer to SAP Note 724545. For DB2, please contact your database administrator, because changing the statistics means changing the system tables.

In live systems, only make use of this option if no other tuning options can be used. In contrast to hints that only refer to the statement with the hint, modifying the statistics affects all statements across the entire system that refers to tables with modified statistics.

When data is supposed to be buffered, you as the application developer are provided with many options to achieve this. This chapter describes these options and compares them regarding the performance.

6 Buffering of Data

Data that is required multiple times should be buffered in the main memory so that the database does not have to repeatedly read this data. For the purpose of buffering data, you as the ABAP developer are given multiple options that are presented in this chapter. Each of these options is also considered with regard to performance aspects.

Initially, it is important to have a look at the SAP memory architecture. Then you learn about the user session-specific and cross-user session buffering techniques. At the end of this chapter, a separate section is dedicated to the SAP table buffer due to its significance in the SAP system, although it ultimately is a cross-user session buffer.

6.1 SAP Memory Architecture from the Developer's Point of View

SAP memory architecture is a complex topic that extends far into SAP system administration. The following sections only describe those topics that are important for the ABAP developer, so you can better classify the different options of buffering in an SAP system. If you are interested in all details and want to familiarize yourself with this topic, read Chapter 8, Memory Management, and Chapter 9, Table Buffering Fundamentals, of *SAP Performance Optimization Guide* by Thomas Schneider (5th edition, Boston, SAP PRESS 2008).

From the technical point of view, SAP work processes have access to the entire memory of an application server. Figure 6.1 shows a diagram of the memory areas of an application server.

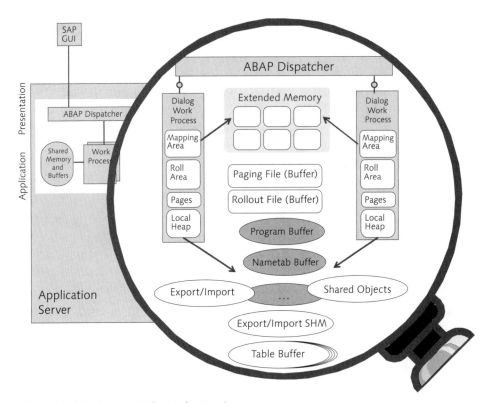

Figure 6.1 SAP Memory in the Application Server

The white areas in Figure 6.1 can be called directly by the ABAP developer. The SAP work process has access to the extended memory via the *mapping area*. All data objects are managed in the extended memory. In the mapping area, you store pointers to the extended memory via which the work process can access the data by a reference without copying the data. Each user can use a specific quota of the extended memory only. The system administrators specify this quota. Usually, the allocation is in blocks with a size of 1 MB or 4 MB. This depends on the `em/blocksize_KB` SAP profile parameter. If this area is used up, there is still the roll area that can then be used for data objects. In contrast to the extended memory, the memory that is allocated in the roll area must be copied to the work process prior to the access if the data is no longer available there. This overhead for copying always incurs if the dispatcher assigns the user to a work process that is different to the one previously used. Before the user leaves the work process again, he must copy back the data if it was changed. If the roll memory is also used up, you can again allocate further memory up to a certain limit in the process-local memory, the *heap memory*. Because this memory is assigned locally to the work process, you cannot leave the work process during the transaction; then, the user is in *PRIV mode,* which indicates that a work process can be used by *one* user only and that it is blocked until the SAP transaction is complete.

Furthermore, the application server has additional memory areas, the *buffers,* which an SAP work process can access and can be called by the ABAP developer. These include the ABAP memory, the SAP memory, the shared buffer, the shared memory, the shared objects, and the SAP table buffer. This chapter discusses all buffers in more detail.

Beyond the control of the ABAP developer, there are various other buffers, such as the nametab buffer that buffers data dictionary information, and the program buffer that buffers executable SAP programs. If these buffers are set too small, this may result in serious performance problems in the SAP system. Such a situation can be detected by a high number of displacements (swaps) for this buffer in Transaction ST02. These buffers are not further discussed in this book because they are relevant for system administrators rather than for ABAP developers.

From the perspective of the ABAP developer, there is a user-specific and a cross-user memory area in which data can be buffered. The cross-user buffering is also referred to as *data sharing* because multiple users use a shared dataset in the main memory. Strictly speaking, the user-specific memory is a user session-specific memory and the cross-user memory is a cross-user session memory (a user can have multiple user sessions, for example, due to multiple logons). For the sake of simplicity, the following uses the terms user-specific and cross-user memory; however, they always refer to user session-specific or cross-user session, respectively.

6.1.1   User-Specific Memory

Within the user-specific memory, no other user session can read data. Consequently, the data is automatically protected against accesses from other user sessions. If data is buffered at this level, this is done at the user session level. For example, if the buffering read modules are executed by multiple users, a separate buffer is created for each single user session.

6.1.2   Cross-User Memory

In the cross-user memory, multiple users have shared access to a dataset. For accesses to this dataset, the data is either copied to user-specific memories or directly processed in the cross-user memory (shared objects). For changing accesses to the cross-user data, the applications involved must ensure the consistency of data.

Figure 6.2 illustrates the different memory areas.

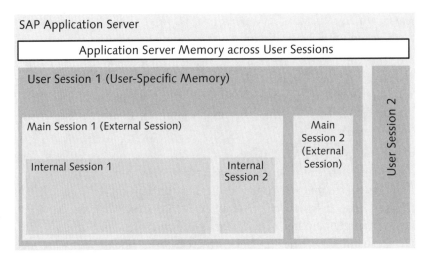

Figure 6.2 Cross-User Session and User Session-Specific Data

A *user session* can contain multiple main sessions. The CALL FUNCTION ... DESTINA-TION... ABAP statement opens a new user session. Of course, new logons to the system are also new user sessions. A data exchange at this level, that is, between the user sessions of different users or one user, is cross-user and is implemented via the memory areas at the application server level. This only works if the new user session is opened on the same application server. Section 6.3, Cross-User Buffering Types, describes the options available for data exchange. If the data is not supposed to be buffered in the main memory, it is also possible to exchange it via the database.

A main session (or external session) is assigned to a user session. You can open a new main session program-controlled using CALL FUNCTION ... STARTING NEW TASK. As of Release 6.10, 16 such sessions are possible; prior to that, only six were available.

> **Note: Number of External Sessions**
>
> The standard setting is still set to six sessions, but the system administrators can change the number to a maximum of 16 using the rdisp/max_alt_modes profile parameter.

Within a main session, there can be up to nine internal sessions. Internal sessions are opened using statements, such as SUBMIT ... [AND RETURN] or CALL TRANS-ACTION. The SUBMIT and LEAVE TO TRANSACTION statements also generate a new internal session, which, in turn, replaces the old internal session from which the statements were called.

The internal session contains the data of the ABAP programs. The global and public data of these programs is only visible to the called programs in this user context (that is, in the internal session). As soon as it is supposed to be visible at another level, the system must user other memory areas, which are described in Sections 6.2.2, Buffering Across Internal Sessions, to 6.3.4, Summary.

The following sections describe the data exchange and buffering at the different levels in more detail.

6.2 User-Specific Buffering Types

Data can be buffered user-specifically at different levels: within an internal session, across multiple internal sessions, or across external sessions.

6.2.1 Buffering in the Internal Session

In the internal session, data can be buffered in variables. Buffering in the internal session should be used if buffering is not possible via the SAP table buffer (see Section 6.4, SAP Table Buffering) and if multiple accesses to the same data (for example, in the database) should be avoided.

The following section describes buffering in the internal session to avoid identical database accesses. As illustrated in Section 5.7 in Chapter 5, SELECT statements in loops can result in identical accesses in the database. The following example shows how such identical accesses can be created:

```
LOOP AT it_order_tab INTO wa_order.
* Search record in the database
   SELECT SINGLE kundenname INTO var_kundenname
   FROM db_kunden_tab
   WHERE kundennr = wa_order-kunnr.
   IF SY-SUBRC = 0.
* If record was found, continue processing
      MOVE var_kundenname TO ...
   ELSE.
      ...
   ENDIF....
ENDLOOP.
```

For a loop via an internal table (it_order_tab) that contains the order headers, the system accesses the customer master data (db_kunden_tab) in the database to determine further customer data not included in the order header. If a customer has multiple orders, this results in multiple accesses with the same customer number to the customer master data in the database.

To avoid such identical accesses, data that was already read should be buffered and repeated accesses to already read data should be performed from the buffer.

If the data is available sorted by customer numbers, you could avoid the SELECT statement by simply checking whether the customer number is still the same:

```
LOOP AT it_order_tab INTO wa_order.
* Only for changed customer number
  AT NEW kunr.
* Search record in the database
      SELECT SINGLE kundenname INTO var_kundenname
      FROM db_kunden_tab
      WHERE kundennr = wa_order-kunnr.
      IF SY-SUBRC = 0.

* If record was found, continue processing
          MOVE var_kundenname TO ...
      ELSE.
      ...
      ENDIF.
  ENDAT.
  MOVE var_kundenname TO ...
  ...
ENDLOOP.
```

If the internal table with the order header is sorted by customer number, only one SELECT statement is executed for each customer number.

If the data is not sorted, the customer data must be buffered in an internal table. Chapter 7 provides comprehensive information on internal tables; the pseudo code examples only illustrate the principle of buffering in internal tables.

The following example illustrates what buffering in an internal table could look like:

```
LOOP AT it_order_tab INTO wa_order.
* First search record in the internal table
READ TABLE it_kunde INTO var_kunde_ex
WITH KEY wa_order-kunnr BINARY SEARCH.
save_tabix = sy-tabix.
* If it is not there...
IF SY-SUBRC <> 0.
```

```
* Search record in the database
       SELECT SINGLE kundennr kundenname
       INTO var_kunde
       FROM db_kunden_tab
       WHERE kundennr = wa_order-kunnr.
       IF SY-SUBRC = 0.
* If record was found, save in internal table
               MOVE var_kunde to var_kunde_ex.
               CLEAR var_kunde_ex-not_found.
               INSERT var_kunde_ex TO it_kunde
               INDEX save_tabix.
* and continue processing
               MOVE var_kunde_ex-kundenname TO ...
       ELSE.
* If record was not found, save customer number and
* NOT_FOUND Flag in the internal table.
               var_kunde_ex-kunnr = it_order_tab-kunnr.

               var_kunde_ex-not_found = 'X'.
               INSERT var_kunde_ex to it_kunde INDEX sy-tabix.
       ENDIF.
ELSE.
       IF var_kunde_ex-not_found = 'X'.
* If no record exists in the database...
               ...
       ELSE.
* If record was found, continue processing
               MOVE var_kunde_ex-kundenname TO ...
       ENDIF.
ENDIF.
ENDLOOP.
```

This example shows how the it_kunde internal table is first searched and how the result is put in the var_kunde_ex variable if a suitable record is found.

If the searched record is not yet available in the it_kunde internal table, the database SELECT is executed. If the searched record is found in the database, it is copied to the internal table. If the searched record was not found in the database and if it is a valid "result" from the application's point of view, the customer number is also copied to the it_kunde internal table, including the comment stating that the data record does not exist in the database. For this purpose, the internal table contains the customer number, the customer name, and the not_found flag, which is also contained in the var_kunde_ex extended structure.

If the search record was found in the it_kunde internal table, the not_found column is used as the basis to check whether the searched record also exists in the database; only then is the customer name continued to be used.

This procedure shows how you can avoid identical accesses to the database completely. You avoid not only identical accesses to existing customer numbers but also identical accesses with customer numbers that don't exist in the database.

Of course, you can also establish the structure of the internal tables using an array interface, for example, by means of the FOR ALL ENTRIES statement (see Section 5.7 in Chapter 5) instead of using individual SELECT statements as in the previous examples.

If possible, this buffering should be implemented in an ABAP Objects class or a function module to ensure the reusability in other programs. If this buffering is implemented directly in a report, other programs cannot use this program-internal buffering.

When you create such a buffering read module, also take the following things into account:

1. You should have the option to delete the buffer "from the outside," that is, the module or the class should provide a parameter or method for deletion. This is also important to invalidate buffered data and to import data that is changed in the meantime from the database.

2. There should be a (changeable) size restriction for the internal table(s) that contain(s) the data.

3. If possible, the data should be transferable without any overhead for copying (transfer of references instead of the data that must be copied).

6.2.2 Buffering Across Internal Sessions

To exchange data between two internal sessions, you can either transfer the data via the interface (call parameter, selection screen, and so on) or use the *ABAP memory*.

Using the EXPORT TO MEMORY ABAP statement, you can export data to the ABAP memory, located in the *ABAP paging area* (paging file in Figure 6.1). Using the IMPORT FROM MEMORY statement, you can import the data from the ABAP memory into another internal session.

For the export, the data is copied from the current internal session to the ABAP memory and for the import from the ABAP memory into the new internal session. Consequently, the data exists up to three times (in both internal sessions involved and in the ABAP memory). To transfer the data from an internal session to another one, you require two copy processes. If you want to retransfer further data, you require four copy processes. These copy processes use CPU time.

The ABAP memory is partly located in the main memory and partly in the file system of the application server. If the configured space in the main memory is not sufficient, this results in time-consuming read operations to the paging file, and it may lead to collisions during the access to this file (indicated by the SEMAPHORE 7 wait reason in the process overview, Transaction SM50). The size of the ABAP memory is determined by the SAP system administrators using the profile parameters, `rdisp/PG_SHM` and `rdisp/PG_MAXFS`.

The ABAP memory was developed for the transfer of relatively small datasets. Larger datasets should rather be transferred at the application server level due to the incurring copying and I/O efforts. This is described later on in Section 6.3.

6.2.3 Buffering Across External Sessions

To exchange very small datasets (parameters) between two external sessions, you are provided with the ABAP statements, `SET PARAMETER ID` and `GET PARAMETER ID`, which write to the *SAP memory* (also referred to as *parameter memory*). The size of the SAP memory is determined by the SAP system administrators using the `ztta/parameter_area` profile parameter.

This memory area is kept small at the application server level because it was developed for user-specific settings or values for parameters only. For larger datasets, select buffering at the application server level.

6.2.4 Summary

All user-specific buffering types have in common that the data is maintained in the internal session. The data in the internal session can be called without any overhead for copying if this is implemented accordingly. Chapter 7 describes the access to internal tables that is free of any copy overhead. For the exchange across multiple sessions, the data is *copied* to special memory areas. If an application implemented a user-specific buffering of data and multiple users use this application, user-specific buffers are created and maintained for each user. Although buffering of data in the internal session enables the fastest possible access, it also means the maximum memory use if multiple users work with the application. If data is supposed to be buffered that is required by more than one user, choose another level.

To exchange data across user limits, that is, between different users, select the application server level discussed in Section 6.3.

6.3   Cross-User Buffering Types

For the cross-user session buffering types, you, as the ABAP developer, are given the following buffers:

1. Buffering in the shared buffer

2. Buffering in the shared memory

3. Buffering in the shared objects

4. Buffering in the SAP table buffer

The SAP table buffer is discussed in a separate section (Section 6.4) due to its significance. In general, it is part of the cross-user buffers.

In addition, there are further buffers that save cross-user data, which cannot be called directly by the ABAP developer, however. These include the nametab buffer, the program buffer, the CUA buffer, the screen buffer, the calendar buffer, and the OTR buffer (Online Text Repository).

All these buffers are located at the application server level and exist exactly once per application server. As a result, the data buffered therein is stored multiple times in an SAP system with multiple application servers. This gives rise to the question whether or how the data is synchronized. The following sections discuss these questions and the specifics of each buffer together with the performance-relevant properties.

6.3.1   Buffering in the Shared Buffer

You can use the shared buffer to store data at the application server level. By means of the EXPORT TO SHARED BUFFER ABAP statement, you can store data in the shared buffer. Using the IMPORT FROM SHARED BUFFER ABAP statement, you can import the data from the shared buffer into the internal session again. By means of the DELETE FROM SHARED BUFFER ABAP statement, you can delete data from the shared buffer again.

The data stored there is visible to *all* user sessions of an application server. As described for the ABAP memory, the data is *copied* from or to the internal session during the export or import and it occupies space in every internal session involved in the import or export as well as in the shared buffer itself.

The shared buffer is completely located in the virtual memory. This memory area is managed by the Least Recently Used (LRU) algorithm. If the space runs short, the oldest data is displaced from the memory and must be provided when it is required again (for example, reimported from the database).

You can use Transaction ST02 to analyze whether displacements took place in this memory area. The Export/Import row relates to the shared buffer. The Swaps column provides information about how many displacements occurred. The monitoring of this and all other memory areas is one of the tasks of the SAP system administrators, and it is described in detail in *SAP Performance Optimization Guide* by Thomas Schneider (5th edition, Boston, SAP PRESS 2008). The size of the shared buffer is determined by the SAP system administrators using the profile parameters, `rsdb/obj/buffersize`, `rsdb/obj/max_objects`, and `rsdb/obj/large_object_size`.

There is no automatic synchronization between the application servers. Apart from the displacement via the LRU algorithm, the shared buffer is managed entirely by the application programs that use it.

> **Note**
>
> The "contexts" that have become obsolete (Transaction SE33) and that are no longer used in new developments were implemented internally via the shared buffer.

6.3.2 Buffering in the Shared Memory

You can also use the *shared memory* to store data at the application server level. Don't confuse the memory area called shared memory, discussed here, with the concept of shared memory because it is used for the memory architecture or from the operating system perspective. The shared memory has been available since SAP Release 6.10. By means of the `EXPORT TO SHARED MEMORY` ABAP statement, you can store data in the shared memory. Using the `IMPORT FROM SHARED MEMORY` ABAP statement, you can import the data from the shared memory into the internal session again. By means of the `DELETE FROM SHARED MEMORY` ABAP statement, you can delete data from the shared memory again.

The data stored there is visible to *all* user sessions of an application server. As described for the ABAP memory, the data is *copied* from or to the internal session during the export or import and it occupies space as long as the data is required in every internal session involved in the import or export as well as in the shared memory itself.

The shared memory is completely located in the main memory (more precisely, in the virtual memory of the operating system). The memory area *doesn't* have an automatic displacement. If data is supposed to be copied there by means of the `EXPORT TO SHARED MEMORY` statement and sufficient space is not available, the statement fails. A catchable runtime error, `EXPORT_NO_SHARED_MEMORY`, occurs. This can be caught as follows:

```
TRY.
EXPORT [...] TO SHARED MEMORY.
CATCH cx-sy_export_no_shared_memory.
ENDTRY.
```

In this context, the DELETE FROM SHARED MEMORY statement plays a particular role: As soon as the data is no longer required in the shared memory, it should be deleted to not occupy the space unnecessarily and to provide the space to other applications. The exported data should also be deleted from the shared memory in program error situations.

In Transaction ST02, the EXPORT/IMPORT SHM row relates to the shared memory. The SWAPS column indicates "0" because no displacements can occur. The monitoring of this and all other memory areas is one of the tasks of the SAP system administrators, and it is described in detail in *SAP Performance Optimization Guide* by Thomas Schneider (Boston, SAP PRESS 2008). The size of the shared memory is determined by the SAP system administrators using the profile parameters, rsdb/esm/buffersize_kb, rsdb/esm/max_objects, and rsdb/esm/large_object_size.

There is no automatic synchronization between the application servers. The shared memory is managed entirely by the application programs that use it.

6.3.3   Buffering via the Shared Objects

The shared objects have been available since SAP Release 6.10. In contrast to the shared buffer and the shared memory, you can only store instances of ABAP Objects but no other data in the shared objects. But you can access these object instances by reference, that is, without any overhead for copying. This is one of the major benefits of shared objects. While in the shared buffer or shared memory, the data must always be *copied* to or from the internal session; you can access the shared objects *directly* without having to copy the data (object instances) to the internal session. This benefit involves increased costs for the object-oriented wrapping. By means of the shared objects, you can load data *directly* to the memory area for shared objects without maintaining the data in the internal session, and other applications can read the data *directly* from there without copying them to the internal session.

Shared objects provide further benefits: For example, a versioning is possible in which new versions of a data area can be created while connected processes can continue to work in the old version. This is done until the transaction is complete because these processes have started reading before the new version was completed. New read accesses that access the object after the new version was completed use the new version. When the last reader of a version interrupts the connection, the old version is removed. Thanks to the object-oriented access, the shared objects integrate seamlessly with the object-oriented programming and therefore represent the latest form of buffering.

The memory area for the shared objects is subdivided into *areas* that the developer creates in Transaction SHMA. You can monitor the created areas in Transaction SHMM. The size of the memory area is determined by the system administrators using the `abap/shared_objects_size_MB` profile parameter.

There is no synchronization between the application servers. Like for the shared memory, there is no displacement for shared objects, that is, the memory area is managed entirely by the applications that use it.

The shared objects are used at different points in the SAP system. For example, one part of the ABAP Workbench (Transaction SE80) is implemented using shared objects by centrally storing the data required by all users of Transaction SE80.

The following provides a small code section that shows the basic part of the access to shared objects that is free of any copy overhead:

```
DATA: shmhandle TYPE REF TO cl_shm_area.
* Connect with shared objects instance
shmhandle = cl_shm_area=>attach_for_read( ).


* Read required data
READ TABLE shmhandle->root->itab
           INDEX i ASSIGNING <fs>.
* and process
*...
* Close connection with shared objects instance
shmhandle->detach( ).
```

6.3.4 Summary

Which of the buffer scenarios described should be used, depends on the usage scenario. If data is required only by one user and can be imported directly from the database without having to be "formatted," buffering in the internal session is advisable. For smaller datasets required by multiple users or for data extracts, you can use the shared buffer or the shared memory. Usually, this involves data that are not required in the relational database format at runtime but must be "formatted." Overheads for copying incur in these buffers; however, in case of smaller datasets they don't impact the performance significantly. The shared buffer is often used to store smaller datasets also required by other user sessions. These find the data in the shared buffer or load it there if it was displaced. The contents of the shared buffer can be displaced. For this reason, use the shared memory for scenarios that expect the contents in the buffer mandatorily. There, the data is kept until it is deleted explicitly. If no sufficient space is available, an error occurs.

For larger datasets or complex structures, you should prefer the use of shared objects. Like for the access to data in the internal session, they can be called without any overhead for copying. The effort is slightly higher due to the object-oriented wrapping. However, this is compensated by saving on overheads for copying when accessing larger datasets. Additionally, shared objects — in contrast to the internal session — enable the sharing of data between multiple users, which can lead to large memory savings on the application server. Furthermore, the shared objects allow for the update of new datasets using versioning. Therefore, shared objects represent the latest variant of data buffering for the shared access of multiple users.

6.4   SAP Table Buffering

The SAP table buffer is another part of the shared memory (the shared memory from the operating system perspective), which is used for the cross-user buffering of data — in principle, it is comparable with the cross-user buffers previously discussed. The table buffer can be accessed by the developer; however, the access is not possible directly but only via Open SQL. Due to the significance of the SAP table buffer in the SAP system, it is discussed separately here.

The SAP table buffer was developed to buffer database tables completely or partially on the application server to achieve a faster access to the data and to decrease the load of the central resource database.

Background: Access Times of SAP Table Buffer versus DB Access

The access to the table buffer is about ten times faster than the access to database. Typical access times to the table buffer are approximately 100μs to 1ms, whereas the access times to the database are approximately 1ms to 10ms. Of course, the access times to the database depend on the capacity of the I/O subsystem, the database cache, and possibly the network times. The access times to the SAP table buffers are based on the speed of the application servers' CPUs. In principle, the access to the SAP table buffer in central instances still involves a faster access if the desired data is in the data cache of the database because the overhead (less software layers) for the access to the table buffer is smaller than for the access to the database. Of course, the difference is not particularly great in this case.

Transaction SE30 provides an example for the different access times in the TIPS & TRICKS under SQL INTERFACE • INDEX AND BUFFER SUPPORT • SELECT WITH BUFFER SUPPORT.

The next section discusses the architecture of the SAP table buffer. There you learn which tables are suitable for the buffering in the SAP table buffer. The subsequent section details the performance aspects of table buffering and particularly why tables selected for buffering cannot be read from the table buffer. This section concludes with a brief overview of the tools available for analyzing the table buffer.

6.4.1 Architecture and Overview

Let's first have a look at the architecture of the SAP table buffer and then discuss the different types of buffering. Then you are provided with detailed information of how read and write accesses to the table buffers are implemented and how the buffers are synchronized. This is followed by the types of buffering and the organization of the data in the table buffer.

Architecture of the SAP Table Buffer

The SAP table buffer is part of the shared memory of every application server. Each SAP work process and consequently every logged-on user can access the data via Open SQL. The tables for which the buffering is activated are maintained in the table buffer. Because a buffer is available on every application server, you can buffer the buffered tables in each of these servers; consequently, they potentially exist multiple times in the buffers in an SAP system if it includes multiple application servers. The buffered data is synchronized with the database at regular intervals. Figure 6.3 shows an overview of the table buffer.

The SAP work processes of an application server have access to the SAP table buffer. The buffers are loaded *on demand* via the database connection (a table selected for buffering is added to the buffer). *On demand* means that the data is loaded when it is first accessed or if it doesn't exist in the buffer. This is done using the "regular" Open SQL commands. The tables selected for buffering are loaded from the database files to the data cache by the database processes or threads. They are then passed on to the SAP table buffer via the SAP work process. The DDLOG database table is used for the synchronization of changes to the buffered tables in the respective application servers.

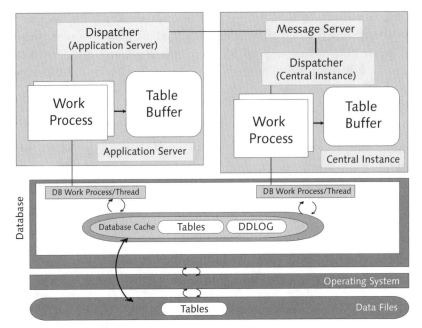

Figure 6.3 SAP Table Buffer

Read Access to the Table Buffer

The access to the table buffer is already integrated with Open SQL in ABAP. You don't require any special ABAP commands like EXPORT or IMPORT to use the table buffer. If a table selected for buffering is read via Open SQL, this is identified by the Database Interface (DBI). Not the entire Open SQL command set is supported by the table buffer. Section 6.4.3, Performance Aspects of Table Buffering, describes the exceptions. If a SELECT statement is executed on a table selected for buffering, the SAP work process initially looks up the desired data in the SAP table buffer. If the data is not available in the buffer, it is loaded from the database, stored in the table buffer, and then *copied* to the ABAP program (in the internal session). Here, many exceptions may occur, which are discussed in Section 6.4.3, Performance Aspects of Table Buffering.

Write Access to the Table Buffer

For the write access to buffered tables, both the contents in the local table buffer of the application server and the contents in the database tables are changed. This mechanism ensures that no changes are lost. The write access to the buffer is not faster than the write access to an unbuffered table due to the implicit access to the database. In both cases, database accesses occur.

Additionally, a log entry is written to the DDLOG database table. The log entries are read by the other (remote) application servers at specific intervals to invalidate the changed tables in their buffers. New read accesses to these application servers then result in a reload of this data. Here, many exceptions may occur, which are discussed in Section 6.4.3, Performance Aspects of Table Buffering. It is also possible that obsolete data is read from a remote table buffer until the synchronization is carried out.

Background: Synchronization

To ensure the synchronization of the buffers in the application servers with the database, you must set the following parameters:

```
rdisp/bufrefmode = sendon,exeauto
rdisp/bufreftime = n seconds
```

The `rdisp/bufrefmode` parameter specifies the synchronization settings per application server. The first part of the parameter specifies whether the synchronization entries should be written to the DDLOG table (`sendon`) or not (`sendoff`). The second part specifies whether the synchronization entries should be read from the DDLOG table (`exeauto`) or not (`exeoff`).

As soon as an SAP system has multiple application servers and doesn't consist of only one central instance, the parameter must be set to `sendon,exeauto` on all servers. Each application server then reads and writes synchronization entries.

If an SAP system only consists of a central instance, the parameter can be set to `sendoff,exeauto`. The system only reads the synchronization entries from the DDLOG table. Because the import of transports also writes synchronization entries, for example, you mustn't deactivate the reading of the DDLOG table for systems with only one instance.

Using the `rdisp/bufreftime` parameter, you can specify for each application server at which intervals the DDLOG table is supposed to be read to invalidate the changed tables. This parameter is usually set to a value between 60 and 120 seconds.

Table Buffering Types

You can set the buffering of a table in Transaction SE13 (Dictionary TECHNICAL SETTINGS) in the BUFFERING area. In principle, you have three different buffering types available:

- Single record buffering
- Generic buffering
- Full buffering

Figure 6.4 illustrates these three types. The light-colored fields indicate the areas that were buffered respectively.

SELECT * FROM table WHERE key1 = '002' AND key2 = 'B' AND key3 = 2

Single Record Buffering (ALL Key Fields)

key1	key2	key3	data
001	A	2	
001	A	4	
001	B	1	
001	B	3	
001	B	5	
002	A	1	
002	A	3	
002	A	6	
002	A	8	
002	B	1	
002	B	2	
002	B	3	
002	C	0	
002	C	1	
002	D	5	
003	A	2	
003	A	3	
003	A	6	
003	B	2	
003	B	4	
003	C	5	
003	D	2	
003	D	6	
003	D	8	

Generic Buffering (TWO Key Fields)

key1	key2	key3	data
001	A	2	
001	A	4	
001	B	1	
001	B	3	
001	B	5	
002	A	1	
002	A	3	
002	A	6	
002	A	8	
002	B	1	
002	B	2	
002	B	3	
002	C	0	
002	C	1	
002	D	5	
003	A	2	
003	A	3	
003	A	6	
003	B	2	
003	B	4	
003	C	5	
003	D	2	
003	D	6	
003	D	8	

Generic Buffering (ONE Key Field)

key1	key2	key3	data
001	A	2	
001	A	4	
001	B	1	
001	B	3	
001	B	5	
002	A	1	
002	A	3	
002	A	6	
002	A	8	
002	B	1	
002	B	2	
002	B	3	
002	C	0	
002	C	1	
002	D	5	
003	A	2	
003	A	3	
003	A	6	
003	B	2	
003	B	4	
004	A	1	
004	D	2	
005	D	6	
005	D	8	

Full Buffering (NO Key Field)

key1	key2	key3	data
001	A	2	
001	A	4	
001	B	1	
001	B	3	
001	B	5	
002	A	1	
002	A	3	
002	A	6	
002	A	8	
002	B	1	
002	B	2	
002	B	3	
002	C	0	
002	C	1	
002	D	5	
003	A	2	
003	A	3	
003	A	6	
003	B	2	
003	C	5	
003	D	2	
003	D	6	
003	D	8	

Figure 6.4 Types of Buffering

You use the buffering type to specify granularity in which the table is buffered.

In single record buffering, buffering takes place at the single record level. The system loads separately only those records into the buffer that were requested by the application.

In generic buffering, buffering takes place for a generic area of the table. Here, you can specify the size of the area to be buffered based on the number of the primary key fields. The fields are always used from the left. For example, if you specify two key fields and the first two primary key fields are MANDT and LANGU, all data records of the queried client and language are loaded to the buffer. For buffering to three primary key fields (MANDT, LANGU, BUKRS), a smaller area is loaded to the buffer, that is, the area that contains the queried client, language, and company code.

Each of these buffering types is able to buffer negative values. If values are queried from a buffered table not available in the database, the value combination is stored in the buffer with a not_found flag. This way, multiple accesses to nonexisting values are read from the buffer without executing a database access each time to determine that the value doesn't exist.

For the full buffering, the complete table is loaded into the buffer at the client level (if the table has a client field, otherwise completely) — regardless of the queried key fields. Because all values or no value of the table are in the buffer, a negative buffer can be mapped here. Nonexisting values can then be determined in the buffer without database access.

Organization in the Table Buffer

A table buffer has two areas — one area for single record buffering and one area for generically buffered tables in which the fully buffered tables are stored, too. In Transaction ST02, the transaction for the SAP buffer and memory analysis, you can view the GENERIC KEY and SINGLE RECORD buffers in the tables' area. You can also view whether swaps occurred in the buffers. A swap occurs if data was displaced from the buffer because not sufficient space was available.

Background: Sizes of the Table Buffers and Swaps

The two table buffers have two parameters each, which you can use to set the size of the buffer area.

For the generic table buffer, these parameters are:

▸ `zcsa/table_buffer_area` = size for this area in bytes

▸ `zcsa/db_max_buftab` = maximum number of objects in this area

For the single record buffer, these parameters are:

▸ `rtbb/buffer_length` = size for this area in KB

▸ `rtbb/max_tables` = maximum number of objects for this area

The size for the two areas should be set in such a way that all tables selected for buffering have sufficient space in the buffer. Ideally, there should be no displacements (swaps) in the buffers in a production system. If these buffers are set too small and many swaps occur, this negatively impacts the performance of the entire SAP system.

A displacement is always asynchronous. If you try to load a table into the buffer and sufficient space is not available, no displacement is implemented at this point in time. Then, the table cannot be loaded into the buffer. The SAP system automatically executes displacement runs at regular intervals using a free work process. The interval of the displacement runs is defined dynamically by the SAP system depending on the load on the table buffer. The number of read accesses to these buffers as well as the available free space play an important role here. In case of a displacement run, the system uses a Least Frequently Used (LFU) algorithm and a Least Recently Used (LRU) algorithm. Objects are displaced that were least frequently or least recently accessed. For this purpose, a read counter is maintained for each object that is automatically reduced in the course of time if the object is not read.

If sufficient space was not made available in a displacement run, for example, because there were no objects to be displaced, the conditions for a new displacement run would still be given and a new displacement run would have to be started immediately. For this reason, the system dynamically increases the interval until the next displacement, in case of a displacement run that cannot make space available. This way, the SAP system is occupied due to continuous displacement runs. The result of table buffers that are set too small are many swaps and/or accesses to tables selected for buffering, which cannot be carried out from the buffer because the tables cannot be loaded into the buffer due to lack of space. In this case, the system administrators must increase the buffer areas if sufficient system resources are available.

Sizes of the Tables in the Table Buffer

The size a database table requires in the SAP table buffer cannot be forecast clearly because negative values that originate from nonpredictable queries are also stored in the buffer. The following lists further reasons for varying sizes of the database and the table buffer.

1. `varchar` **on the database versus fixed length in SAP NetWeaver AS ABAP**
   Whereas on the database a character-like field only occupies the required length and administration information, SAP NetWeaver AS ABAP requires the maximum length for this field in the buffer. A character-like field with a length of 40 can occupy 0 to 40 characters plus administration information on the database (depending on the length of the field content), whereas 40 characters are required in the SAP table buffer (even if the field is empty, 40 spaces are stored in the buffer).

2. **Unicode**
   In SAP NetWeaver AS ABAP, Unicode is mapped using UTF16. That is, each character occupies 2 bytes. Some databases map Unicode using UTF8 in which the characters require 1 or 2 bytes (depending on the character).

3. **Fragmentation**
   The database table can be fragmented and consequently occupy more space than the data actually requires.

Based on this information, you can approximately specify the space required for a table. The maximum length of a data record (in Unicode the character-like fields are multiplied by 2) multiplied by the number of data records to be buffered results in the minimum space requirement. Additionally, you must consider the administration information that the table buffer needs and the space required for the buffering of negative values. Chapter 3 describes a technical analysis option.

This should suffice as a technical overview for developers. The next section discusses the tables suitable for buffering.

6.4.2 What Tables Can Be Buffered?

The most essential criteria for buffering tables are the following.

Due to the synchronization between the application servers, it may be possible that changed data is available to other users with a time delay. This must be acceptable from the application's perspective. Therefore, tables for which you always require the most recent status should not be buffered.

Tables that are changed frequently must not be buffered either because the performance is rather decreased than increased due to the synchronization effort and the reload processes. However, tables that are changed rarely and read frequently can be buffered if they are not too large. Here, the change rate should not be above 1%. The larger the generic areas, the more the change rate should approximate to 0.1%. Transaction ST10 indicates the change rate in the CHANGES/TOTAL (%) column if you select the statistics of the unbuffered tables.

The size of a table is another criterion. Only tables that are not too large should be buffered. If possible, avoid absolute size specifications at this point. A buffered table should occupy only a small percentage (up to 5%) of the table buffer. If you consider what tables can be buffered, always take into account the memory available for the table buffer.

The type of access is also a criterion. Because the tables in the table buffer are always managed using the primary key, only the access via the primary key is supported efficiently. For fully buffered tables, you can also search in the table buffer via non-primary key fields; however, this search is not efficient.

The monitoring of the buffer areas, the buffer efficiency of the buffered tables, and the technical analysis of the unbuffered tables with regard to the buffer option is a task of the system administration and is implemented using Transactions ST02 and ST10. This is described in great detail in Chapter 9, Table Buffering Fundamentals, of *SAP Performance Optimization Guide* by Thomas Schneider (5th edition, Boston, SAP PRESS 2008).

The logical analysis whether a table can be buffered from the application perspective and the analysis of the table contents are within the responsibility of the application developer.

6.4.3 Performance Aspects of Table Buffering

This section presents the aspects of table buffering that can negatively impact the performance when accessing buffered tables as experience has shown.

Overhead for Copying

Just like for the other buffers at the application server level, the selected data is *copied* from the table buffer into the internal session. In this respect, the table buffer behaves like a cross-user buffer at application server level (for instance, the shared memory or the shared buffer). However, the overheads for copying are of secondary importance.

Low Performance Accesses to Fully Buffered Tables

Buffered tables are managed using the primary key and can only be searched efficiently using this key. There are no secondary indexes in the table buffer; therefore, possibly existing secondary indexes on the database have not effect in case of buffer accesses.

For fully buffered tables, however, accesses to field combinations that don't correspond to the primary key (or an initial part of the primary key) are read from the buffer. As a result, the entire memory area that is occupied by the fully buffered table is scanned for the suitable data record. This involves a sequential read in the main memory in which the system reads the table record by record and checks it against the WHERE condition. This basically corresponds to a full table scan on the database.

Once the table has reached a certain size, such an access can negatively influence the performance. The scan of a larger dataset in the main memory can take longer than an efficient database access using a secondary index.

For large, fully buffered tables, always implement the access via the primary key (or an initial part thereof). If this is not possible and if there are long running accesses with other fields in the WHERE condition, you can check the buffering and change it where necessary. An alternative is to force the problematic accesses to not execute the table buffer but instead the more efficient database access via a secondary index. You can achieve this by using the BYPASSING BUFFER addition of the SELECT clause.

In principle, all buffered tables (not only the fully buffered tables) should always be accessed via the buffered primary key area. Only the access via the primary key area ensures an efficient access in the table buffer.

Changes to the Buffered Tables

Changing accesses (DML—Data Manipulation Language) to buffered tables behave differently depending on the buffering type. The following discusses these differences briefly, before you learn more about the changing accesses to buffered tables. The respective tables indicate which areas are affected and invalidated by the change. You can also find this information in SAP Note 47239.

Examples for single record changes:

```
INSERT [INTO] dbtab [VALUES wa]
UPDATE dbtab
DELETE dbtab
```

Buffering Type	Local Buffer	Remote Buffer
Single record	Changed record	Changed record
Generic	Changed record	Changed generic area
Full	Changed record	Entire table

Examples for array changes:

```
INSERT dbtab FROM TABLE itab
UPDATE dbtab FROM TABLE itab
DELETE dbtab FROM TABLE itab
```

Buffering Type	Local Buffer	Remote Buffer
Single record	Changed records	Changed records
Generic	Changed records	Changed generic areas
Full	Changed records	Entire table

Examples for generic changes:

```
UPDATE dbtab SET ... WHERE...
DELETE dbtab ... WHERE ...
```

Buffering Type	Local Buffer	Remote Buffer
Single record	Entire table	Entire table
Generic	Changed generic areas	Changed generic areas
Full	Entire table	Entire table

However, do not change your DML statements from UPDATE dbtab SET ... to UPDATE dbtab based on the facts mentioned previously. As described in Chapter 5, an UPDATE statement only for certain fields has major advantages on the database side that compensate the disadvantages of the local buffer invalidation.

In principle, implement a precise analysis in case of changes to the buffered tables. If the change of a buffered table is necessary and must be implemented regularly, consider whether the table should be buffered at all because you should only buffer tables that are changed *rarely*.

Caution: Escalation for Many Changes in a Transaction

In extreme cases, a high number of changes to buffered tables within a transaction may result in an escalation. All changes within a transaction are collected in a special buffer area for the synchronization.

If the number of changes exceeds the memory space available, the system first tries to bundle the changes in one table by invalidating the entire table in the remote buffers instead of the changed records (level 1). This way, you only require one entry for the entire table and not an entry for each individual record.

If this measure is not sufficient and you still require more memory for the changes within a transaction, the entire remote table buffer is invalidated (level 2). This is indicated in the system log (Transaction SM21) with the BSO message (memory overflow in buffer synchronisation).

So, if you discover changing accesses to buffered tables, check carefully under which conditions and how often the changes are implemented. Frequent changes to buffered tables result in a higher system load due to the frequent reloading and negatively affect the performance of the entire system. In extreme cases, a full buffer reload may take place. In this case, an unbuffering of the tables that are changed frequently can result in an increased performance. To avoid identical accesses to such tables, select another buffering type, for example, in the internal tables.

Accesses that Bypass the Buffer

Accesses that bypass the buffer can be identified easily in the statement summary of Transaction ST05 because the BFTP (BUFFER TYPE) column includes the entry, FUL, GEN, or SNG. Then this refers to an access to a full (FUL), generic (GEN), or single-record buffered (SNG) table. The fact that the access was recorded in the SQL trace means that the data is read from the database and not from the buffer. Accesses to the table buffer can be also recorded using Transaction ST05; for this purpose, however, the TABLE BUFFER TRACE option must be activated. Then, accesses to the table buffer are highlighted in blue in the extended trace list, whereas accesses to the database are highlighted in yellow. In the statement summary, accesses to table buffers are generally not displayed.

There are many reasons for accesses that bypass the table buffer. But they can be divided into two categories: Firstly, that they are not in the buffer when accessing a table that is selected for buffering. Secondly, that the used SQL statement prevents a buffer access. The following sections describe the various reasons for these two situations.

You can analyze the state of a buffered table using Transaction ST10 (see Chapter 3). By means of Transaction ST10, you can create a list of the single-record buffered (SNG) or generically buffered (GEN, FUL) tables.

For generically buffered tables, the ABSENT, DISPLACED, or ERROR status indicates that the table is not in the buffer at present. This may have various reasons — for example, that the table has not been accessed yet, that it was displaced, or that sufficient space was not available in the buffer while the table was being loaded. For single-record buffered tables, the ERROR status indicates insufficient space is available in the buffer. If a table gets the ERROR status because it didn't fit into the buffer due to lack of space, the system will not automatically retry to load the table into the buffer until the next start of the application server. The system administrators should analyze space problems in the table buffer in more detail.

The INVALID status indicates that the table contents were changed and that there are open transactions that concern this change. For generically buffered tables, you are also given the LOCKED status, indicating that the change involves multiple generic areas. Accesses to tables with this status always bypass the buffer and directly address the database.

As soon as the change is complete, the single-record buffered tables adopt the LOADABLE status and the generically buffered tables first adopt the PENDING status and then LOADABLE. To prevent a high load caused by reload processes, changed buffered tables are reloaded into the buffer only after a specific number of accesses (five by default).

The MULTIPLE status for generically buffered tables indicates that there are multiple different, generic areas that each have different statuses. Here, it is important whether the queried areas exist in the buffer.

The VALID status indicates that a table exists in the buffer and that the system can read from it if the statement that uses this table permits access to the buffer.

Background: Displacement and Invalidation of Tables

At this point, again, note that the displacement in the table buffer does *not* occur when the tables are loaded but asynchronously at specific points in time that depend on the system load. Such displacements are referred to as *swaps* and must be monitored separately for single-record buffered and generically buffered tables using Transaction ST02. A table that was displaced for reasons of space is reloaded directly with the next access if sufficient free space is available in the buffer.

If database accesses to buffered tables occur due to space problems in the table buffer, the system administrators should examine this more closely.

For the invalidation of tables, the buffered table is marked as `pending` or `loadable` after a change. To prevent a high database load caused by reload processes, for each changed table the system waits a specific number of accesses before it reloads the table into buffer. This wait time is based on the assumption that a change to buffered contents usually does not occur for a single record but for multiple records. The aim is to prevent unnecessary reload processes triggered by accesses to these tables while the records are changed. Multiple reload processes during the change periods result in an increased system load.

You can control the number of accesses before the reload is started using the following parameters:

- `zcsa/inval_reload_c = n`
- `zcsa/sync_reload_c = n`

Here, the first parameter is evaluated for a "normal" invalidation in which one or more data records are changed in the tables, whereas the second parameter is evaluated for a complete synchronization of the entire table buffer. Usually, the two parameters don't need to be changed.

To actually read a table that is selected for buffering from the buffer, it may be necessary to access it up to *n* times before it is loaded into the buffer. For the load process, the space required for the table must be freely available in the buffer.

A buffer access can also be prevented by the SQL statement if the statement uses keywords that cannot be processed in the SAP table buffer. Another reason could be that the number of specified key fields is less than the number of buffer key fields of the buffered table. *Buffer key* means the number of primary key fields entered in the technical settings (this can be less fields than the entire primary key).

If an SQL statement for a buffered table proves to be critical for the runtime, it should be reprogrammed in such a way that the table buffer can be used. In the following cases, it is not possible to use the buffer due to a specific keyword.

The JOIN keyword prevents the processing of the statement in the buffer completely regardless of whether only one, multiple, or all tables are buffered in the join. For simple joins, it is therefore recommended to switch to nested SELECT statements to use the already buffered data in the table buffer and to place less load on the database. In these cases, the higher number of SQL statements is less important than the database access to the data available in the table buffer anyway. It can be avoided completely by using the table buffer. This case is checked by the SAP Code Inspector.

The same as for the join applies to queries with *subqueries*. Therefore, a programming in ABAP with individual SQL commands should occur for simple statements that access buffered tables to enable a buffer access for the buffered tables. This case is checked by the SAP Code Inspector.

Aggregate functions (such as MAX( ), MIN( ), SUM( ), AVG( ), COUNT( ), and so on) cannot be mapped in the table buffer. Frequently, a COUNT is used for the existence check, which should generally be avoided (see Section 5.4, in Chapter 5). For aggregate functions to buffered tables that are required, program the aggregate function in ABAP, for example, using SELECT/ ENDSELECT, to use the table buffer. This case is checked by the SAP Code Inspector.

An ORDER BY is only supported by the table buffer in the case of the ORDER BY PRIMARY KEY keyword or if an initial part of the primary key is used in the ORDER BY clause. An ORDER BY according to other fields is not supported by the table buffer. To still use the table buffer, the sorting according to non-primary key fields should be carried out in a separate step using the SORT ABAP command. This case is checked by the SAP Code Inspector.

Groupings using GROUP BY are not supported by the table buffer. To use the table buffer, they should be programmed using ABAP. This case is checked by the SAP Code Inspector.

The DISTINCT keyword prevents the processing of statements in the table buffer. For this example, code the function in ABAP to use the table buffer. This case is checked by the SAP Code Inspector.

The BYPASSING BUFFER keyword explicitly bypasses the table buffer. Here, it is decisive whether the bypassing of the buffer is really necessary.

The FOR UPDATE keyword usually starts an intended change to the data records by setting a lock at database level while reading the data. This access also bypasses the table buffer. Here, you must check whether a change to the buffered tables is really necessary. This should not be the case for buffered tables by definition.

The use of IS NULL or IS NOT NULL in WHERE conditions prevents a table buffer use because NULL is not known in ABAP and is replaced by type-specific initial values. If such a query is really necessary, it can only be checked on the database. This case is checked by the SAP Code Inspector.

Native SQL accesses, whether static (EXEC SQL/ENDEXEC) or dynamic (ADBC), cannot make use of the table buffer because they are transferred by the DBI to the database by definition.

Accesses to the single record buffer always bypass the table buffer if the SINGLE keyword was not indicated, even if all other key fields were specified completely. This case is checked by the SAP Code Inspector.

Accordingly, a SELECT statement with FOR ALL ENTRIES that specifies all key fields in the WHERE condition cannot be mapped in the single record buffer because the SINGLE keyword cannot be used in combination with the FOR ALL ENTRIES keyword.

All comparisons for key fields that use an operator other than the equal operator (=) cannot be carried out on the single record buffer. So all comparisons with LIKE, BETWEEN, >=, and so on bypass the single record buffer. For generically buffered tables, all accesses that don't use = on the key fields bypass the buffer.

In case of the key fields in the WHERE condition to generically buffered or single-record buffered tables, the buffer cannot be used whenever the number of the specified keys in the WHERE condition is less than the number of keys indicated in the buffer settings. A buffer key that is not fully specified always results in database accesses for generically buffered and single-record buffered tables. An incomplete buffer key also exists if the SQL statement contains CLIENT SPECIFIED and the client is omitted in the WHERE condition. This case is checked by the SAP Code Inspector.

In many cases, comparisons between database fields like in the following example also bypass the buffer:

```
SELECT SINGLE *
FROM tabelle
WHERE feld1 = tabelle~feld2.
```

For fully buffered tables, however, every access (which doesn't contain any of the previously mentioned keywords) is processed on the table buffer. Exceptions are accesses using CLIENT SPECIFIED for which the client is not specified in the WHERE condition, and comparisons between database fields like in the previous example. Otherwise, an incomplete specification of the key fields results in an inefficient search in the table buffer. This case is checked by the SAP Code Inspector.

Accesses to Tables That Could be Buffered

In the SQL trace (Transaction ST05), the buffer types, DEACT, DEFUL, DEGEN, and DESNG, enable you to identify accesses to tables that are not buffered but could be buffered. For tables with this status, it was not possible to decide at the time of development whether buffering is possible or not because the future data volume in these tables could not be assessed and is different from system to system. For these tables, the system administrators should check the size and the change frequency of the tables. Based on the given situation, the system administrators and the application support can then decide for or against buffering.

Furthermore, you also have the option to also use your individually developed tables for buffering, provided that they meet the criteria for table buffering (see Section 6.4.2, What Tables Can be Buffered?).

6.4.4 Analysis Options

The following lists the tools for the performance analysis of buffer accesses.

1. **SQL and buffer trace** (see Sections 3.3.8 and 3.3.11, in Chapter 3)
   For recording the accesses to the database or the table buffer

2. **Transaction ST10 — Table Call Statistics** (see Section 3.3.6 in Chapter 3)
   For monitoring the statuses of buffered tables

3. **Transaction DB05 — Selectivity Analysis** (see Section 3.3.2 in Chapter 3)
   For the selectivity analysis and size determination for tables that should be buffered

In addition, Transaction SE17 must also be mentioned at this point, which in contrast to Transaction SE16, enables an access to generically buffered and fully buffered tables in the table buffer. Transaction SE16 is bypassing the buffer by default to always access the database. This is not the case in Transaction SE17. However, you cannot simulate accesses to single-record buffered tables in Transaction SE17 because no SELECT SINGLE is defined there.

6.5   Summary

The aim of all buffering types is to temporarily store data of the database for reuse in order to have faster access to the data and to decrease the load on the database by reducing repeating queries. Which type of buffer should be preferred depends on many factors, for example, whether it is "simple" table data, calculated data, or extracts. Another decisive factor is the data volume as well as the question whether the data is required by only one user or multiple users. In principle, use the buffering types discussed here instead of repeating accesses to the database, if this is permitted by the application logic. But there are also application cases in which you cannot avoid the repeating queries to the database. To reduce the load of the central resource database, implement a buffering of the repeatedly required data wherever possible. Finally, Tables 6.1 and 6.2 provide an overview of all buffer types.

	Internal Session	**ABAP Memory**	**SAP Memory**
Possible Usage	Small sets of master data	Extracts, metadata	Parameters
Copy-free Access	Yes, if implemented accordingly	No	No
Compression	Yes, if implemented accordingly	Optional	No

Table 6.1 User-Specific Buffering

	Table Buffer	**Shared Objects**	**Export/ Import**	**Export/ Import SHM**
Possible Usage	Simple table data	Complex data, objects	Extracts, metadata	Extracts, metadata
Copy-free Access	No	Yes	No	No
Compression	No	No	Optional	Optional
Synchronization	Yes	No	No	No

Table 6.2 Cross-User Buffering

Inefficient accesses to internal tables are a frequent cause of long-running ABAP programs. This particularly applies to the processing of large data volumes. This chapter describes the most critical aspects for ABAP developers for the processing of internal tables.

7   Processing of Internal Tables

Internal tables are among the most complex data objects available in the ABAP environment. The use of internal tables lets you store dynamic datasets in the main memory. Internal tables are comparable to arrays and they spare the programmer the effort of program-controlled memory management thanks to their dynamic nature. The data in internal tables is managed per row, whereas each row has the same structure.

In most cases, internal tables are used for the buffering or formatting of contents from database tables. The type of access to internal tables plays an important role for performance, as is the case with database tables. Experience shows that the tuning of internal tables enables similarly major effects as the tuning of database accesses. The negative effects of inefficient accesses to internal tables for the overall system can be compensated more easily than inefficient database accesses by adding further CPUs or application servers. Inefficient database accesses affect the database as a central resource, whereas inefficient accesses to internal tables impact the better scalable application layer (see Chapter 2).

The following sections first provide a general overview of the internal tables. This is followed by a description of how the internal tables are organized in the main memory. The subsequent section discusses the different types of internal tables. The major part of this chapter then details the performance aspects for the processing of internal tables. Typical problematic examples and solution options are presented here.

7.1   Overview of Internal Tables

Internal tables are completely specified by four properties:

1. **Table type**
   The access type to the table type determines how ABAP accesses the individual table rows. Section 7.3, Table Types, discusses this topic in great detail.

2. **Row type**
   The row type of an internal table can be any ABAP data type.

3. **Uniqueness of the key**
   The key can be specified as unique or non-unique. In case of unique keys, there are no multiple entries (regarding the key) in the internal tables. The uniqueness is based on the table type. Standard tables only allow for non-unique keys and hashed tables only for unique keys.

4. **Key components (taking the sequence into account)**
   The key components and their sequence specify the criteria based on which the table rows are identified.

Figure 7.1 illustrates this syntactically.

Field1	Field2	Field3
A	1	10
A	2	5
B	1	7
B	2	25

```
TYPES: <itabtype> TYPE <tablekinddef> of <linetype>
       [WITH [UNIQUE | NON-UNIQUE] <keydef> ]
       [INITIAL SIZE <n>].

DATA:  <itab> TYPE <tablekind> of <linetype>
       WITH [UNIQUE | NON-UNIQUE] <keydef>
       [INITIAL SIZE < n>] .
```

```
<tablekinddef>:                                        <keydef>
[STANDARD] TABLE | SORTED TABLE | HASHED TABLE         KEY f1 ... fn |
for types also:       INDEX TABLE  | ANY TABLE         KEY TABLE LINE |
                                                       DEFAULT KEY
```

Figure 7.1 Internal Tables — Declaration

The combination of access type and table type is mainly relevant for the performance. Section 7.3, Table Types, discusses the various access types and table types.

Before describing the table types in detail, let's first discuss the organization of internal tables in the main memory.

7.2   Organization in the Main Memory

In the main memory, the internal tables, just like the database tables, are organized in blocks or pages. In the context of internal tables, the following sections use the term *pages*.

When an internal table is declared in an ABAP program, the system only creates a reference (table reference) in the main memory initially. Only when entries are written to the table does the system create a table header and a table body. Figure 7.2 shows a schematic diagram of the organization in the main memory.

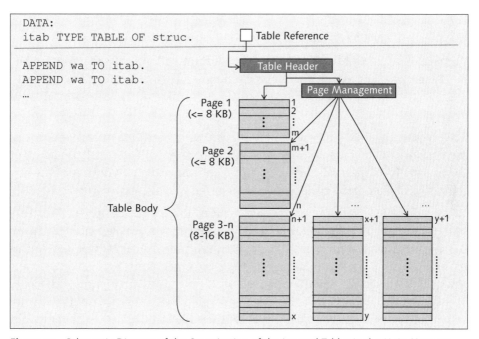

Figure 7.2 Schematic Diagram of the Organization of the Internal Tables in the Main Memory

The table header has a reference to the first page of the table body and another reference to page management. Page management manages the addresses of the pages in the main memory.

The table reference currently occupies 8 bytes of memory space. The table header occupies about 100 bytes of memory space depending on the platform. The space required for page management depends on the number of pages.

The table body consists of pages that can include the table rows. The first two pages are — depending on the row length and other factors — usually smaller than the pages 3 to *n* (if the row lengths are not so long that the maximum page size is reached already at the beginning).

As of the third page, the pages are created with the maximum page size, which is usually between 8 KB and 16 KB. This depends on the length of the row. Unlike database tables, the access is not per page but per row. So if you access a row of an internal table, the system reads only one row. The effort for searching table entries (or data records) is comparable to the database tables. For this purpose, the index or hash administration provides support for the internal tables. You learn more about internal tables in Section 7.3, Table Types, for the table types because they are directly related to this topic.

The table header includes the most important information about an internal table. For example, you can quickly query the number of rows using DESCRIBE TABLE <itab> LINES <lines> or the integrated function, LINES(itab), from the table header.

As very small internal tables with only a few rows can result in wastage due to the memory use of the automatically calculated first page, INITIAL SIZE is added for the declaration of internal tables. It can provide information on the size of the first page, so a smaller memory allocation than in the standard case occurs.

However, if considerably more rows are required than originally specified for INITIAL SIZE, the third page is created faster with the maximum page size. For example, if 4 was specified for INITIAL SIZE, the third page may already be required as of the 13th row if the second page is twice as large as the first page. Relatively few rows (13, for example) require relatively much memory (three pages, third page with a size of 8 to 16 KB), whereas one page would have been sufficient if a higher value (for example, 14) had been specified for INITIAL SIZE. Consequently, for small tables it is important that INITIAL SIZE is not selected too small. Select a value that provides sufficient space in the first (or first and second) page for most cases.

INITIAL SIZE should always be specified if you require only a few rows and the internal table exists frequently. For nested tables, if an internal table is part of a row of another internal table, this is likely for the inner internal table. It can also occur for attributes of a class if there are many instances of this class.

> **Caution: INITIAL SIZE and APPEND SORTED BY**
>
> In conjunction with the `APPEND wa SORTED BY comp` command, the `INITIAL SIZE` addition not only has a syntactic but also a semantic meaning (see documentation). However, don't use the `APPEND wa SORTED BY comp` command; instead, work with the `SORT` command.

Depending on the table type or type of processing, you also require a management for the access to the row, that is, an index for the index tables and a hash administration for the hashed tables. At this point, memory may be required for the management of entries in addition to the pages. This management also occupies memory. Both in the Debugger and in the Memory Inspector, this memory is added to the table body and not displayed separately. Compared to the user data, this management can generally be neglected.

But how can you release allocated space in the internal tables again? The deletion of individual or multiple rows from the internal table using the `DELETE itab` command doesn't result in any memory release. The rows concerned are only "selected" as deleted and not deleted from the pages.

Only when you use the `REFRESH` or `CLEAR` statements the system does release the pages of the internal tables again. Only the header and a small memory area remain.

> **Note**
>
> In this context, *released* means that the occupied memory can be reused. As the memory allocation from the Extended Memory (EM) for a user is usually done in blocks (see Section 6.1 in Chapter 6), which are considerably larger than the pages of an internal table, this is referred to as a two-level release. Release initially means that the pages within an EM block are released and this space can then be reused by the *same* user. Only if the EM block is completely empty and doesn't contain any data (variables, and so on) of the user any longer is this block returned to the SAP memory management and available for the other users again.

The `FREE itab` ABAP statement, however, results in the complete de-allocation of the table body, that is, *all pages* and the index (if available) of the internal tables are released. Additionally, the table header is added to a system-internal "free list" for reuse.

If an internal table should be reused, it is advisable to use `REFRESH` or `CLEAR` instead of `FREE` because this way the creation of the first page can be omitted. If a large part of the rows of an internal table was deleted using DELETE and the occupied memory should be released, it is recommended to copy the table rows. A simple copy to another internal table is not sufficient because of table sharing, which is discussed in Section 7.4, Performance Aspects. Alternatively, you can revert to ABAP statements (INSERT or APPEND) or to the EXPORT/IMPORT variants (see Section 6.2.2 in Chapter 6) for copying. In the context of performance, the "release" of memory only plays a secondary role (as long as no memory bottleneck exists in the system). In contrast to fragmented database tables, fragmented internal tables have no negative effects on the performance because the entries can always be addressed efficiently because internal tables are always managed per row.

Background: Difference between Internal Tables and Database Tables

Internal tables can be compared to database tables in many respects, but there is one major difference:

Internal tables are always processed on a row basis, whereas database tables are always processed on a set basis. A set-based processing, possible with Open SQL on database tables, is not possible on internal tables because the single row is the main processing criterion for internal tables, whereas a set of data records is the main processing criterion for database tables. Set-based accesses to internal tables, for instance, LOOP ... WHERE or DELETE ... WHERE, are emulated by the ABAP VM and can be mapped in an optimized way for some table types (see Section 7.4, Performance Aspects). More complex, set-based operators, such as joins and aggregates,... are not possible on internal tables. They must be programmed using the existing ABAP language techniques.

After you've learned about the organization of internal tables in the main memory, the next section focuses on the organization of internal tables and discusses the different types of internal tables.

7.3   Table Types

Internal tables can be subdivided into index tables and hashed tables. The index tables, in turn, can be divided into standard tables and sorted tables. Figure 7.3 shows an overview of the table types.

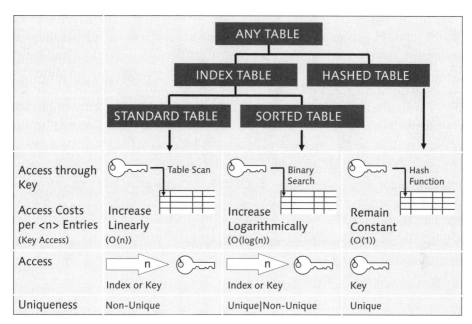

Figure 7.3 Overview of the Table Types

The table type specifies how you can access individual table rows via ABAP.

For *standard tables,* the access can be implemented via the table index or a "key." For a key access, the response time depends linearly on the number of table entries because the read access corresponds to a linear scan of the entries, which is canceled after the first hit. The key of a standard table is always non-unique. If no key is specified, the standard table receives the *default key,* which is a combination of all character-like fields.

Sorted tables are always sorted by the key. The access can be carried out via the table index or the key. For a key access, the response time depends logarithmically on the number of table entries because the read access is carried out via a binary search. The key of sorted tables can be unique or non-unique. On sorted tables, you can process partial keys (initial parts of the complete key) in an optimized manner. An over-specification of the table key is also possible; only the components of the key are used for the search and the remaining components are then utilized for the filtering.

Standard tables and sorted tables are also referred to as *index tables* because both tables can be accessed using the table index.

The read access to *hashed tables* is only possible by specifying a key. Here, the response time is constant and doesn't depend on the number of table entries because the access is carried out via a hash algorithm. The key of hashed tables must be unique. Neither explicit nor implicit index operations are permitted on hashed tables. If a hashed table is accessed with a "key" that is different to the unique table key, the table is handled like a standard table and searched linearly according to the entries. This is also the case for a partial key. Different to the sorted table, this partial key cannot be optimized for the hashed table. Over-specified keys are processed in an optimized manner.

By means of the DESCRIBE TABLE <itab> KIND <k> statement, you can determine the current table type at runtime. Of course, this is also possible using Run Time Type Identification (RTTI).

An index or a hash administration is available for the efficient management or access optimization of internal tables. The following section describes which types are available and when they are created.

Index Tables

Indexes for index tables are only created when the physical sequence no longer corresponds to the logical sequence, that is, when one of the INSERT, DELETE, or SORT statements is executed on the table and the following conditions apply:

1. INSERT
   The entry to be inserted should be inserted before an already existing entry. (An INSERT statement that inserts *behind* the last record largely corresponds to an APPEND statement.)

2. DELETE
   The entry to be deleted is not the last entry of the table.

3. SORT
   The table has a certain size and is sorted.

An index is used for the efficient index access in the "logical sort sequence" or the efficient finding of "valid rows" if the table pages have gaps due to deletions. By means of the index, the logical sequence of the table is mapped on the physical memory addresses of the entries.

An index is available in two types:

1. As a linear index

2. As a tree-like index

The index structure is always maintained without any gaps, whereas the table pages may have gaps due to the deletion of records. In comparison to the management of the index without gaps, the management of the table pages without gaps would be too time consuming for larger tables.

Due to the management of the index structure without gaps, the insertion and deletion of records incur movement costs because the existing entries must be moved. Strictly speaking, these costs are overheads for copying. For large indexes (as of about 5,000 entries), they get dominant; this is why a tree-like index is created for large tables.

In addition to the index, a free list exists that manages the addresses of the entries that were deleted using DELETE for reuse.

Figure 7.4 shows a schematic diagram of a linear index.

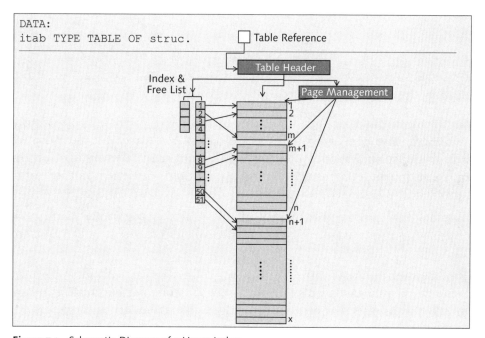

Figure 7.4 Schematic Diagram of a Linear Index

Whether a tree-like index is created depends on system-internal rules, for example, the number of entries (to be expected), and other factors. Figure 7.5 shows a schematic diagram of a tree-like index.

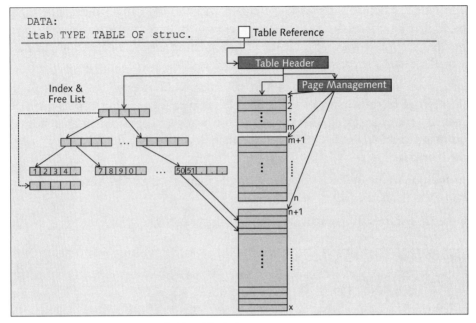

Figure 7.5 Schematic Diagram of a Tree-Like Index

For the tree-like index, the index entries are organized in *leaves*. The previously mentioned movement or copy costs only incur at the leaf level. The index doesn't have to be allocated at once; you only require continuous memory at leaf level. In return, you must first navigate through the tree structure when you access the index to reach the respective index entry.

Apart from that, the tree-like indexes on index tables are comparable to the database indexes presented in Chapter 5. A tree-like index requires about 50% more space than a linear index.

If the logical sequence of entries corresponds to the physical sequence in the main memory when the index tables are processed, you don't need to create an index. In this case, the insertion sequence corresponds to the physical sequence, and the table was filled with a sorting and not deleted or sorted. If no index is necessary, the internal table requires less memory.

Hash Administration

The hash administration is based on the unique key of the table. The hash administration is created for hashed tables only. It is established using the unique key of the internal table. Index accesses (for example, second entry of the internal table) are not possible, hashed tables can only be accessed with the key.

For the hashed table, each key value is assigned to a unique number using a hash function. For this number, the memory address of the respective data record is stored in a corresponding hash array.

If a DELETE or SORT is executed on a hashed table, you must create a double-linked list (previous and next pointer), so sequential accesses (LOOP) via the data are still possible according to the insertion sequence (or in a sort sequence generated using SORT). The double-linked list requires about 50% more space for the hash administration.

Figure 7.6 shows a schematic diagram of a hash administration.

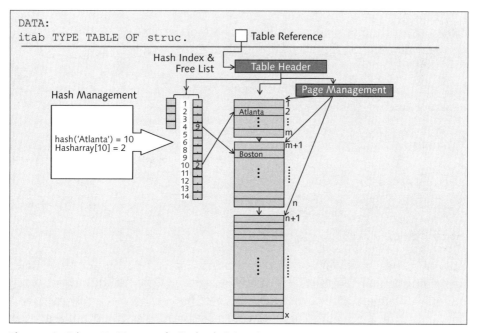

Figure 7.6 Schematic Diagram of a Hash administration

Limitations

Besides the memory that is available to the user, there are further limitations for internal tables:

A limit for the number of rows in internal tables results because they are addressed internally and in ABAP statements via 4 byte integers, which limits them to 2,147,483,647 entries.

The size of hashed tables is further limited by the biggest memory block available at once. The maximum size is 2 GB, but it is usually further limited by the `ztta/max_memreq_MB` *profile parameter*. The maximum number of rows of hashed tables depends on the required size of the hash administration that must be stored there.

The actual maximum size of internal tables is usually smaller than specified by the previous limits because the overall available memory is usually not only used by a string or an internal table (see ABAP documentation: MAXIMUM SIZE OF DYNAMIC DATA OBJECTS).

Summary of the Table Types

Table 7.1 lists the most important characteristics of the table types. This is followed by a recommendation for when you should use which table type.

	Standard Table	Sorted Table	Hashed Table
Possible Accesses	Index access or key access	Index access or key access	Key access
Uniqueness	Non-unique	Non-unique or unique	Unique
Optimal Access	Index or binary search (if the table is sorted by the search components)	Index or key	Key

Table 7.1 Characteristics of Table Types

Standard tables should only be used if all entries should be processed sequentially after filling or if the internal tables should be accessed flexibly and efficiently using multiple different keys. For this purpose, the table must be sorted by the search field and scanned using the binary search. The resorting is carried out only as often as necessary. If a resorting is only required for one or a few read accesses, the sort times far outweigh the time savings for reading. Use key accesses without binary search only for small tables or better avoid them completely. If you search only via a specific field, use a sorted or hashed table.

Sorted tables are particularly suited for partially sequential processing, for example, when a small part of a table should be processed via key accesses for which only the initial part of the key is given. Key accesses to the table key can also be carried out efficiently by the sorted tables.

Hash tables are optimal if you access only via the table key. If the key has a high left significance, you can also use a unique sorted table because in this case performance benefits arise for the binary search when you access individual rows. In this context, *left significance* means that the selective part of a key should be positioned at the beginning of the key (as far to the left as possible).

7.4   Performance Aspects

This section discusses all performance-relevant aspects when working with internal tables. For this purpose, the most important commands for internal tables are discussed. The examples are indicated with a work area (wa). Processing with header lines is still supported but should not be used any longer because the header lines of internal tables are obsolete and prohibited in the OO context.

7.4.1   Fill

Like for the database accesses, array operations and single record operations are also available for the internal tables.

Array Operations

ABAP documentation generally describes this type of processing as block operation, whereas the SELECT statement uses the term array operation with regard to the database.

When internal tables are filled from database tables, the INTO TABLE itab keyword causes the SELECT statement to insert the data records en bloc to the internal tables (see Section 5.7 in Chapter 5).

An array interface is also available for filling internal tables from other internal tables. The corresponding ABAP statements are:

```
APPEND LINES OF itab1 TO itab2.
INSERT LINES OF itab1 INTO  TABLE itab2.
```

For hashed tables, you can only use the INSERT statement, and for index tables you can use both APPEND and INSERT. If you append rows using APPEND, for sorted tables you must ensure that the sort sequence of the internal tables is maintained.

Assignments using MOVE and = also belong to the array operations to internal tables.

Here, minor runtime differences arise between the table types, which depend on the insertion position and the quantity of inserted entries. The management of indexes incurs relatively low costs.

Prefer array operations on internal tables to single record operations (next section) wherever possible because the kernel can process administrative work (for example, memory allocation) more efficiently.

Note that in contrast to the database tables the sequence of the rows in internal tables is always well defined:

▸ For duplicates and non-unique keys, the sequence in the target table and within the duplicates in the source table will always be the same for array operations. This is not the case for single record operations; here, the sequence of the duplicates can change.

▸ For duplicates and unique keys, the block operations result in non-catchable runtime errors, whereas the single record operations only set the sy-subrc return code.

> **Real-Life Example — Transaction SE30, Tips & Tricks**
>
> In the TIPS & TRICKS under Internal TABLES • ARRAY Operations, Transaction SE30 provides various examples whose runtime you can measure.

Single Record Operations

The ABAP statements, APPEND and INSERT, are also available for the single record operations:

```
APPEND wa TO itab.
INSERT wa INTO itab INDEX indx.
INSERT wa INTO TABLE itab.
```

Whereas you can use an APPEND and an INSERT statement with the INDEX addition only in index tables, the third variant is available for all tables.

For standard tables, an INSERT statement without INDEX mostly corresponds to the APPEND statement. (For APPEND, the row to be appended must be convertible, while for INSERT, the row to be inserted must be compatible; see ABAP documentation.) The costs for the APPEND statement are constant. An APPEND is the fastest variant for inserting single records because in this process only one entry is appended to the end of the table.

The insertion at a specific position (INSERT ... INDEX) incurs movement costs depending on the insertion position. These costs increase the "closer" the entry is inserted to the beginning (more movement costs) and decrease the "farther" the entry is inserted to the end (less movement costs). Up to a certain limit (currently 4,096), the costs for inserting depend on the insertion position and linearly on the number of entries. As soon as the index table has more entries, the system switches to a tree-like index internally in which the movement costs and the insertion position are only relevant at leaf level. When a tree-like index is present, the costs don't scale linearly any longer but logarithmically with the number of entries.

An insertion with an index for the standard tables is useful to structure them in a sorted manner. For this purpose, you must first determine the correct insertion position if it is not known. The best way to achieve this is by using a binary search (see next section).

For sorted tables, you can only use an APPEND and an INSERT statement with the INDEX addition if the sort sequence remains unchanged. In this case, you must check whether the key of the new entry is suitable for the desired position in the table.

A binary search is carried out for a generic INSERT (without the INDEX addition), which determines the correct insertion position internally. The costs for finding the position correspond to a read access to this table using a key and scale logarithmically with the number of entries. Like for the standard table, movement costs also occur. These costs depend on the insertion position and the index (linear or tree-like).

For hashed tables, the insertion is based on the table key. The costs are constant here and don't depend on the number of entries. Using the hash administration is somewhat more complex than appending entries to the standard table.

In summary, use array operations for insertion wherever possible. However, note the previously mentioned behavior of these operations.

Table 7.2 provides an overview of the costs for the single record statements. The costs for the reorganization of the index or hash administration when extending the internal memory or managing the tree-like index are not considered here.

	Standard	Sorted	Hashed
APPEND	O(1) Constant	O(1) Constant (higher than standard, check required)	–

Table 7.2 Costs of Single Record Operations for Filling Internal Tables

	Standard	Sorted	Hashed
INSERT ... INTO ... INDEX	Linear index: O(1) – O(n) Constant—linear Tree-like index: O(1) – O(log n) Constant—logarithmic (depending on the position)	Linear index: O(1) – O(n) Constant—linear Tree-like index: O(1) – O(log n) Constant—logarithmic (depending on the position) Constant (a bit higher, check required)	–
INSERT ... INTO TABLE	O(1) Constant	O(log n) Logarithmic	O(1) Constant (higher than standard, hash administration)

Table 7.2 Costs of Single Record Operations for Filling Internal Tables (Cont.)

7.4.2 Read

For read accesses, you differentiate reading of multiple and individual rows.

Multiple Rows (LOOP)

Here, you differentiate between reading all rows and reading a specific section of rows.

All rows are read using the LOOP AT itab ABAP statement. In this process, all rows of an internal table are read. The costs for reading all data records scales linearly with the number of data records. These costs are independent of the table type because each entry in the internal table must be processed. Without any further specification, each entry is *copied* into the work area specified with INTO.

A part of the rows in an internal table is read with LOOP ... FROM ix1 TO ix2 (for index tables) or generally with LOOP ... WHERE. The costs for reading a subarea of the internal table depend on the size of this part and whether the part to be read can be found efficiently. Costs for providing the resulting set in the output area

(LOOP ... INTO) accrue. However, the costs for finding the relevant entries are far more important.

For standard tables, the costs are linear to the number of entries.

For hashed tables, you can implement a search via the hash administration if the complete key of the table is specified in the WHERE condition. Then the LOOP ... WHERE corresponds to a read of a unique record. The costs are constant then. In all other cases, the read accesses to the hashed table are linear, depending on the number of entries because the table is searched completely.

When you access sorted tables, the kernel can optimize an incomplete key because the table is available in a sorted manner by definition. For this purpose, the following conditions must be met:

1. The WHERE condition has the form, WHERE k1 = b1 AND ... AND kn = bn.

2. The WHERE condition covers an initial part of the table key.

In contrast to hashed tables, partially sequential accesses are optimized for sorted tables, too. This way, you can find the starting point for the searched area in an efficient manner.

If standard tables are sorted by the key, you can also achieve an optimization by first searching for the first suitable entry using the binary search and then starting a loop from this position. This loop is exited as soon as the system determines with an IF statement that the search condition no longer applies. The costs for this procedure correspond approximately to the costs of the sorted table and scale logarithmically to the table entries. The following listing provides a pseudo code example for this procedure:

```
READ TABLE itab INTO wa WITH KEY ... BINARY SEARCH.
   INDEX = SY-TABIX.
   LOOP AT itab INTO wa FROM INDEX.
   IF ( key <> search_key ).
      EXIT.
   ENDIF.
   ENDLOOP.
```

Mass access incurs the following costs, which are also listed in Table 7.3. The costs include both search costs for finding the relevant entries (as shown in the table) and costs for providing the hit list (for example, in the work area or a data reference). The costs for providing the hit list are of secondary importance in case of small hit lists. Only for LOOP ... FROM ... TO, for which the search costs are constant, can the provision of the hit list dominate the costs.

For longer hit lists or the extreme case that all rows of the internal table are included in the hit list due to duplicates relating to the key, the costs on index tables are dominated by the provision costs, which scale linearly with the number of hits.

	Standard	Sorted	Hashed
LOOP ... ENDLOOP (all rows)	O(n) Linear (full table scan)	O(n) Linear (full table scan)	O(n) Linear (full table scan)
LOOP ... WHERE ENDLOOP (complete key)	O(n) Linear (full table scan)	O(log n) Logarithmic	O(1) Constant
LOOP ... WHERE ENDLOOP (incomplete key, initial part)	O(n) Linear (full table scan) Can be optimized manually using a sorted standard table and a binary search O(log n).	O(log n) Logarithmic	O(n) Linear (full table scan)
LOOP ... WHERE ENDLOOP (incomplete key, no initial part)	O(n) Linear (full table scan)	O(n) Linear (full table scan)	O(n) Linear (full table scan)
LOOP ... FROM ... TO	O(1) Constant	O(1) Constant	–

Table 7.3 Costs for Reading Multiple Rows from Internal Tables

Single Rows

The following statements are available to read single rows from internal tables:

```
READ TABLE itab INTO wa INDEX ...
READ TABLE itab INTO wa WITH [TABLE] KEY ...
READ TABLE itab INTO wa FROM wa1
```

Index accesses can only be executed on index tables and have constant costs.

Usually, you want to access an internal table using the key and not using the index. In this case, the costs depend on the effort required to find the correct entry.

For standard tables, the costs depend linearly on the number of entries because the table is scanned entry by entry until the proper entry is found. If the entry is positioned at the beginning of the table, the search finishes earlier than if the entry is positioned at the end of the table.

The use of the binary search is an option to accelerate the search in a standard table. For this purpose, the standard table must be available sorted by the search term and an initial part of the sort key must be provided. With the READ itab WITH KEY ... BINARY SEARCH statement, a binary search is used for the standard table. In this case, the costs scale logarithmically with the number of entries.

Background: Binary Search

The binary search on standard or sorted tables uses the bisection method. For this purpose, the table must be available sorted by the respective key. Here, the search doesn't start at the beginning of the table but in the middle, and then the half that contains the entry is bisected again, and so on, until a hit is available or no record can be found. If duplicates exist, the first entry is returned in the duplicate list.

Ensure that the standard table is not sorted unnecessarily because the sorting of a standard table is also an expensive statement (see Section 7.4.6, Sort); for this reason, the number of sorting processes must be kept as small as possible.

Real-Life Example — Transaction SE30, Tips & Tricks

In the TIPS & TRICKS under INTERNAL TABLES • LINEAR SEARCH VS. BINARY SEARCH, Transaction SE30 provides an example whose runtime you can measure.

The binary search can also be used for the optimization of partially sequential accesses as shown at the beginning of this section for the LOOP ... WHERE to standard tables. You can also use a binary search to establish a standard table in a sorted manner. For this purpose, have another look at the example from Section 6.2.1 in Chapter 6:

```
READ TABLE it_kunde INTO var_kunde
WITH KEY it_order_tab-kunnr BINARY SEARCH.
save_tabix = sy-tabix.
IF SY-SUBRC <> 0.
        SELECT *
        INTO var_kunde
        FROM db_kunden_tab
      WHERE kundennr = it_order_tab-kunnr.
          IF SY-SUBRC = 0.
            INSERT var_kunde INTO it_kunde INDEX save_tabix.
          ...
```

The `it_kunde` table is scanned for a suitable entry using the binary search. If no suitable entry can be found, the `sy-tabix` table index is positioned on the row number on which the entry is. You can use this index to insert the entry at the correct position. This way, the standard table is organized in a sorted manner without requiring a `SORT` statement.

For read accesses to sorted tables, a binary search is used internally if an initial part of the table key is available. The costs scale logarithmically with the number of entries.

For hashed tables, the hash administration is used in case a fully specified key access exists. The costs are constant then. If the system accesses the hashed table with a key that is not fully specified, the costs depend linearly on the number of entries.

For all accesses, it is irrelevant for the performance whether the access is carried out using the table key (`...WITH TABLE KEY...`) or a free key (`...WITH KEY...`). The only decisive factor for the performance is that the key fields referred to comply with the beginning or the entire table key. So, over-specified keys (with more fields than the key fields) can also be used to optimize to internal tables.

Single record access incurs the costs listed in Table 7.4. As already mentioned for `LOOP ... WHERE`, a linear share is added for duplicates in the binary search for the index tables, which can exhibit a linear runtime behavior in extreme cases (all entries relate to the duplicates key).

	Standard	Sorted	Hashed
READ ... INDEX	O(1) Constant	O(1) Constant	–
READ ... WITH KEY ... (Complete key)	O(n) Linear Binary search: O(log n) Logarithmic	O(log n) Logarithmic	O(1) Constant
READ ... WITH KEY ... (Incomplete key, initial part)	O(n) Linear Binary search: O(log n) Logarithmic	O(log n) Logarithmic	O(n) Linear
READ ... WITH KEY ... (Incomplete key, no initial part)	O(n) Linear	O(n) Linear	O(n) Linear

Table 7.4 Costs for Reading Single Rows from Internal Tables

7.4.3 Modify

Internal tables are changed using the MODIFY command. MODIFY to internal tables *only* involves a change and not a change or insertion as is the case for the MODIFY command to a database table.

Multiple rows of an internal table are modified with the following statement:

```
MODIFY itab FROM wa TRANSPORTING ... WHERE ...
```

The costs are the same as for the LOOP ... WHERE statement and depend on the number of entries to be modified and the effort for finding the entries.

Single entries in internal tables can be modified as follows:

```
MODIFY itab [INDEX n] [FROM wa]
MODIFY TABLE itab [FROM wa]
```

The costs are constant if you access index tables via the index (variant 1). Within loops, you can also use this variant for the sequential modification of multiple rows without INDEX. In this case, the current row where the loop is used is modified. This is an implicit index operation that is only permitted for index tables.

For the key accesses (variant 2) with a complete key, the costs scale linearly for standard tables and logarithmically with the number of entries for sorted tables. The costs are constant for hashed tables. Because this variant includes a separate search of the proper entries, it shouldn't be used in the loop via the same table. This could result in a nonlinear runtime behavior.

The costs for MODIFY correspond to those of the LOOP; the same restrictions apply for the duplicates (see Table 7.5).

	Standard	Sorted	Hashed
MODIFY ... TRANSPORTING ... WHERE (complete key)	O(n) Linear (full table scan)	O(log n) Logarithmic	O(1) Constant
MODIFY... TRANSPORTING... WHERE (incomplete key, initial part)	O(n) Linear (full table scan)	O(log n) Logarithmic	O(n) Linear (full table scan)
MODIFY... TRANSPORTING... WHERE (incomplete key, no initial part)	O(n) Linear (full table scan)	O(n) Linear (full table scan)	O(n) Linear (full table scan)

Table 7.5 Costs for Modifying Internal Tables

	Standard	Sorted	Hashed
`MODIFY ... [INDEX n] FROM wa` (index access)	O(1)	O(1)	–
`MODIFY TABLE... FROM wa` (search effort as for `WHERE`)	O(n) Linear (full table scan)	O(log n)	O(1) Constant

Table 7.5 Costs for Modifying Internal Tables (Cont.)

7.4.4 Delete

The following statements are available to delete multiple entries from internal tables:

```
DELETE itab FROM ix1 TO ix2
DELETE itab WHERE...
```

The costs depend on the effort for finding and the quantity of rows to be deleted. For the index access, the costs for finding are constant; for the key access, they correspond to the costs of `MODIFY`.

Accesses to individual entries are implemented using the following statements:

```
DELETE itab [INDEX n].
DELETE TABLE itab WITH TABLE KEY .../DELETE TABLE itab FROM wa
```

For the accesses to individual rows, the costs correspond to those of `LOOP` or `MODIFY` (see Table 7.6).

	Standard	Sorted	Hashed
`DELETE ... FROM ... TO`	O(1)	O(1)	–
`DELETE ... WHERE` (complete key)	O(n) Linear (full table scan)	O(log n) Logarithmic	O(1) Constant
`DELETE ... WHERE` (incomplete key, initial part)	O(n) Linear (full table scan)	O(log n) Logarithmic	O(n) Linear (full table scan)
`DELETE ... WHERE` (incomplete key, no initial part)	O(n) Linear (full table scan)	O(n) Linear (full table scan)	O(n) Linear (full table scan)

Table 7.6 Costs for Deleting Entries from Internal Tables

	Standard	Sorted	Hashed
DELETE ... INDEX	O(1)	O(1)	–
DELETE FROM WA / DELETE TABLE WITH TABLE KEY	O(n) Linear (full table scan)	O(log n)	O(1) Constant

Table 7.6 Costs for Deleting Entries from Internal Tables (Cont.)

7.4.5 Condense

Using the COLLECT command, you can create condensed datasets in internal tables. For this purpose, the numeric data of all fields that aren't key fields are added to already existing values with the same key in the internal table. For standard tables without explicit key specification, all non-numeric fields are handled as key fields. The costs of the command are significantly determined by the effort of finding the relevant row.

A temporary hash administration is created for standard tables if a standard table is filled with COLLECT only. This is rather unstable compared to other modifying statements (APPEND, INSERT, DELETE, SORT, MODIFY, changes using the field symbols/ references). However, this optimization has become obsolete because of the implementation of key tables (sorted tables, hashed tables) and therefore the COLLECT command to standard tables, too.

If the temporary hash administration is intact, the finding of entries is a constant process just like for hashed tables. If the hash administration is destroyed, the effort for searching entries depends linearly on the number of entries in the internal table. You can use the ABL_TABLE_HASH_STATE function module to check whether a standard table has an intact hash administration.

For sorted tables, the entry is specified internally using a binary search, whereas the effort for searching entries depends logarithmically on the number of entries in the internal table.

In hashed tables, the entry is determined using the hash administration of the table. The costs are constant and don't depend on the number of entries.

COLLECT should be used mostly for hashed tables because they have a unique table key and a stable hash administration.

Real-Life Example — Transaction SE30, Tips & Tricks

In the TIPS & TRICKS under INTERNAL TABLES • BUILDING CONDENSED TABLES, Transaction SE30 provides an example whose runtime you can measure.

7.4.6 Sort

Standard and hashed tables can be sorted by any field of the table using the SORT command. Sorted tables cannot be sorted using the SORT command because they are already sorted by the key fields by definition and cannot be resorted by other fields.

During the sorting process, the data is sorted in the main memory (in the process-local memory of a work process) if possible. If the space in the main memory is not sufficient, the components are sorted in the file system. For this purpose, the blocks are first sorted in the main memory and then written to the file system. Subsequently, these sorted blocks are reimported using a merge sort.

Sorting is a runtime-intensive statement regardless of whether the sorting is implemented in the main memory or in the file system. (Of course, the sorting in the file system is even more expensive than the sorting in the main memory.) Therefore, only sort if this is absolutely required by the application or, in the case of the standard table, if you can achieve runtime gains for the reading from these tables using the binary search. For example, it is possible to sort an internal standard table first by one key field and then by another one and to browse it using the binary search. In this case, the achieved runtime gains via the binary search are not canceled out by the increased effort of sorting. The sorting is only worthwhile if you can optimize a large number of subsequent read accesses this way. For a table with about 1,000 rows, a sorting process should be followed by at least 40 to 50 read accesses.

If the internal standard table is processed in such a way that a search access to a field is implemented alternately to a search access to another field, and consequently a sorting process for the respective resorting would be necessary for each search access, it would be counterproductive to carry out the sorting. In this case, only optimize one of the two search processes by means of a one-time sorting and a binary search. Optionally, you could consider the use of a second internal table, which acts as a secondary index (see Section 7.4.8, Secondary Indexes).

> **Note**
>
> The assignments in sorted tables could also require implicit sorting processes if these have a key that is different to the source table. These sorting processes are not evident in the ABAP trace directly because assignments are not assigned to events and are not recorded separately. The time required for these sorting processes is added to the net times of the calling modularization unit.

7.4.7   Copy Cost-Reduced or Copy Cost-Free Access

If you use the LOOP ... WHERE and READ statements, the results are *copied* to the work area. If you use the MODIFY statement, the changes are copied from the work area back to the table.

In case of READ and MODIFY, the costs for copying can be limited to the required fields. For this purpose, you must specify the TRANSPORTING f1 f2 ... addition. Then only the fields are copied, which are indicated after the addition. You can also avoid the costs for copying for LOOP ... WHERE and READ if you specify a TRANS-PORTING NO FIELDS. In this case, the system fills only the corresponding system fields and no result is copied to the header or the work area. This is used to check whether a specific entry is available in an internal table. For LOOP ... WHERE, this access corresponds to a read access instead.

You can also avoid the costs for copying if the reference to a table row is copied to a reference variable or if the memory address of a row is assigned to a field symbol. Figure 7.7 illustrates this.

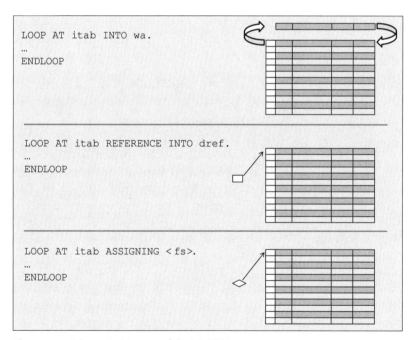

Figure 7.7   Schematic Diagram of the LOOP Variant

The first variant, LOOP AT itab INTO wa, copies the itab internal table row by row into the wa work area. If the row should be modified, you must copy it back using MODIFY (see Section 7.4.3, Modify).

The second variant, LOOP AT itab REFERENCE INTO dref, provides the memory address of each row — row by row — to the dref data reference variable.

The third variant, LOOP AT itab ASSIGNING <fs>, assigns the memory address of each row to the <fs> field symbol, again row by row.

The second and the third variant are more efficient due to the reduced cost for copying. For large datasets, the runtime can be reduced by means of these options. For very small datasets — when the internal tables have less than five rows and no excessively long rows (more than 5,000 bytes) — the regular copy process is faster because both the management of the data reference variable and the field symbols constitute a certain overhead for the system. In case of nested internal tables (internal tables in which a column of the row structure is another table), it is always worthwhile to use the copy-free techniques. If the changes to the row in the internal table should be written back, it pays off to use the copy-free techniques because you don't require the MODIFY command any longer.

The basic rule here is that the larger the dataset to be copied, the more worthwhile it is to use the copy-free techniques.

An access to *one* entry via LOOP ... WHERE or READ is suitable for wide rows (more than 1,000 bytes). If the read row should be modified and written back into the table (MODIFY), the copy-free access already pays off for shorter rows.

> **Real-Life Example — Transaction SE30, Tips & Tricks**
>
> In the Tips & Tricks under Internal Tables • Using the Assigning Command • Modifying a Set of Lines Directly, Transaction SE30 provides an example whose runtime you can measure.

7.4.8   Secondary Indexes

Up to and including Release 7.0 EhP1, internal tables cannot include secondary indexes. If you require efficient accesses via different fields, secondary indexes are implemented in the form of custom internal tables. In this process, an additional internal table is created for each secondary key, which includes a reference to the main table in addition to the field that represents the secondary key. This reference can be the position of the data record in the main table (only for index tables) or the key in the main table. But you can also define a separate unique number for it. All solutions entail additional memory requirement but allow for an efficient access via multiple key fields in return. When processing the internal table, you must ensure with utmost accuracy that the secondary index tables are maintained with every change of the main table. Generally, such a procedure is error prone because of its complexity and should be used in special situations only.

Real-Life Example — Transaction SE30, Tips & Tricks

In the TIPS & TRICKS under INTERNAL TABLES • SECONDARY INDICES, Transaction SE30 provides an example whose runtime you can measure.

As of Release 7.0 EhP2 and 7.1, you are provided with secondary indexes which are described in Chapter 10.

7.4.9 Copy

Table sharing is another performance aspect that you should be aware of. For assignments and value transfers (import and export per value) of internal tables *of the same type*, whose row types don't contain a table type, only the internal administration information (table header) is transferred because of performance reasons. Figure 7.8 illustrates this.

Background: Internal Tables of the Same Type

Tables with the same structure are referred to as internal tables of the same type. Table sharing is possible between tables of the same type if the table in the target table has the same or a more generic type as the source table. The following combinations are possible, for example:

`itab_standard = itab_sorted`

`itab_standard = itab_hashed`

`itab_sorted_with_nonunique_key = itab_sorted_with_unique_key`

The sharing works for the same or a more general key of the target table (on the left-hand side of =).

In the following cases, the table sharing is not possible because the target table is not more generic than the source table:

`itab_sorted = itab_standard` (with same key definition)

`itab_sorted_with_unique_key = itab_sorted_with_nonunique_key` (with same key definition)

Table sharing is possible with any number of tables and cannot be influenced by the ABAP developer.

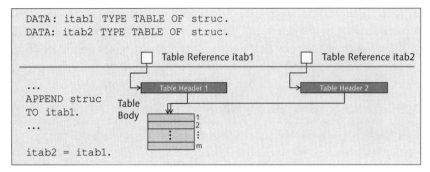

Figure 7.8 Table Sharing — Assignment

Table sharing is canceled if one of the internal tables involved in the sharing is modified. Only then does the actual copy process take place. Figure 7.9 shows the situation after the table sharing was canceled.

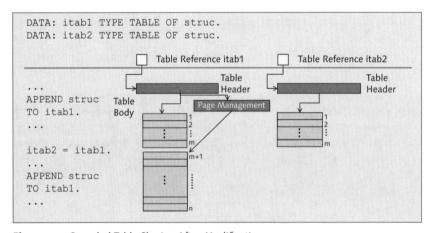

Figure 7.9 Canceled Table Sharing After Modification

The copy process after the cancellation of the table sharing (also referred to as *copy on write* or *lazy copy*) can result in situations that look "strange" at first:

For example, it can be possible that not sufficient memory is available if an entry of an internal table should be deleted because the table sharing can only be canceled in case of change accesses to one of the tables involved. Only then does the actual copy process take place. If sufficient memory is not available for the copy, then the short dump will inform you that not sufficient memory was available for executing the current operation (DELETE).

Another example is that a fast operation, such as an APPEND statement, can become eye-catching in the runtime measurement, because it has a considerably higher time than comparable operations. This may be due to the cancellation of the table sharing.

In principle, each changing access to an internal table can possibly cancel a previously existing table sharing. However, these are not additional but only deferred costs.

Change accesses to internal tables include the statements, APPEND, INSERT, MODIFY, DELETE but also assignments to fields or rows of tables implemented via data references or field symbols. A DETACH for shared objects also results in cancellation of table sharing. Likewise, the transfer of a table per value as a parameter of a method/function/form can cancel the sharing if the parameter is changed.

Table sharing is also displayed in the Debugger or in the Memory Inspector. In Figure 7.10 below the memory objects, the respective table headers point to the memory object. In this example, the internal tables, ITAB2A and ITAB1, are shared.

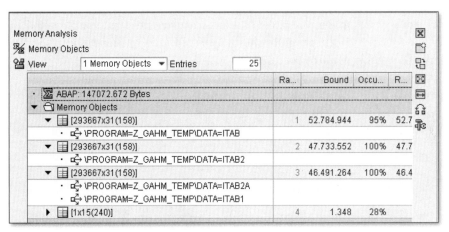

Figure 7.10 Table Sharing in the Debugger

In the Memory Inspector (see Figure 7.11), you can already view the name of the respective internal table next to the table bodies. Table bodies without a name (for example, the second table body in Figure 7.11) indicate shared tables. In this case, too, these are the internal tables, ITAB2A and ITAB1.

281

Memory Object	Seq.	Value 1	Value 2	Value 3	Value 4
▼ 🗂 Roll Area		ABAP_TOTAL	MM_TOTAL delta	MM_TOTAL (GC)	
•		147.073.084	147.796.728	0	
•		Number of Programs	Number of Classes	Number of Instances	Number of Tables
•		29	3	0	5
▶ 🗀 29 Programs		Global Data	Number of Instances	Number of Tables	Number of Strings
▶ 🗀 3 Classes (ABAP Objects)		Number of Instances	Bound (Allocated)	Bound (Used)	Referenced (Alloc.)
▼ 🗂 4 Table Bodies		Lines (Allocated)	Lines (Used)	Usage - Lines (%)	Bound (Allocated)
• Σ Total		881.019	881.002		147.011.108
▼ 🧮 [293667x158] : ITAB	1	293.680	293.667	100	52.784.944
• ᵛ₊ \PROGRAM=Z_GAHM_TEMP\DATA=ITAB	1				
▼ 🧮 [293667x158]	2	293.667	293.667	100	46.491.264
• ᵛ₊ \PROGRAM=Z_GAHM_TEMP\DATA=ITAB2A	1				
• ᵛ₊ \PROGRAM=Z_GAHM_TEMP\DATA=ITAB1	2				
▼ 🧮 [293667x158] : ITAB2	3	293.667	293.667	100	47.733.552
• ᵛ₊ \PROGRAM=Z_GAHM_TEMP\DATA=ITAB2	1				
▶ 🧮 [1x240] : SCREEN_PROGS❘	4	5	1	20	1.348
▶ 🗀 1 Strings		Bound (Allocated)	Bound (Used)	RefCount	

Figure 7.11 Table Sharing in the Memory Inspector

7.4.10 Nested Loops and Nonlinear Runtime Behavior

Inefficient accesses to internal tables have a particular impact in case of large datasets. The following little example shows a nested loop in which the respective orders of the customer are processed:

```
LOOP AT it_customers REFERENCE INTO dref_customer.
  LOOP AT it_orders REFERENCE INTO dref_order
  WHERE cnr = dref_customer->nr.
...
  ENDLOOP.
ENDLOOP.
```

Let's assume that the internal table, it_customers, has 1,000 entries. An average of two orders exists for each customer; consequently, the internal table, it_orders, has 2,000 entries. If these are standard tables, respectively, the two internal tables must be fully processed: the external table, it_customers, because no restriction exists and because all data records should be processed semantically; the internal table, it_orders, is restricted, but the corresponding entries for each customer cannot be searched efficiently. Therefore, the entire table, it_orders, must be browsed for the internal table. This is done for each entry of the external table, that is, 1,000 times in this example.

Let's assume that the external loop requires approximately 200 μs and the internal loop a total of 140,000 μs. If you now double the datasets, the runtime of *each* loop doubles as well because the two loops scale linearly with the number of entries. So, in case of 2,000 entries in the external table, it_customers, this results in ~400 μs and for 4,000 entries in the internal table, it_orders, in ~560.000 μs for all 2,000 runs. The internal table must be run through for each entry of the external table, but the system doesn't need to process all entries of the internal table for each external entry but only the two entries that belong to a customer.

As a result, the runtime is four times longer in case of a double dataset. The runtime behavior is not linear but quadratic. (The internal loop is twice as long as previously — scaled with n — and is executed twice as often as previously.)

In this case, the reason is an inefficient access to the inner internal table. To avoid this, you must optimize the access to the inner internal table. For a linear runtime behavior, the access to the inner internal table has to be constant, so the runtime doubles if the access frequency doubles. Because no unique key is possible in the previous example, you can achieve a logarithmic runtime behavior for the inner access using a sorted table. The sorted table allows for a binary search in the inner internal table and consequently ensures an efficient finding of the two suitable entries in the inner internal table for each entry of the outer table. The result of the entire code fragment is O(n x log n).

At this point, a brief comparison to the nested loop join for databases (see Section 5.4.5 in Chapter 5): Like for the nested loop joins on databases, the number and the efficiency of the access to the internal table are significant for the optimization of nested loops.

Nonlinear runtime behavior is not always due to inefficient accesses to internal tables but can also result from a quadratic increase of the call frequency of an efficient access to an internal table, for example.

In general, the effects of nonlinear programming can be reduced by using smaller data packages. However, the packages should not be too small to not generate a too large overhead at other points (see Section 4.1.3 in Chapter 4).

Because in most cases only a small test dataset is available for the development of programs in the development system, it may occur that a nonlinear runtime behavior can only be discovered with difficulty because nested loops with small datasets only account for a smaller portion of the entire program runtime. For small test datasets, it often appears as if the program behaves linearly to the number of processed datasets.

To detect a nonlinear runtime behavior already during the development with small datasets, you must compare the runtime behavior at ABAP statement level. Here, the times for the accesses to internal tables with two variants — for example, with ten or with 100 data records to be processed — is measured and compared with one another using Transactions SE30 or ST12. This way, you can detect a nonlinear runtime behavior already with small datasets.

In Release 7.0 EhP1, there is no tool available that you can use to automatically implement this comparison. However, the following links of the SDN provide tools and descriptions of how you can automate such a comparison:

▶ Nonlinearity: The problem and background
  https://www.sdn.sap.com/irj/sdn/weblogs?blog=/pub/wlg/5804

▶ A Tool to Compare Runtime Measurements: Z_SE30_COMPARE:
  https://www.sdn.sap.com/irj/sdn/weblogs?blog=/pub/wlg/8277

▶ Report Z_SE30_COMPARE:
  https://www.sdn.sap.com/irj/sdn/wiki?path=/display/Snippets/
  Report%2bZ_SE30_COMPARE

▶ Nonlinearity Check Using the Z_SE30_COMPARE:
  https://www.sdn.sap.com/irj/sdn/weblogs?blog=/pub/wlg/8367

In Release 7.00 EhP2, you can implement the comparison of trace files using the standard SAP means (see Chapter 10).

7.4.11 Summary

When you work with internal tables, the selection of the right table type and the access type is important.

Standard tables should only be used for small tables or tables that can be processed using the index accesses. For larger standard tables, ensure an efficient processing with the binary search if you want to process some parts of the table only. It can be used both for single record accesses and for mass accesses. If possible, the standard tables should be sorted in the same way or only sorted as often as absolutely necessary. For accesses to different key fields using the binary search, which requires a resorting, you must check whether the effort for sorting is justified (is amortized by the improved read accesses).

Sorted tables can be used uniquely or non-uniquely for most application cases. They are particularly useful for partially sequential processing in which the initial part of the table key is used, for example.

Hashed tables should only be used where the unique key access is the only type of access, particularly if you must process very large tables.

In general, internal tables should be filled using array operations if possible to avoid the overhead of single record accesses.

Wherever reasonable, reduce the copy costs for providing the results using `TRANS-PORTING fieldlist/NO FIELDS` or completely avoid it by means of `ASSIGNING` or `REFERENCE INTO`. This is particularly essential for nested tables.

If possible, internal tables should not be too large to save the memory space of the SAP system.

The Remote Function Call (RFC) programming plays a significant role for data transfers to other systems. This chapter describes the most important performance aspects of RFC programming.

8   Communication with Other Systems

This chapter discusses the performance aspects of the communication with other systems (SAP or non-SAP systems). Here, you must differentiate direct and indirect communication. *Direct communication* means the communication of two systems via a direct call. *Indirect communication* is the communication using SAP NetWeaver Process Integration (PI), formerly Exchange Infrastructure (XI), for which the calls are carried out via a "communication partner." The advantage of indirect communication is higher flexibility. The "detour" via the communication partner can be a disadvantage regarding performance, however. This chapter describes the direct communication. Process integration is a separate topic that goes beyond the scope of the ABAP topic and is therefore not discussed within this book.

Different protocols are given for direct communication. Table 8.1 shows three typical protocols that can be used in an SAP system.

Protocol	Implemented via
RFC	Client: CALL FUNCTION func DESTINATION dest Server: func, remote-enabled function module
HTTP	Client: CL_HTTP_HANDLER, for example Server: IF_HTTP_EXTENSION~HANDLE_REQUEST
SMTP	Client: SAPconnect APIs (CL_SMTP_CLIENT) Server: SAPconnect APIs (IF_SMTP_EXTENSION~HANDLE_REQUEST)

Table 8.1 Communication Protocols and Their Implementations

In addition, there are further protocols that don't play any role in this chapter.

The mentioned protocols contain rules and guidelines that must be observed by different processes that want to communicate with one another via a protocol.

The following description details the communication between ABAP systems with RFC because this protocol is the traditional protocol for the communication with other systems for ABAP developers.

8.1 RFC Communication Between ABAP Systems

For the RFC communication, you always require a remote-enabled function module in the target system and the following call in the source system:

```
CALL FUNCTION func DESTINATION dest
```

You must differentiate between synchronous and asynchronous RFC calls.

8.1.1 Synchronous RFC

For the synchronous RFC, the RFC client (sender) waits for the execution of the function in the RFC server (receiver). A close coupling exists between the sender and the receiver. If the receiver is not available, the sender must have implemented a suitable error handling to handle this situation. In this regard, synchronous read accesses to other systems ensure the easiest handling because they can simply be repeated. For synchronous write accesses, you must first determine whether the error occurred before or after the execution of the function in the server before this error can be handled accordingly in the sender. Therefore, the reliable asynchronous RFC is more useful for write accesses (see next section). The advantage of the synchronous RFC is that it doesn't generate any additional load (for example, through persistence) on the client and the server.

8.1.2 Asynchronous RFC

For asynchronous RFC, you must differentiate between asynchronous RFC without data persistence and asynchronous RFC with data persistence.

Asynchronous RFC Without Data Persistence

The asynchronous RFC without data persistence is used mostly for parallel processing (see Section 4.2 in Chapter 4). With regard to the error handling and the availability of the RFC server, it corresponds to the synchronous RFC. The only difference is that the remote function is executed asynchronously and that the RFC client can continue processing in parallel directly after the call. There is no data persistence, and the asynchronous RFC can implement a CALLBACK in the RFC client after the execution in the RFC server is complete. This type is not further discussed here. However, the general recommendations also apply to this type.

Asynchronous RFC with Data Persistence

This is the transactional RFC (tRFC) or queued RFC (qRFC). Here, all calls for an RFC server are grouped, so an "all-or-nothing" execution of the functions is enabled.

For the reliable asynchronous RFC, the RFC client (sender) doesn't wait for the execution of the function in the RFC server but only until the data is persisted in the local system. The transfer and error handling in case of communication problems are implemented by the basis layer. If the RFC server is temporarily not available, the transfer is carried out at a later point in time. Hence, the systems are loosely coupled.

It is ensured that the data is transferred completely and exactly once (EO) to the RFC server. The qRFC additionally allows for a transfer of the data in the call order (EOIO = *exactly once in order*), which is not possible with the tRFC.

The decoupling and reliability is ensured with the persistence in the RFC client system. An additional overhead for the management of these RFCs is also necessary in the RFC server. A reliable asynchronous RFC enables the independence of the availability and response time of the RFC server but generates additional load on both systems.

> **Note**
>
> In Release 7.0 as of SP14, you are also provided with the background RFC (bgRFC [type T] as the transactional RFC and bgRFC [type Q] as the queued RFC). The bgRFC is a further development of the tRFC and the qRFC.

The schematic diagram in Figure 8.1 illustrates the differences between the synchronous and the asynchronous reliable RFC.

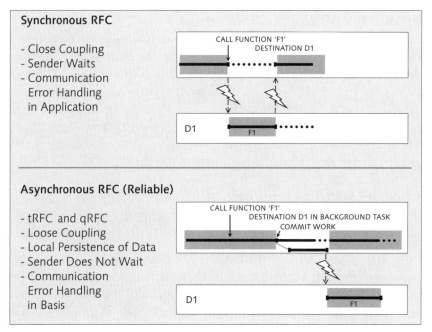

Figure 8.1 Schematic Diagram of Synchronous and Asynchronous RFCs

8.2 Performance Aspects for the RFC Communication

Usually, the requirements should decide which type of RFC should be used.

The synchronous RFC is usually used when you require a close coupling between the client and the server or if the result of an RFC is required immediately. The asynchronous RFC is used if you don't require a close coupling or if the RFC can be executed with a time delay. In case of an asynchronous RFC, the client can usually be reused more quickly for further requests.

In addition to the decision regarding which type of RFC is used, there are further aspects to consider regardless of this.

Each RFC entails an overhead, for example, for establishing the connection and the transfer time, which you must add to the actual runtime of the function. Figure 8.2 illustrates the course of a synchronous RFC call.

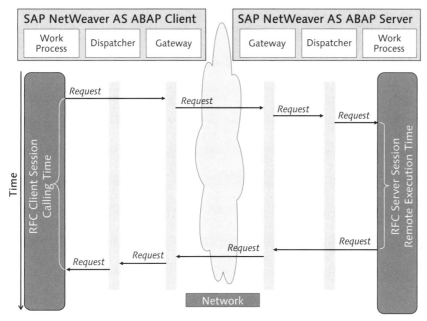

Figure 8.2 Course of a Synchronous RFC Call

The overall time for the RFC consists of the runtime for the function on the server (remote execution time) and the communication time (difference of the calling time and the remote execution time; see Section 3.3.15 in Chapter 3).

The communication time includes fixed and variable portions.

The fixed portions are independent of the data volume to be transferred and consequently constant. The time required depends on the latency time of the network connection (LAN, WAN, and so on) and the CPU speed of the computers involved. The fixed portions include:

1. Round-trip time

2. Logon to the system (for the first call)

3. Initialization of a new session on the server

The variable portions depend on the type and data volume to be transferred, the time required by the bandwidth of the network connection, and the CPU speed of the computers involved.

The variable portions include:

1. Data transfer time

2. Copy costs of data (no call by reference possible)

3. Encoding and/or compression

4. Serialization and deserialization of data

You as the developer cannot influence most of the components of the communication time (CPU speed, type of network, and so on). However, in some cases you can influence the *volume of transferred data* and in most cases the *number of data transfers*.

Volume of Transferred Data

Just as in the case of database accesses in which only the required data should be read, it also applies to RFC calls that only the data that is actually required should be transferred. However, the data volume to be transferred is frequently predefined by the requirements. An option to reduce the data volume is to read data that is also available on the RFC server directly instead of transferring it.

Number of Data Transfers

The number of data transfers involves the packaging. Instead of sending a single "object" in a call, collect multiple objects and send them in a package.

Of course, this means that the called function on the RFC server must be able to process such a package. If the function on the server was implemented using such an array ability, this results in further benefits in addition to the reduction of the communication costs. For example, the array functions can be used against the database and for internal tables (see Sections 5.7 in Chapter 5 and 7.4.1 in Chapter 7). The packages should not be too large as already mentioned for working with arrays against the database. Otherwise, this would result in timeouts on the RFC server because the RFC is executed in a dialog process. At this point, error handling for package processing can be more tedious than for single record processing.

A brief example should illustrate the effect of the execution frequency. Let's assume you have a function that reads the customer data for a customer number.

For one single customer number, the system requires approximately 20 ms (milliseconds). This function is called remotely. If this is done in a local area network (LAN), about 10 ms must be added additionally. So the communication overhead is 50%. If you read 1,000 of such customer numbers individually, you obtain a response time of approximately 30 seconds (10 seconds for the communication overhead and 20 seconds for the remote execution time).

If you carry out this scenario in a network in which the remote system is only accessible via a wide area network (WAN) and a satellite connection, for example, the communication time is considerably higher — for example, about 1,000 ms. For 1,000 individual calls, this results in about 1,000 seconds of communication time and 20 seconds of remote execution time.

In case of a package transfer, for example, if you send ten packages with 100 customers each, in the local area network this results in 100 ms of communication time (plus additional effort for the data transfer) and 20 seconds for the remote execution time.

For a network via a satellite connection, this results in ten seconds for the communication time (plus additional effort for the data transfer) and 20 seconds for the remote execution time.

The examples provided here don't take the additional effort for larger data volumes and the possible reduction of the remote execution time in case of array processing into account. However, it becomes clear that the communication time accounts for a large portion of the overall response time for short runtimes on the RFC server.

The larger the portion of the communication time in the execution time for a call and the more calls are required within a short period of time, the larger the portion of the communication time is in the overall response time. This particularly applies to network connections that have a high latency time anyway (WAN, satellite connection, and so on). In such scenarios, the reduction of the calls is one of the most critical aspects that must be considered.

Therefore, the packaging is important not only for the remote execution of an application (see Sections 5.7 in Chapter 5 and 4.1.3 in Chapter 4) but also for the communication time because you can reduce the number of round trips this way. This reduction saves processing time for the synchronous and asynchronous RFC.

8.3   Summary

For the communication with other systems, the selection of the protocol and the RFC type in case of RFCs plays an important role for the performance. However, they are frequently predefined by the application case.

The transferred data volume and the number of calls for the data transfers (round trips) have a major influence on the performance. For this reason, check the transferred data volume and the number of round trips with regard to optimization potential.

This chapter summarizes further, very specific yet important topics with regard to ABAP performance.

9 Special Topics

This chapter discusses special topics, such as the local updates, and further aspects that are critical for the ABAP performance.

9.1 Local Update

The *local update* is an option to optimize the management overhead of the traditional update in mass data processing. Let's first discuss the essential points of the asynchronous update from the performance perspective once again and then the local update.

9.1.1 Asynchronous Update

In the asynchronous update, the names and parameters of the called update modules are written to special database tables, the *update tables* (VBDATA, VBLOG, and so on). When a COMMIT WORK is triggered, the dialog part of the update ends. Consequently, the work process is released again for further requests, that is, the dialog user can directly continue working. The COMMIT WORK starts an update process. The SAP locks set during the processing are inherited to the update process if the corresponding _SCOPE parameter was specified. The update process reads the data (parameters, ...) from the update tables and then executes the update function modules using the corresponding parameters. In this process, the data is written to the application tables. At COMMIT WORK in the update process, the inherited SAP locks are released again.

> **Note: Synchronous Update**
>
> For the synchronous update, a `COMMIT WORK AND WAIT` is triggered instead of `COMMIT WORK`. In this case, the dialog process waits until the update was completed in the update process. Only then can one continue with the dialog process. This scenario is usually used if the result of the update must be evaluated before you can continue with your work.

The asynchronous update is usually used in dialog applications, which require a fast response time. The benefit that the user can directly continue work after the data has been entered and that the data is updated asynchronously involves an increased database load for storing the update modules and their parameters temporarily. The simplified illustration in Figure 9.1 shows the steps of the asynchronous update.

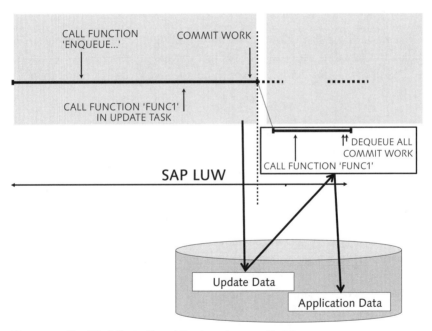

Figure 9.1 Simplified Illustration of the Asynchronous Update

Because the decoupling of the update involves a higher resource consumption on the database side, it is desirable for the mass data processing, which uses the update functionality, to avoid the higher resource consumption. The local update can be used for this purpose.

9.1.2   Local Update

In the local update, the names and parameters of the update modules are not written to the database but to the ABAP memory (EXPORT TO MEMORY ...). At COM-MIT WORK, the update is implemented by the same process, and the data is read from the ABAP memory (IMPORT FROM MEMORY) and then written to the application tables. The management of the SAP locks remains the same as for the synchronous or asynchronous update. Figure 9.2 shows a simplified illustration of the local update.

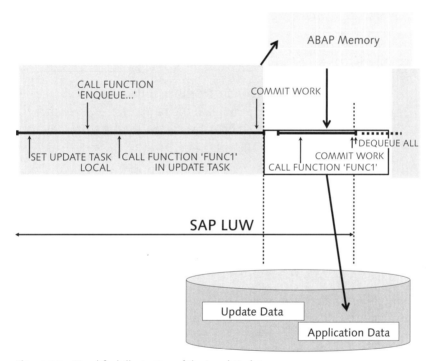

Figure 9.2 Simplified Illustration of the Local Update

By writing the update data to the ABAP memory instead of to the database, you can save database accesses and decrease the load on the central resource database.

> **Caution: Local Update**
>
> If an error occurs during the processing using a local update — for example, a system crash — the update data in the ABAP memory is lost. For this reason, you can use the local update only for scenarios in which the update data can be recovered. For mass data processing, this is usually the case because the data to be processed is often available in database tables or files. Therefore, the local update is not an option for the online update with dialog users. In this case, you don't have any time benefit: In contrast to the asynchronous update, the local update results in longer response times for the dialog user because the data is processed completely before the user can continue working — just as in the synchronous update.
>
> Here as well, the local update may result in longer locks on number range objects than in the asynchronous update because in the asynchronous update the system triggers a database commit prior to the update part, which is not the case in the local update.

The local update is usually used in situations where mass data must be processed in parallel processes. This applies, for example, to data transfers. Experience has shown that you can increase the throughput by up to 20% by using the local update.

An alternative to the local update is the complete omission of the update functionality by writing the data directly to the application tables. However, this involves a high programming effort and a good knowledge of the application tables if no special data transfer programs are available.

9.2   Parameter Passings

If you use subroutines, function modules, and methods, you can select either pass by reference or pass by value for the parameter passing.

Exceptions are:

1. For TABLES parameters in subroutines and function modules, you always require a pass "by reference."
2. For RETURNING parameters of methods, any parameters of event handler methods, parameters for RFC modules, and update function modules, you always require a pass "by value."

In ABAP, the parameter pass "by value" is determined by the costs for copying, among others. The data transfer "by reference" only transfers the memory address of the data object. So it is generally recommended to transfer all data by reference wherever possible.

In general, transfer as few data as possible and implement the data transfers as often as necessary.

The consistent selection of the pass "by reference" for large datasets or a large number of data transfers enables you to save runtime.

9.3 Type Conversions

When you assign data objects, it may be possible that a type conversion is necessary if the data objects don't have the same data type. Dynamic assignments of data references or field symbols may additionally require a type determination for generic or non-typed assignments. The type conversion involves effort for the system, which you can avoid if you use suitable data types. You should use non-typed or generically typed field symbols or data references only if this is absolutely necessary. This applies to dynamic programming, for example, in which the data type is unknown during development. In all other cases, ensure the correct typing to avoid unnecessary type conversions.

> **Real-Life Example — Transaction SE30, Tips & Tricks**
>
> In the TIPS & TRICKS under TYPING, Transaction SE30 provides two examples whose runtime you can measure.

9.4 Index Tables

Secondary indexes are not provided for some important transaction data tables. Instead, in the system, you maintain proprietary index tables that enable an alternative, efficient access. To use them, you require some basic knowledge of the SAP data model.

Table 9.1 describes the existing index tables and their uses:

Note Number	Description
185530	Performance: Customer Developments in SD
191492	Performance: Customer Developments in MM/WM
187906	Performance: Customer Developments in PP and PM

Table 9.1 SAP Notes on Index Tables

Consider these notes when you develop applications that access these tables. Instead of creating secondary indexes on transaction data tables, select the alternative access path wherever possible.

9.5 Saving Frontend Resources

Two points should be noted with regard to frontend resources: the transferred data volume and the number of data transfers to the frontend, the *round trips*.

In principle, send as few data as possible to the frontend, because a limitation exists there with the CPU and the main memory, as discussed in Section 2.2.1 in Chapter 2. For large data volumes, the network connection to the frontend can also become a limiting factor. The data must be transferred, formatted, and displayed by these resources.

> **Example**
>
> Initially, display the header data of an object only. Ensure that detail data is read and transferred only on demand if the detail data is not necessarily required in the frontend. If a large set of data is requested, you must form packages and transfer the first <n> entries only, for example, only as many entries as fit on the screen. Then you can send further packages only upon request.

Equally important is the number of data transfers to the frontend (round trips), particularly in cases in which the frontend is not connected via a LAN but via a WAN. Here, the signal runtimes (latency times) can account for a considerable portion of the response time if many communication steps are executed toward the frontend.

> **Example**
>
> Don't execute the status display using the SAPGUI_PROGRESS_INDICATOR function module too often, for example, by percentage or for each record but at specific intervals, for instance, after 20%, 40%, 60%, and so on.

> **Tip**
>
> If you use the *Advanced List Viewer* (ALV) for your lists, an optimized data transfer is already implemented. That means that even if you transfer large datasets to the ALV, it only transfers data to the frontend that is currently visible on the screen. If you scroll, sort, and search, the system sends a request to the backend to execute the action.

Only transfer data to the frontend that the end user really requires. Ensure that detailed information can be obtained as needed if it is not directly required. Transfer data in packages to keep the round trips low.

9.6   Saving Enqueue and Message Service

The enqueue service manages the locks that are set by the ABAP programs.

To not overload the enqueue service of the central instance, you as the developer can use the *array interface*. Here, you don't send the lock requests individually but collect them in a container and then transfer them en bloc to the enqueue service. By means of the _COLLECT parameter, you can trigger the collection in a container, which is then transferred to the enqueue service using the FLUSH_ENQUEUE function module:

```
LOOP AT itab.
CALL FUNCTION 'ENQUEUE_OBJECT1'
EXPORTING var1 = itab-field1
_COLLECT = 'X'.
ENDLOOP.

CALL FUNCTION 'ENQUEUE_OBJECT2'
EXPORTING var2 = wa-field2
_COLLECT = 'X'.

CALL FUNCTION FLUSH_ENQUEUE.
```

The FLUSH_ENQUE function module can be used to implement locks according to the "all or nothing" principle. If only one lock request cannot be met in the container, the entire package fails. Be careful with locks that don't have logical interdependency. If you must request large containers with locks multiple times to obtain the locks, these failures affect the enqueue service, too.

> **Warning**
>
> In case of the X lock mode (extended exclusive lock), don't write the locks to the container if many locks refer to the same lock table as the probability of lock collisions is high. In comparison to direct sending of locks, this results in considerable performance losses.

With this procedure, you save communication steps and requests to the enqueue service. Particularly if your programs don't run on the central instance, but on an application server, this saves valuable communication steps and decreases the load on the message service and the dispatcher via which the lock requests are sent from and to the application servers. In contrast, the processes on the central instance can communicate directly with the enqueue service using the shared memory communication.

In case of central services (for which the enqueue service runs on a separate instance), the previously mentioned points also apply with regard to the communication because the communication effort accrues with the SCS instance.

Figure 9.3 illustrates schematically the lock requests of the application server and the central instance.

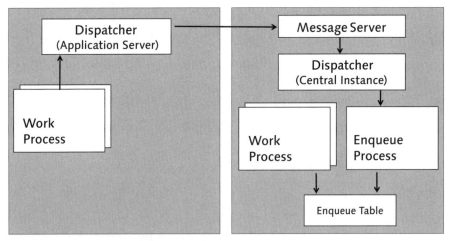

Figure 9.3 Lock Requests of the Application Server and the Central Instance

For some of the topics discussed within the scope of this book, SAP NetWeaver Release 7.0 EhP2 provides innovations presented in this chapter.

10 Outlook

With SAP Business Suite 2009 (SAP NetWeaver Release 7.0 EhP2), there will be some significant changes to the topics discussed within the scope of this book. This chapter outlines them. The changes refer to the tools, performance trace (Transaction ST05) and ABAP trace, and to the internal tables. The topics presented here were not officially available at the time of press and may be subject to change for this reason.

10.1 Important Changes to the Tools for the Performance Analysis

The major changes refer to the performance trace and the ABAP trace. The interfaces of the two tools appear completely different, but several changes were also implemented behind the interface.

10.1.1 Performance Trace (Transaction ST05)

The most obvious change in Transaction ST05 is the new user interface. You can view them already in the first selection screen (see Figure 10.1).

In the PERFORMANCE TRACE menu, you can find the ACTIVATE STACK TRACE or DEACTIVATE STACK TRACE option. The stack trace is an option that you can activate in addition to the traces. If you activate the stack trace, you can display the call stack in the trace for each call (regardless of whether it is an SQL trace, enqueue trace, RFC trace, or table buffer trace). Of course, this option requires more space in the trace and therefore is deactivated by default. It should only be activated if this analysis functionality is required. The evaluation of the stack trace is discussed later in this chapter. The HTTP trace is another new functionality, which is briefly discussed at the end of this section.

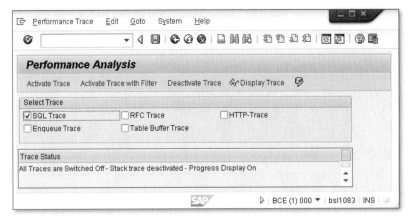

Figure 10.1 Transaction ST05 — Initial Screen

The display of a trace is now implemented via a selection screen as is common for reports. Figure 10.2 shows the selection screen.

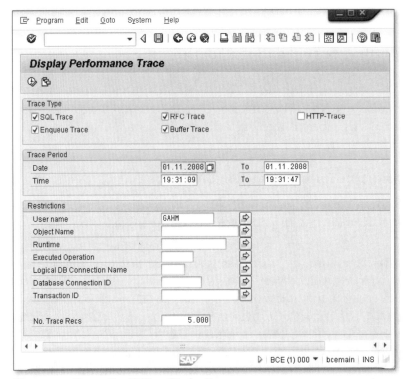

Figure 10.2 Transaction ST05 — Display Trace

> **Tip**
>
> As a traditional selection screen exists, you can store selections for traces as variants. This facilitates the work within a team because not all the details (user, start time, end time, server, and so on) must be communicated but only the name of the variant. To ensure that the server can be stored within the variant, you must store an existing RFC connection to this server. You can display the input field for the RFC connection in the selection screen using the EXPM OK code.

The trace list (see Figure 10.3) is now displayed in the ALV. The block record display with a separate row for fields of the block record is no longer available. Instead, the fields of the block record are part of each trace record so that you can still search and sort according to values of the block record. The display in the ALV provides some benefits. For example, you can create layouts for the lists and store them user-specifically. This way, you can show or hide fields depending on your requirements. Another benefit is that the sorting, filtering, summary, and so on can be used for all supported fields of the list.

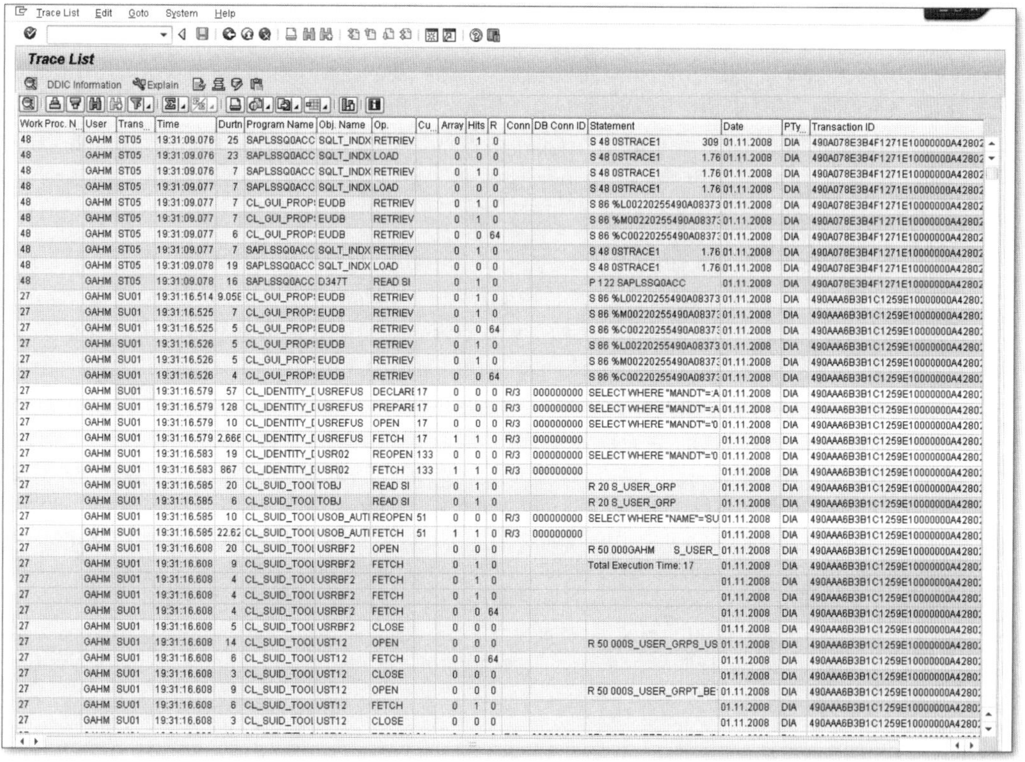

Figure 10.3 Transaction ST05 — Trace List

The trace summary is also displayed in the ALV and contains the new field, REDUNDANCY, in which the system displays the absolute number of superfluous accesses. In case of three identical accesses, the REDUNDANCY column displays two superfluous accesses. The IDENTICAL field still contains the percentage value.

All other lists of Transaction ST05 are also displayed in the ALV but don't have any new functions.

Let's now discuss the two useful functions in the basic list: the evaluation of the stack trace and the evaluation of the SQL trace in the SAP Code Inspector.

Stack Trace

The activated stack trace lets you trace the call of the respective trace record via the ABAP call stack.

Based on the basic list, you can use the 🗄 icon (stack trace) to have the system display an ABAP call stack for each call. From this list, you can navigate to the respective call in the call stack by double-clicking the row.

This is very useful for identical accesses from function modules, for example. This way, you can trace who has called the function module. Previously, this analysis was only possible in Transaction SE30 for non-aggregated traces or via Transaction ST12 for aggregation per call position. If you know the calling program, for example, you can use the Debugger to check whether the function module is called multiple times with the same parameters. This enables you to find the appropriate level for a buffering, for example. Figure 10.4 shows a corresponding example.

The stack trace is also useful for enqueue trace entries. Previously, you could only view the generic enqueue call when you navigated to the source code for the enqueue trace entries; however, you could not determine who triggered it. By means of the call stack from the stack trace, you can now trace the calling program as it is shown in Figure 10.5.

> **Warning**
>
> If the trace is displayed in a filtered manner, it is possible that the stack trace doesn't work any longer. To keep the space required for the stack trace as low as possible, for each entry in the trace only the delta information is written, but not the complete stack. The complete stack is then created dynamically during the evaluation (click on the 🗄 button). This is only possible if all trace records that were recorded are displayed. If entries were filtered in the display, you are not provided with all the information for the dynamic creation of the stack trace.

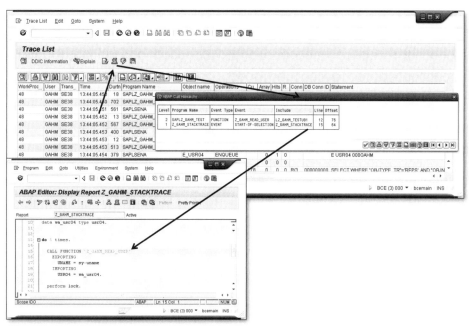

Figure 10.4 Transaction ST05 — Call Stack

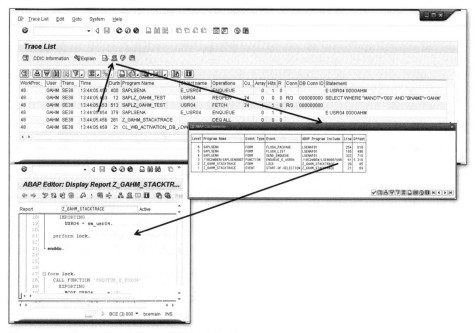

Figure 10.5 Transaction ST05 — Call Stack for Enqueue

SQL Trace in the SAP Code Inspector

Another function in the basic list is the check of the executed SQL statements using the SAP Code Inspector. In this scenario, the SAP Code Inspector checks dynamically executed coding. Within the SAP Code Inspector, all known functions are given, which were described in Section 3.3.1 in Chapter 3. This check is called from the basic list via the GOTO • TRACE ANALYSIS USING CODE INSPECTOR menu as shown in Figure 10.6.

HTTP Trace

In addition to the known traces, the new Transaction ST05 enables you to create an HTTP trace. Here, the system logs the inbound and outbound HTTP requests. The information in the trace is approximately the same as in the RFC trace; it includes the calling program and the called program, duration and the transferred dataset, as well as the relevant HTTP-specific information (URL, method, etc.).

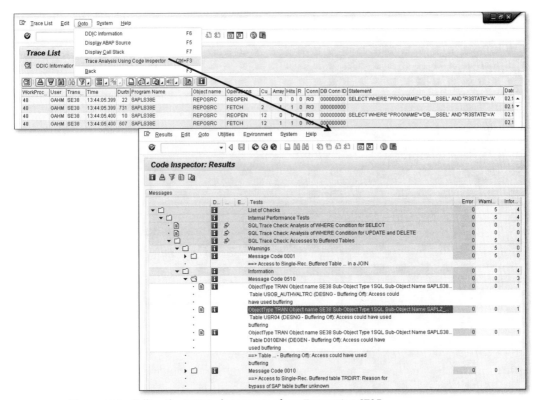

Figure 10.6 Calling the SAP Code Inspector from Transaction ST05

10.1.2 ABAP Trace (Transaction SAT)

The new release provides a new transaction (Transaction SAT) for the ABAP trace. The known ABAP trace can still be called using Transaction SE30.

In contrast to Transaction SE30, Transaction SAT persists extracts from the trace files in the database.

The trace recording using variants in the trace files is unchanged and corresponds to the procedure of Transaction SE30. Therefore, you can immediately find your way in the initial screen of Transaction SAT (see Figure 10.7). Optionally, you can import the created trace files to a trace container in the database at the end of the trace.

In the MEASUREMENT tab, you can define the measurement variants and record the measurements. Here, you can find the two new options, EVALUATE IMMEDIATELY and WITH NAMES OF INTERNAL TABLES. The former navigates to the analysis immediately after the measurement and deletes the trace file after the conversion of the data in the trace container. The latter option displays the names of the internal tables as they are used in the ABAP program (as is the case in Transaction ST12, for example).

Figure 10.7 shows the initial screen of Transaction SAT.

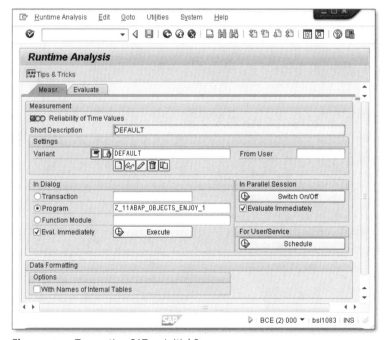

Figure 10.7 Transaction SAT — Initial Screen

In the EVALUATE tab, you manage the measurements (see Figure 10.8).

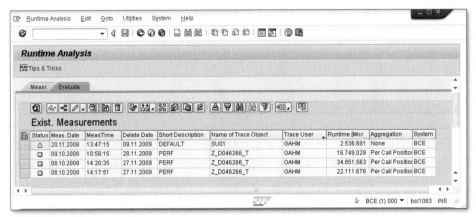

Figure 10.8 Transaction SAT — Managing Measurement Data

Some new functions are available here. They enable you to:

1. Delete traces

2. Send traces to other systems via RFC

3. Change the retention periods of traces in the database

4. Convert trace files (for example, from other systems) into the SAT-specific, system-independent format and store them

5. Display traces as UML sequence (only for non-aggregated traces)

6. Compare traces with each other

The last option is discussed later on in this section.

As soon as you start the evaluation (either automatically immediately after the measurement or by double-clicking a saved measurement), Transaction SAT presents itself with a new, modern user interface as you already know from the ABAP Debugger, for example.

Like in the Debugger, Transaction SAT also provides desktops in which you can display and arrange different tools. You can save this arrangement user-specifically like in the Debugger.

There are two default desktops (desktop 1: time consumption, desktop 2: program flow) and six different tools. The following tools are available:

1. Hit list
2. DB tables
3. Profile
4. Times
5. Processing blocks (only for non-aggregated traces)
6. Call hierarchy (only for non-aggregated traces)

If the trace was recorded per call position in an aggregated manner, only one desktop and four tools are displayed. Transaction SAT does not support fully aggregated traces. By default, the tools for time analysis are displayed in the first desktop and the tools for the program flow analysis in the second desktop.

The hit list, the call hierarchy, and the DB tables largely correspond to the views known from the old Transaction SE30, whereas Transaction SAT partly provides more information and functions. For example, the DB tables view displays the type and status of the table buffering and a short description of a database table, or you can directly navigate to the DDIC. In the call hierarchy, you can conveniently navigate to the calling or the called program or display the call stack for an entry, for example.

The processing blocks present the program flow grouped by the processing blocks (for example, dynpros and modularization units). Here, you are provided with a function for the automatic determination of critical processing blocks. This determination is carried out either according to a user-defined percentage limit for the runtime (gross or net) or via the memory use.

Profile and Time Tool

The profile tool generates a time profile that can display the time allocation grouped by the different levels. By default, the grouping is set by trace event. But you can also group by packages, components, programs, or software layers.

The time tool displays the times of the selected section. By default, the system displays all times, but you can also select a specific event (or another level, for example, a program) based on the profile tool; then you can view all times within this selection. Figure 10.9 shows the profile and the time tool.

All tools are linked with each other, so you can navigate from any tool to the position in another tool for a selected entry or have the system display the selected range in another tool. In doing so, the system displays a new window with the new tool, so the two tools are available in parallel.

In some tools, you can display additional columns, such as software package, person responsible, transport layer, and so on. Another function available is the restriction to subsections. This way, you can handle a subsection (for example, a modularization unit) as if it was the complete measurement. All other tools receive this subsection as the common basis as if only this section had been measured.

Filter Tool

Another important function is the filter tool for non-aggregated traces. This tool lets you suppress the display of details and to add the times of these filtered details to the calling program (that was not filtered out). This way, you can filter out the database accesses (or RFC calls) and not display them; the times of these database accesses (or RFC calls), however, are optionally added to their visible calling programs.

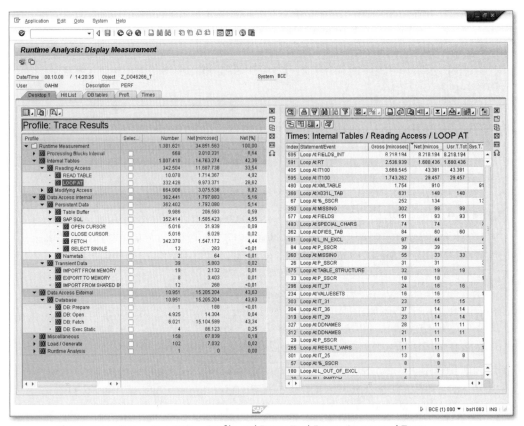

Figure 10.9 Transaction SAT — Profile and Times Tool For an Aggregated Trace

It is also possible to filter for specific programs or software layers to have the system display their program flow or time consumption only.

For aggregated traces, a function for suppressing the display of database times (second icon from the left in the toolbar of Figure 10.9) is given. This enables the analysis of the pure ABAP times. In the same toolbar, you can find the filter tool for non-aggregated traces.

Measurement Data Overview

In the measurement data overview, you can select two measurements and compare them (see Figure 10.10).

Such a comparison lets you quickly identify a nonlinear runtime behavior. In the figure, for example, the first entry (READ TABLE) in the second measurement doesn't depend linearly on the dataset. The processed data volume was increased ten-fold (see No. 2 and No. 1). In contrast, the last entry (READ TABLE) behaves linearly.

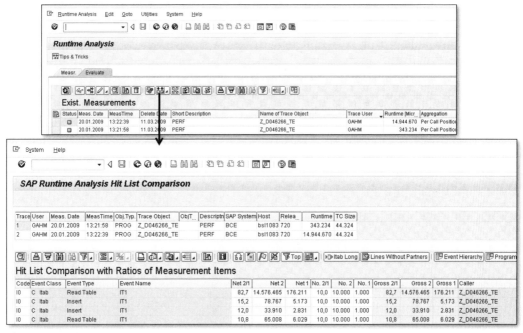

Figure 10.10 Comparing Runtime Measurements

10.2 Important Changes to Internal Tables (Secondary Key)

In the upcoming SAP NetWeaver Release 7.0 EhP2, you can define *secondary keys* on internal tables. Based on the secondary key, it is possible to access internal tables efficiently and directly via different fields.

Up to now, internal tables had to be re-sorted without secondary keys by the respective key or you had to manually create and manage internal tables (as secondary keys) for an efficient access.

Analogous to the database tables, multiple secondary keys (up to 15) are possible for an internal table. The major difference to the database tables with secondary keys is that *no* automatic selection of the suitable key is carried out at runtime based on an optimizer. Instead, you must always explicitly specify the key that is supposed to be used for the access. This facilitates the changeover for existing applications to secondary keys and prevents unpleasant surprises. However, within the scope of the syntax check, a warning exists if secondary keys are available, which seem to be better suited for access. This warning indicates which positions of the program could potentially be optimized and also contributes to the easier changeover. You can obtain further information from the long text of the warning, for example, how you can suppress this warning using *pragmas* if you want to use another key for the access.

10.2.1 Definition

Secondary keys are part of the table definition and are statically defined via a name, the access type (sorted or hashed), the uniqueness (unique or non-unique), and the key components of the key. PRIMARY_KEY and LOOP_KEY are reserved names for keys. The former mustn't be used for secondary keys; the latter mustn't be used in general.

The following provides some examples for the definition of table types with secondary keys in ABAP:

```
TYPES:
BEGIN OF t_struc,
  a TYPE i,
  b TYPE c LENGTH 3,
  c TYPE i,
  d TYPE string,
END OF t_struc,

* standard table with default key
t_itab TYPE TABLE OF t_struc
       WITH NON-UNIQUE DEFAULT KEY,
```

```
* hashed table with unique key b
* and sorted key a,c (name k1)
t_itab2 TYPE HASHED TABLE OF t_struc
        WITH UNIQUE KEY b
        WITH UNIQUE SORTED KEY k1 COMPONENTS a c,

* same as t_itab2 (new syntax for primary key)
t_itab3 TYPE HASHED TABLE OF t_struc
        WITH UNIQUE KEY primary_key COMPONENTS b
        WITH UNIQUE SORTED KEY k1 COMPONENTS a c.
```

If you define redundant secondary keys, this results in a warning in the syntax check.

Of course, you can also define the table types with secondary keys in the DDIC in the SECONDARY KEY tab.

10.2.2 Administration Costs and Lazy Index Update

Like secondary indexes on the database, secondary indexes on the internal tables require more space in the main memory.

The higher administration effort for change accesses to internal tables is postponed in case of non-unique indexes as far as this is possible. *Lazy index update* postpones the changes up to a point in time at which the change must actually be carried out, for example, if the internal table is accessed with this key. This feature can result in a lower memory use if the secondary index is not used. All unique keys on internal tables must be maintained directly due to semantic reasons to trigger the respective exception in case of duplicates. As described in Section 7.4, in case of duplicates in the primary key, a sy-subrc 4 is carried out for the single record processing; for block processing, it results in a runtime error that cannot be handled. For duplicates in the unique secondary index, a treatable exception (CX_SY_ITAB_DUPLICATE_KEY) is triggered in single record processing; for block processing, it also results in a runtime error that cannot be handled.

10.2.3 Read Accesses

When you access internal tables with secondary keys, you must explicitly specify the key you want to use.

Here are some examples of read accesses to internal tables:

```
READ TABLE it3 WITH KEY b = 1 INTO wa.
* use key k1 for access
READ TABLE it2 FROM wa USING KEY k1 ASSIGNING <fs>.
* use primary key for access
READ TABLE it INDEX 1 USING KEY primary_key ASSIGNING <fs>.
* use key k1 for access
READ TABLE it2 WITH KEY k1 COMPONENTS a = 2 INTO wa.
* use key k1 for access
READ TABLE it3 WITH KEY k1 COMPONENTS a = 2 c = 1 INTO wa.

* use key k1 for access
LOOP AT it2 USING KEY k1 ASSIGNING <fs>.
...
ENDLOOP.

* use key k1 for access
LOOP AT it3 USING KEY k1 ASSIGNING <fs>
WHERE a = 2 AND c =  1.
...
ENDLOOP.
```

Further examples of changing accesses are:

```
* use primary key for access
DELETE it INDEX 1 USING KEY primary_key.
DELETE TABLE it2 FROM wa USING KEY k1.
* use key k1 for access
DELETE it3 USING KEY k1 WHERE a = 2 AND c = 1.
* use key k1 for access
MODIFY TABLE it3 FROM wa USING KEY k1 TRANSPORTING d.
```

For accesses to secondary keys of the hashed type, you must always specify all components of the key; for the sorted type, you must always define an initial part of the key. This is verified by the syntax check. For dynamic WHERE conditions, which are also possible in this release, this cannot be checked statically, of course; a violation of these rules then results in a runtime error that cannot be caught.

Tip
Avoid DELETE statements with secondary keys to standard tables. The entry to be deleted can be found quickly in the secondary index; then, however, it must also be deleted in the primary key. The primary key must be scanned linearly for standard tables. Therefore, the runtime behavior of such a command is linear.

10.2.4 Active Key Protection

By means of the active key protection, the system doesn't allow for changes to the primary key and the active secondary keys. The table key(s) used for the access is/are considered as the active key.

The following rules apply for the changing access via field symbols or data references to internal tables:

1. The components of the primary keys of sorted or hashed tables are write-protected and cannot be changed.

2. In a loop carried out via a secondary key, the components of the active secondary key (which is used for the loop) are also write-protected.

3. In nested loops via the same table with different keys, the union of all active keys is write-protected.

4. All key fields that are not active can be changed.

10.2.5 Delayed Index Update for Incremental Key Changes

To not receive a duplicate error message for incremental changes with field symbols or data references to unique keys, changes are delayed. The change is carried out with the next access (loop, read) to this table or when the table is transferred as a parameter. The following example illustrates this:

Contents of the table:

...	B	D	...
...	16	5	...
...	17	5	...

ABAP code example:

```
DATA:
ref TYPE REF TO t_struc,
wa TYPE t_struc,
* hashed table with unique key b,d (name k)
it TYPE TABLE OF t_struc WITH UNIQUE HASHED KEY k
COMPONENTS b d.
* read table it using key k for access
READ TABLE it WITH KEY k COMPONENTS b = 16 d = 5
REFERENCE INOT ref.
```

```
* next statement
* would result in duprec dump if immediate update
* no index update
ref->b = 17.
* no index update
ref->d = 4.
* loop triggers secondary index flush -> key is updated
* index update
LOOP AT it INTO wa.
...
```

10.2.6 Summary

Secondary keys for internal tables were developed mostly for large internal tables, which are rarely changed after the creation. The performance benefits result from the read accesses to different key fields. These prevail if the additional administration costs remain low in such a scenario. Secondary keys should not be used for tables with less than 50 entries due to the administration overhead. Don't define secondary keys for internal tables for which the change processing predominates.

Unique secondary keys form an exception here to ensure the data integrity. Of course, this scenario also applies to small internal tables with less than 50 entries.

The execution plans basically depend on the database used. Due to the big differences in appearance, this chapter provides an example of the typical execution plans for each database.

A   Execution Plans of Different Databases

The following sections provide an example of the typical execution plans and access strategies for each database, as discussed in Section 5.4. This should make it easier for you to navigate within your platform after reading Chapter 5.

A.1   General Information on Execution Plans

Execution plans are given either as lists or in a tree structure. If they are mapped as lists, the system processes them from top to bottom. If they have a tree structure, the general processing sequence is as follows:

```
SELECT STATEMENT
  |
  ---       Result
    |
    ---        Join2
      |
      |--        Join1
      |  |
      |  |--        Table access Table1
      |  |  |
      |  |   ------    Index acess Table1
      |  |
      |  ---     Table access Table2
      |     |
      |      ------    Index acess Table2
      |
      ---      Table access Table3
        |
         ------    Index acess Table3
```

There is not always a numbering scheme that indicates in which sequence the steps should be processed. Sometimes, the numbering can be confusing because it differs from the processing sequence. This chapter briefly explains how you should read execution plans.

Usually, the system begins at the top with the first statement in the rightmost position. In our example, this is `Index access Table1`. From there, you go one step to the top to `Table access Table1`.

The results of `Table1` are then joined with `Table2` via `Join1` (again, one step to the top) where first `Index access Table2` and then, one step to the top, `Table access Table2` are implemented for `Table2`.

The resulting set from `Join1` and `Join2` is joined with `Table3` — again, first via `Index access Table3` and then via `Table access Table3`.

This leads to the result of the `SELECT STATEMENT`.

This example used a heap table with separate indexes. For index-organized tables, the index accesses are omitted if no secondary indexes were used (see also joins for MS SQL Server and SAP MaxDB in Figures A.20 and A.30).

The following sections provide the respective execution plans and additional notes.

A.2 IBM DB2 (IBM DB2 for zSeries)

The Sequential Tablespace Scan access corresponds to a full table scan (see Figure A.1).

The Index (Matching Index) with 1 matching columns of 3 index columns access corresponds to an index range scan that only uses the first index column (see Figure A.2). It is not clear which additional columns are used as a filter.

The Index (Matching Index) with 4 matching columns of 4 index columns access corresponds to an index unique scan (see Figure A.3). All columns of the unique index are used.

The Index (Non Matching Index) access corresponds to the index full scan (see Figure A.4). The entire index is read.

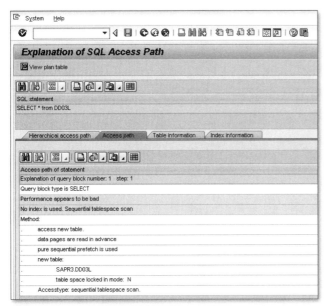

Figure A.1 Full Table Scan

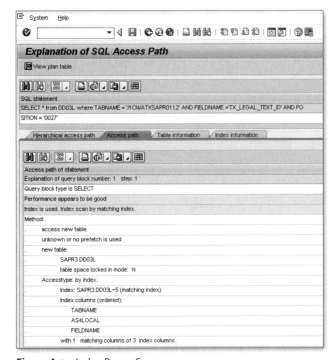

Figure A.2 Index Range Scan

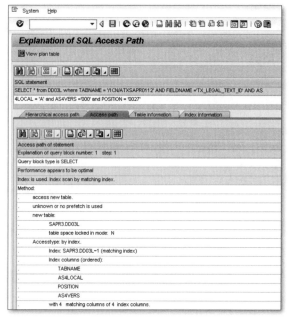

Figure A.3 Index Unique Scan

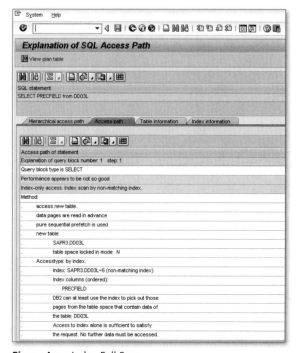

Figure A.4 Index Full Scan

A join consists of several successive steps (STEP1, STEP2, and so on) of which each contains an access as described previously (see Figure A.5).

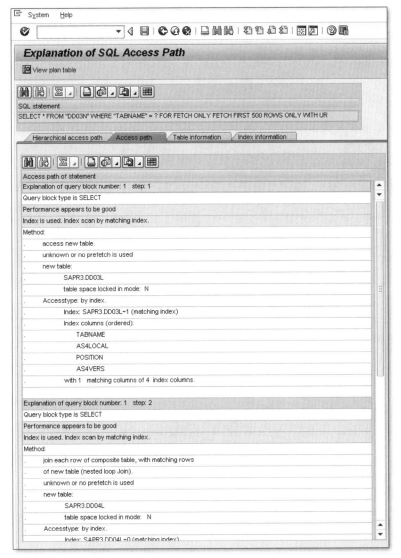

Figure A.5 Join

A.3 IBM DB2 (DB2 for iSeries)

The TABLE SCAN ON... access corresponds to a full table scan (see Figure A.6).

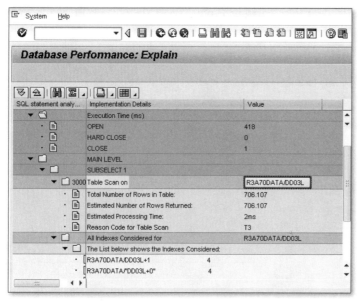

Figure A.6 Full Table Scan

The INDEX ... WAS USED BY QUERY ON access with the INDEX SCAN – KEY POSITIONING USING 2 KEY COLUMN(S) supplement corresponds to an index range scan that uses two columns (see Figure A.7). It is not visible which columns are used or which columns are used as filters.

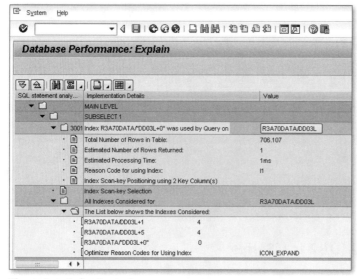

Figure A.7 Index Range Scan

The INDEX ... WAS USED BY QUERY ON access with the INDEX SCAN – KEY POSITION-ING USING 5 KEY COLUMN(S) supplement corresponds to the index unique scan (see Figure A.8). All of the five columns of the unique index are used.

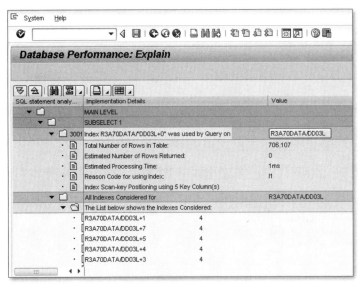

Figure A.8 Index Unique Scan

The INDEX ... WAS USED BY QUERY ON access corresponds to the index full scan (see Figure A.9). The entire index is read.

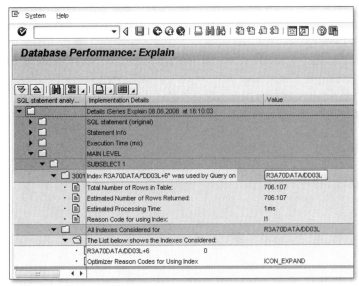

Figure A.9 Index Full Scan

A join consists of several successive steps (POSITION 1, POSITION 2, ...) of which each contains an access as described previously (see Figure A.10).

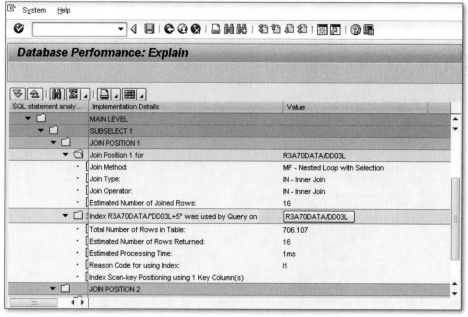

Figure A.10 Join

A.4 IBM DB2 (DB2 for LUW)

The TBSCAN access corresponds to a full table scan (see Figure A.11).

The IXSCAN #KEY COLUMNS 2 access corresponds to an index range scan with two columns. If you position the mouse pointer on the IXSCAN row and click the DETAILS button (in the top left corner of Figure A.12), a dialog box opens that displays in the predicates area which column is used for what. Here, USED AS START CONDITION or USED AS STOP CONDITION corresponds to a restricting condition that restricts the number of leaf pages that should be read. A sargable predicate (sargable = Search ARGument Able), in contrast, is a filter, that is, these restrictions are used as a filter after the reading process.

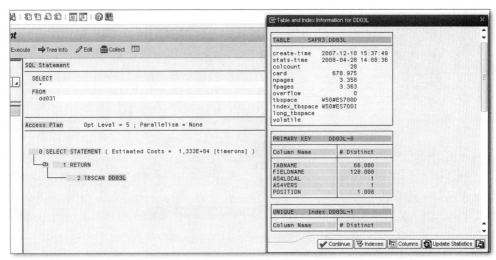

Figure A.11   Full Table Scan

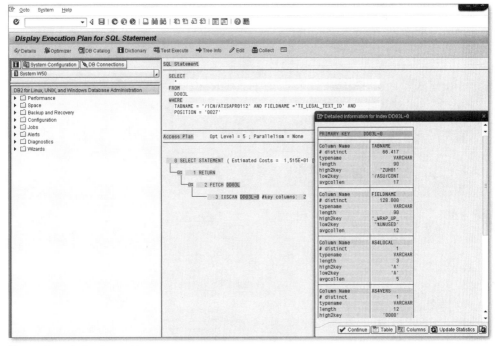

Figure A.12   Index Range Scan

The IXSCAN #KEY COLUMNS 4 access corresponds to an index unique scan with all four columns (see Figure A.13).

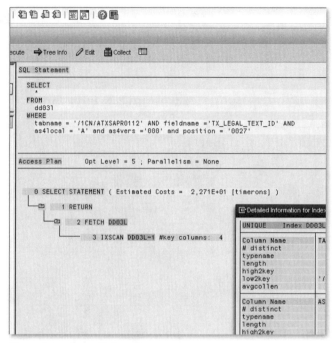

Figure A.13 Index Unique Scan

The IXSCAN #KEY COLUMNS 0 access corresponds to an index full scan (see Figure A.14). The entire index is read.

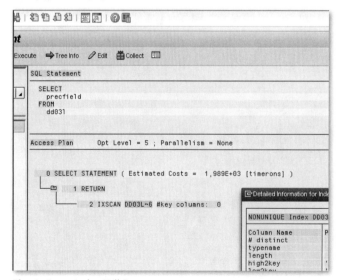

Figure A.14 Index Full Scan

A join is mapped as a tree whose nodes and leaves contain a join category (NLJOIN) and an access as described previously (see Figure A.15).

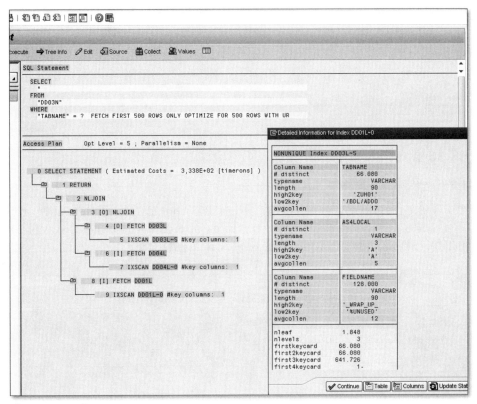

Figure A.15 Join

A.5 SAP MaxDB

The TABLE SCAN access corresponds to a full table scan (see Figure A.16). An access that only has the CLIENT or MANDT field in the WHERE condition usually corresponds to a full table scan (provided that there aren't multiple clients in the system), although SAP MaxDB will most likely execute an index range scan (see next access) for the first column of the primary key.

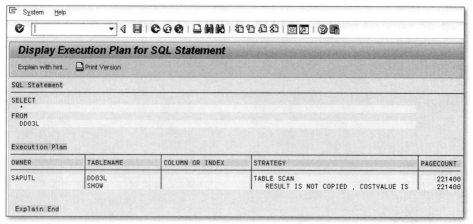

Figure A.16   Full Table Scan

The RANGE CONDITION FOR KEY access corresponds to an index range scan that only uses two index columns in this case (see Figure A.17). The COLUMN OR INDEX column indicates which index fields are used for the range scan.

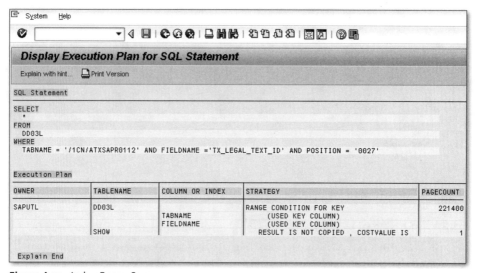

Figure A.17   Index Range Scan

The EQUAL CONDITION FOR KEY access corresponds to an index unique scan with all five columns (see Figure A.18).

The INDEX SCAN – ONLY INDEX ACCESSED access corresponds to an index full scan (see Figure A.19).

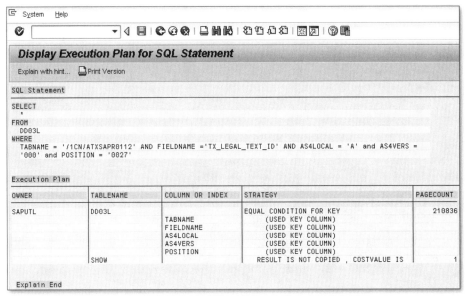

Figure A.18 Index Unique Scan

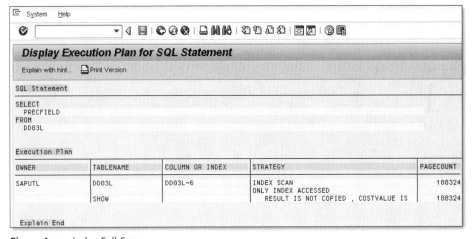

Figure A.19 Index Full Scan

A join is mapped as a list with join category and access type (JOIN VIA KEY RANGE). The access types correspond to the access types discussed previously (see Figure A.20).

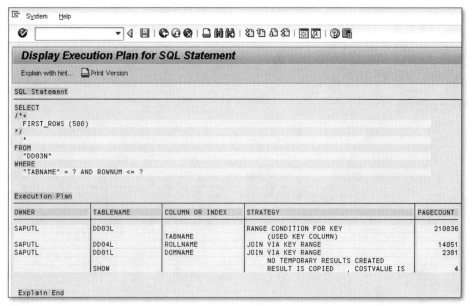

Figure A.20 Join

A.6 Oracle

The TABLE ACCESS FULL access corresponds to a full table scan (see Figure A.21).

The INDEX RANGE SCAN SEARCH COLUMNS 3 access corresponds to an index range scan with three columns (see Figure A.22). If you click on the ACCESS PREDICATES or FILTER PREDICATES fields highlighted in dark blue, the system displays which columns are used to restrict the range scan or which fields can be used as filters (not shown here).

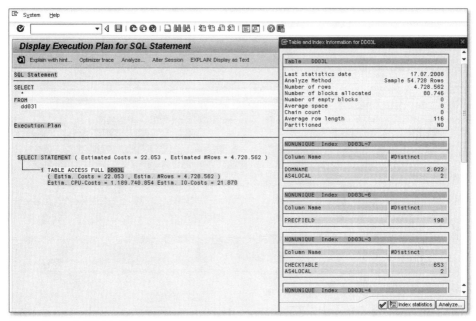

Figure A.21 Full Table Scan

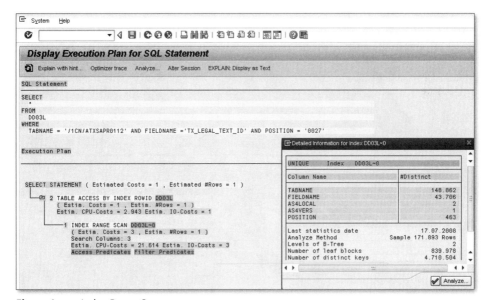

Figure A.22 Index Range Scan

The INDEX UNIQUE SCAN Search Columns 5 access corresponds to an index unique scan with five columns (see Figure A.23).

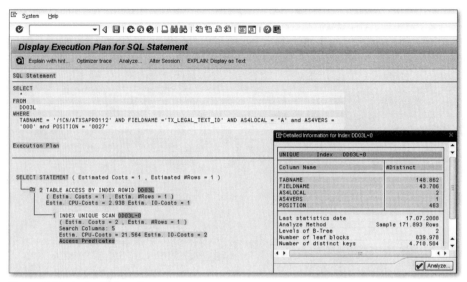

Figure A.23 Index Unique Scan

The INDEX FULL SCAN access corresponds to an index full scan. The entire index is read (see Figure A.24).

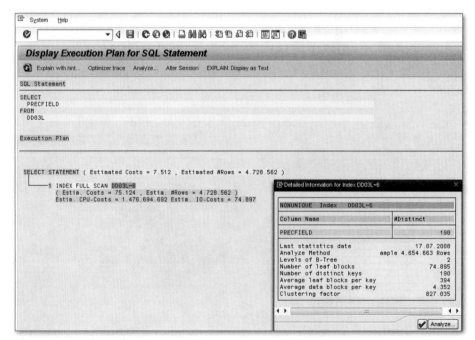

Figure A.24 Index Full Scan

A join is mapped as a tree whose nodes and leaves contain a join category (NESTED LOOP) and an access as described previously (see Figure A.25).

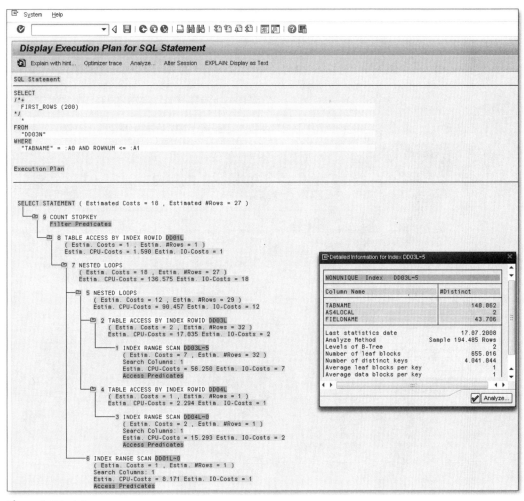

Figure A.25 Join

A.7 Microsoft SQL Server

The CLUSTERED INDEX SCAN access corresponds to a full table scan (see Figure A.26). An access that only has the CLIENT or MANDT field in the WHERE condition usually corresponds to a full table scan (provided that there aren't multiple clients in the system), although Microsoft SQL Server will most likely execute an index range scan (see next access) for the first column of the primary key.

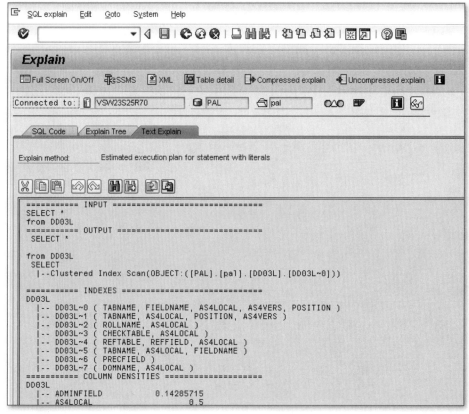

Figure A.26 Full Table Scan

The CLUSTERED INDEX SEEK access corresponds to an index range scan with two columns (two columns for SEEK, see Figure A.27). The columns after SEEK indicate which columns can be used for the range scan (SEEK). The columns after WHERE indicate which columns can be used for filters.

The CLUSTERED INDEX SEEK access corresponds to an index unique scan with five columns (five columns for SEEK, see Figure A.28).

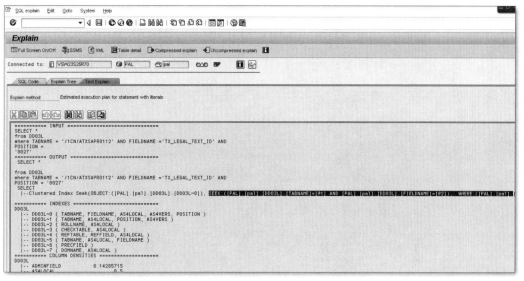

Figure A.27 Index Range Scan

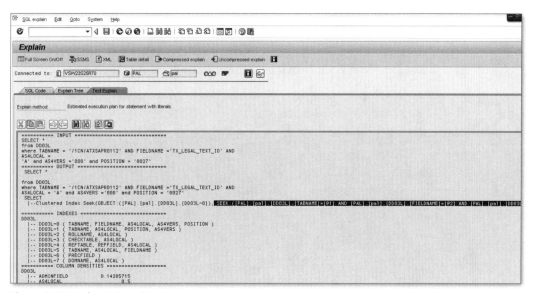

Figure A.28 Index Unique Scan

The INDEX SCAN access corresponds to an index full scan (see Figure A.29). The entire index is read.

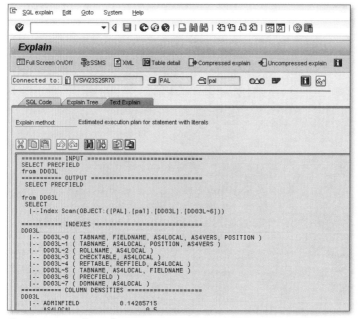

Figure A.29 Index Full Scan

A join is mapped as a tree whose nodes and leaves contain a join category (NESTED LOOPS) and an access as described previously (see Figure A.30).

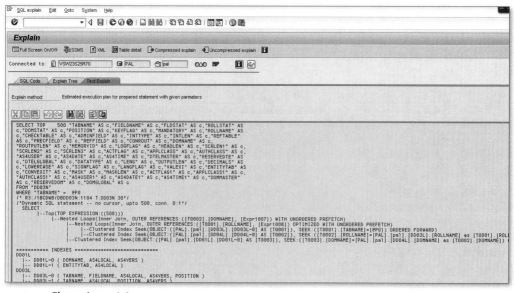

Figure A.30 Join

B   The Author

 **Hermann Gahm** is an SAP Support Consultant in the Technology & Performance area, and he has worked in the Active Global Support department of SAP AG since 2007. His tasks focus on the support of major SAP customers with regard to performance problems within the scope of ABAP developments for CPO (Customer Program Optimization) and BPPO services (Business Process Performance Optimization).

While working as an ABAP developer at one of the largest commercial enterprises in Germany and as an SAP system administrator at the industry-leading enterprise for processing industrial credit and building society savings products, he finished his further training as an expert in business data processing at the IHK (German Chamber of Commerce and Industry). Here, his work focused on the performance analysis and optimization of mass data processing in SAP systems.

He then joined SAP SI AG as an SAP technology consultant where he took over responsibility for various system, database, and ABAP program tuning projects for national and international customers.

Index

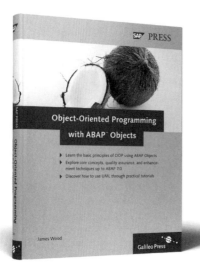

Learn the basic principles of OOP using ABAP Objects

Explore core concepts, quality assurance and enhancement techniques up to ABAP 7.0

Discover how to use UML through practical tutorials

James Wood

Object-Oriented Programming with ABAP Objects

This book provides a gentle (and yet, comprehensive) start to programming object-oriented ABAP! What are objects? How to define and write classes? What's polymorphism all about? The book helps you to venture the switch to object-oriented programming, and brings your skills up to date: First learn about all essential OO concepts, then see examples from daily development work. Exception handling, object debugging and unit testing are demystified here, plus, you get advice on enhanced techniques and tools in ABAP 7.0.

357 pp., 69,95 Euro / US$ 69.95
ISBN 978-1-59229-235-6

>> www.sap-press.de/1859

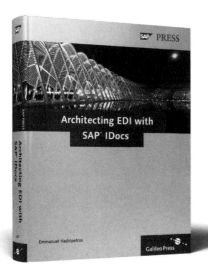

Covers the requirements, standards, and capabilities of EDI and IDocs

Teaches how to design the architectural blueprint of the EDI systems

Provides a sample scenario for implementing order-to-cash in a real-world project

Emmanuel Hadzipetros

Architecting EDI with SAP IDocs

This book is your project-based guide to architecting Enterprise Data Interchange (EDI) with SAP IDocs. Following a large sample scenario of an order-to-cash process from blueprint to code, you'll get an A-to-Z explanation of what an EDI system or architecture looks like. The book explains the basics of the process, shows a real-life implementation, and introduces utilities, test strategies, monitoring and troubleshooting activities. Following the sample project, you'll learn everything you need to know about SAP EDI.

approx. 600 pp., 69,95 Euro / US$ 69.95
ISBN 978-1-59229-227-1, July 2009

>> www.sap-press.de/1850

Interested in reading more?

Please visit our Web site for all
new book releases from SAP PRESS.

www.sap-press.com